'Tom has the rare ability of capturing the true nature of parenthood. Reading The Search for Sanity *transported me back to the fun, fear and sometimes pure frustration it is to be a dad'*

Neil Sinclair, AKA Commando Dad

'When you think nothing sucks harder than a Henry Hoover, along come the terrible twos'

(not so) Secret Dads Business

'Immediately engaging with genuine laugh-out-loud moments, The Search for Sanity *will have you simultaneously laughing and sighing in relief, because now you know you're not alone'*

Toddle About

'Sanity seekers unite! Embrace the toddler tornado with this gem'

MANtenatal

'Toddler storytelling at its best – filled with humour and the odd swear word, The Search for Sanity *perfectly documents the whirlwind that is life with a toddler'*

The Modern Fatherhood Club

'Behind every young child who believes in themselves is a parent who believes first'

From Lads to Dads

'Discover the amazing adventures you can have with your kids and learn to see the world through their eyes. Tom's writing style is easy and fun to engage with, and if you're good with F-bombs and the hard-hitting truth that is parenting, then this book is for you'

MANDAD MEDIA

'Whether you're a parent, a soon-to-be parent or simply someone who cherishes the beauty of life's little moments, The Search for Sanity *will leave you with a heart full of warmth*'

Be a Super Dad

'If you are a new parent and looking to learn more about your soon-to-be toddler, Tom's book is one you should pick up!'

Art Eddy – *The Art of Fatherhood*

'Heartfelt, funny and truly touching'

Rays Your Mental Health

THE SEARCH FOR SANITY

Life with a Two-Year-Old

TOM KREFFER

Charlie Cat Books
Kemp House, 160 City Road
London, EC1V 2NX

First published in Great Britain in 2023 by Charlie Cat Books

Copyright © 2023 Tom Kreffer
All rights reserved.
www.tomkreffer.com

Tom Kreffer has asserted his right to be identified as the author of this Work in accordance with the Copyright, Designs and Patents Act 1988.

No parts of this publication may be reproduced, stored in a retrieval system, or transmitted in any form or by any means, electronic, mechanical, photocopying, recording, or otherwise, without the prior written permission of the copyright owner.

This book is sold subject to the condition that it shall not, by way of trade or otherwise, be lent, resold, hired out, or otherwise circulated without the publisher's prior consent in any form of binding or cover other than that in which it is published and without a similar condition including this condition being imposed on the subsequent purchaser. Under no circumstances may any part of this book be photocopied for resale.

Some names and identifying details have been changed to protect the privacy of individuals.

Cover Design and layout by MiblArt
Illustrations and cover artwork by Chandana Wanasekara
The image on page 80 is by The Hub
A CIP catalogue record for this book is available from the British Library

ISBN 978-1-7395902-4-6

For Mum
I don't know how you did it alone

Also by Tom Kreffer

Adventures in Dadding

DEAR DORY: JOURNAL OF A SOON-TO-BE FIRST-TIME DAD

DEAR ARLO: ADVENTURES IN DADDING

TODDLER INC.

Table of Contents

Toddler Inc.: We've Only Just Begun. 9

November. 15

December. 53

January 103

February 147

March. 189

April 223

Toddler Inc.: We're In For One Helluva Show 241

May 247

June. 291

July 311

August 353

Toddler Inc.: Panic Stations 383

September 389

October. 431

November (Again) 451

Toddler Inc.: Goodbyes 479

Arloisms: A Guide To Toddler Talk 484

Acknowledgements 486

A Note From The Author 488

About Tom Kreffer 489

Want Free Stuff? 490

terrible twos
noun

1. A period in a child's life where they deem it appropriate and acceptable to throw tantrums and objects periodically throughout the day – especially when out in public.

2. A period in a child's life when they are prone to arseholery.

The Parenthood Dictionary
Adventures in Dadding Edition

Toddler Inc.:
We've Only Just Begun

Toddler Inc.
proper noun

A toddler-training facility specialising in the art of parent warfare.

Toddler Inc. Employee Handbook
Third Edition

It was done. The job complete, the renovations finished – on time and under budget. I mean, of course it was: Mr Jacobs had personally been at the helm, overseeing the project from concept to design and then right through to the red-ribbon-cutting inauguration ceremony. And if Mr Jacobs was in charge, then you could guarantee unrivalled performance and delivery of the highest results.

In his late fifties, Mr Jacobs, CEO of Toddler Inc., was a handsome man and well presented too. If you typed his name into an online thesaurus, the search would throw up words like 'accomplished', 'consummate' and 'reliable'. He was the man who got the job done – and he still is.

He stood outside the newly redesigned and developed headquarters of Toddler Inc., admiring the façade, especially the sign at the front: *Toddler Inc.: Helping infants to emotionally (and sometimes physically) tear Mummy and Daddy a new one since the dawn of man.*

The building had been meticulously designed to cater for the needs of toddlers: the reinforced octuple-glazed windows that could withstand the screams of toddlers in tantrum training; the exposed steels, painted in shiny handprint-and-dribble-absorbing matt-black paint that reduced the cleaning budget by two thirds; and, of course, a large, open atrium where toddlers had space to roam, skid and otherwise practise their showing-Mummy-and-Daddy-up-in-public skills.

But for all of Mr Jacobs' stern posture and serious approach to life, he was, above all else, very fond of children. For them, he wore a different demeanour, one of kindness and warmth. As he marched into the building, his body language softened and his pace slowed to a leisurely stroll. He arrived at the visitors' desk and met his first appointment of the day: a toddler by the name of Arlo.

'Arlo, my lad, so good to see you. What do you think of the new digs? Impressive, aren't they?'

'YEAH!' Arlo exclaimed. He certainly was impressed, particularly with the open-plan foyer that stretched the length of the building. He could see some of his similar-aged colleagues tearing the place up, arms stretched out behind them jet-plane style. To the right was the food court that boasted vibrant-coloured snack trucks with well-known Pixar Animation Studios film characters painted on the side. There was a truck serving Weetabix, where Mr Jacobs personally took breakfast each morning; another serving every kind of milk; and yet another offering recycled, barely nibbled-on apples, sliced up and transformed into apple-and-peanut-butter wedges.

Mr Jacobs permitted Arlo to take a few seconds to enjoy the view. 'Come, let me show you around – no, not that way,' he said, halting Arlo in his tracks as he steered him down a side entrance that had a sign overhanging it: *Terrible Twos Induction Centre*.

'Arlo, you've had a wonderful start to your career as a toddler, and we here at Toddler Inc. couldn't be prouder. But ...' Mr Jacobs stopped short in front of a pair of large, colourful doors: '... things are about to get interesting.' He pushed the doors open to reveal a wide, well-lit corridor. The floor was made of white marble decorated with primary-coloured geometric shapes. The ceiling was arched and adorned with an exquisite fresco, a homage to Raphael's *The School of Athens*, which featured many toddlers learning how to push their parents beyond their limits.

Glass-walled offices lined either side of the corridor – each of them in use. In the first office, a Toddler Inc. employee showed two brothers – twins – how to climb over a stair gate by working together. A girl, an only child, was in the next. She couldn't rely on the aid of a sibling, so another employee was showing her how to drag objects over and create 'stepping stones', helping her achieve the same goal. Every toddler was expected to master stair-gate ascension. But how they did this was up to them.

In the next cubicle, Peter, a preschooler, was presenting to a group of seven toddlers. He used a stick he had found at the park as a pointer, directing his audience to a large projector screen behind him. On it was a video that was currently paused on the still of a tall kitchen cupboard. The audience looked perplexed as they stared at the screen. The handle on the cupboard was out of reach, and there were no objects nearby that were light enough for a toddler to drag over and stand on. Peter had asked the group to figure out how they would breach this snack-containing vault. After a while, one small female hand gently rose. Peter nodded, encouraging the little girl to answer. She squatted low, got her arms *under* an imaginary door in front of her and then pulled. Her peers were impressed and so was the proud preschooler. Peter unpaused the video and, sure enough, it showed a toddler running over to the cupboard, dropping to their knees, gripping the underside of the exposed door and pulling it open towards them – without needing to use the handle at all. They now had access to whatever treats lay within.

'You see,' Mr Jacobs said as he walked the length of the corridor with Arlo, 'everything about this term has to be bigger, louder and dialled up. Last year, I instructed you to give Mum and Dad hell, self-immolating grief-stricken hell. This year, you're to do the same but to a higher order of magnitude. Keep them guessing, don't give them even a second to relax, and never, ever let them believe that they are in control. Two-year-olds rule the world, and it's the responsibility of every one of you to let parents know this. Do you understand?'

'Yeah, I do,' Arlo said.

'Excellent stuff. You know, Arlo, in my opinion, toddlers have never had it better.' Mr Jacobs, having reached the end of the corridor with Arlo, pushed open a new set of double doors that opened into a sizeable state-of-the-art surveillance room. The far wall was full of monitors, each of them displaying footage of toddlers doing what toddlers do best: wreaking havoc.

Arlo's eyes widened. He saw within those monitors ... inspiration. Toddlers were tipping cereal boxes upside down, unravelling toilet rolls, throwing tantrums in the middle of a restaurant, dropping F-bombs, biting, scratching and hitting parents, and mastering the art of generally opposing Mum and Dad.

'Arlo, every member of your adult support network thinks you're cute and adorable. Let's you and I see if we can't force them to reshape their definition of what's cute and adorable, shall we?'

'Yeah!'

'In that case, I wish you the very best of luck. I'll be checking in again with you in six months' time. And may I end our appointment by wishing you a very happy birthday. Welcome to the terrible twos.'

November

pass the parcel
noun

1. A birthday party tradition that desperately warrants going the way of the dodo.
2. Something that is falsely advertised as fun.

The Parenthood Dictionary
Adventures in Dadding Edition

A Birthday Party For A Two-Year-Old
Friday, 19 November 2021

'DADDA! DADDA!'

Christ, what's the time? I look at my phone – 6.15 a.m.

'DADDA! MAMMA!'

Here we go again – welcome to parenthood: Year Three.

At least we got a lie-in. Your mother and I get out of bed and traipse to the other side of the house, responding to the calls of a young man on his special day. 'Good morning, Arlo,' I say. 'Do you know what day—'

'I'm twooooooo!'

'That's right, baby boy,' Mummy says.

We sing 'Happy Birthday' to you, and then you hold your arms up, telling us to take you out of your cot. At some point this year, you'll transition to your very own big-boy bed, and you won't be so dependent on a parent to grant you freedom. But not yet – *we're not ready for that.*

Last night, I devoted a considerable part of my evening to setting up your birthday present, a VTech Toot-Toot Drivers set. It has electronic cars that light up and play sounds, all manner of track parts, a parking tower – and even a car wash. Mummy found the bundle for sale second-hand on Facebook Marketplace, a platform that has become a financial ally in the battle to keep parenthood costs down. It was priced at £30. Had it been brand new, we would have spent over £200.

Other than your second-hand Toot-Toot set, we've got you a scooter. But that's it. We're putting a lesson we learnt last Christmas into practice and ensuring you don't have too many presents. This is so that you're not overwhelmed and the appreciation factor doesn't diminish as a result of us piling gift after gift in your arms, replacing the one you've barely opened with another.

We're seeing the value of this lesson immediately. You are 100 per cent absorbed in the world of your new car set. In fact, you spend so long playing with it that we cancel our plans to go to the park and test out your new scooter.

But that doesn't mean Mummy can't give it a try, so she takes it for a spin up and down the hallway, until you steamroll your way into her path, yelling, 'No, Mamma!'

'What do you mean, "No, Mamma"? You're playing with your cars!'

November

You shake your head. Then you shuffle your body next to Mummy and barge her out of the way. I wonder if 'sharing' is on the curriculum this year. If it is, it's apparently not scheduled for today.

Usually, you wear an eyepatch on your right eye for a couple of hours every morning to strengthen what doctors have said is the 'weaker left eye' – one that suffered from a congenital abnormality affecting the cornea. Patching the stronger eye forces the brain to work and rely on the weaker eye, and in doing so, strengthens it. Don't ask me to go into any more detail than that, but what I can tell you is that we used to patch you for a lot longer than two hours. However, the treatment is working, and the performance of your weaker left eye continues to improve, and thus, the patching periods have reduced. But, like last year on your birthday, we've given you a hall pass from having to wear one today.

Knock knock.

'Nana. Ooofer?' you say.

'It might be. Shall we take a look?'

You toddler sprint-waddle to the front door in time to welcome Nana Hoover into the house. She's carrying a big bag of presents for you, which is another reason for parents not to go mad on gifts, because you can be assured everyone else will – especially grandmothers.

Nana Hoover is my mum. We originally named her Granny Smurf, but then you learnt to talk, and you claimed ownership of grandmother-naming conventions. Your first act was to change 'Granny' to 'Nana', so she became Nana Smurf. And now, 'Smurf' is out too, and 'Hoover' is in. Nana Hoover gets her latest title because you are obsessed with vacuum cleaners, and Nana owns a Hetty Hoover. She also allows you to watch YouTube videos of Hetty, Henry and other members of the same Numatic vacuum-cleaner family. If that sounds beyond fucking nuts, it's because it is, both the obsession with Hoovers and the fact that there are so many YouTube videos dedicated to the topic.

My dad has never been involved in our lives (yours and mine), so there's no Grandad Hoover, but Nana Hoover has the strength and capacity to love and care for you with the power of a million grandparents, so I promise you, neither of us is missing out.

Your favourite present from Nana Hoover is a tractor pulling a trailer that houses a chicken, a cow, a pig and a 'baa-baa'. Getting it out of the packaging is fraught with frustrations. Seriously, what goes on in a manufacturing and marketing meeting? I suppose the marketing manager says something like, 'We want the toy to be completely on show so it's more appealing on the eye and therefore likely to sell, but we also want it to be impossible to unbox.'

After presents, it's time for your nap. I'm about to put you down when a frightening thought invades my consciousness. *Holy shit.* 'Will Arlo drop his midday nap this year?' I say to Mummy.

'No, don't worry. He should nap now until he starts school.'

Is it me, or has a quartet of angels just appeared and begun singing ear-pleasing melodies?

November

Your mother is a wonderful mummy. She is quite simply superb at the job in every respect. She works in childcare, which means other children benefit from her maternal warmth too. I once referred to her as the Mona Lisa of motherhood, a title she embodies every waking minute. As with Nana Hoover, you and I are fortunate to have her.

Last year, Covid-19 restrictions meant you couldn't have a party, so as I write this at midday, I'm wonderfully ignorant of the carnage that a two-year-old's bash so often wreaks. However, I've heard horror stories recounted by other traumatised parents who were stupid enough to think that hosting a bunch of toddlers was a good idea. They're still attending therapy. Luckily, we're not hosting; that delight falls to Nana and Grandad See-See. Mummy is heading over there right now to finish hanging birthday decorations and set everything up while I stay at home with you, dreading the upcoming festivities and the destruction they're sure to bring.

Nana and Grandad See-See are Mummy's mummy and daddy. The naming – or renaming – of your second set of grandparents is just as charming as the renaming of your paternal grandmother. We used to call them Nana Feeder and Grandad Tools. Why Nana Feeder? Because she overfeeds all guests and house residents. Also, she was a 'Granny', but, like Nana Hoover, you changed that to 'Nana'. Why Grandad Tools? Because he owns 50 per cent of the entire planetary stock of them. Tools, that is. So then, why the change of name? When we were in lockdown, you would often ask Mummy to video-call Nana, and she would oblige. But as soon as Nana answered, you would repeatedly say, 'See?' – which was your way of asking to 'see' your grandad. Over time, Grandad Tools became Grandad See-See, and even though you've just turned two, you've learnt the highly archaic – not to mention sexist – tradition that the woman takes the man's name upon marriage. And that's how Nana Feeder and Grandad Tools became Nana and Grandad See-See. Confused?

'Arlo, what is it?'

'Hooverrrrrr,' you say. Your face brightens, irradiating your surroundings with the power of a million suns.

'Is that a red toy Henry Hoover?'

'YEAH!'

You are so bloody chuffed with this. Hat tip to Nana See-See for procuring a present that trumps all those that came before and probably a long list of others that will come after.

I guess now is the perfect time to tell you that the theme of your party is ... wait for it ... Henry Hoover! But also with a few *Bing* balloons thrown in, as up until a week ago, *Bing* was your favourite children's television show (currently, it's *Cocomelon*). But the headline act is the mischievous, smiling, red fella, as he's the one who's on the cake.

November

Guests arrive, and children soon warm up to the new environment. They begin a frenzied exploration of the house, searching for toys and sweets. Arguments are unavoidable. Luckily, every parent automatically qualifies as a hostage negotiator when their children reach toddler age. A quick tour of the room reveals half a dozen conversations at varying points. Parents take different approaches in defusing and placating angry little people who want things that other angry little people have taken from them either because they're theirs or because they just want them. Here are a few snippets:

'You mustn't snatch. It's not yours.'

'Can you let Oakley have a turn now?'

'You can have one more sweet, then that's it.'

'You can play with anything in the house – the cutlery, the tools in the shed, any of the glassware – but please don't go near Arlo's Hoover as he will rage.'

More guests.

'Happy-birthday-Arlo-I-got-you-a-dinosaur,' says your cousin Haylee, who's holding out a big wrapped-up box that I presume contains a dinosaur.

Soon, it's time for you and me to battle through a negotiation of our own. Fortunately, we've got the living room all to ourselves so that we can conduct our business in private. Why is it in private? Because everybody else has moved to the kitchen in readiness to sing 'Happy Birthday' and watch you blow out your candles. You haven't noticed a single thing, because you're immersed in playing with your Henry Hoover toy.

Enter (evil) Daddy.

'Arlo, shall we have a look at what's in the kitchen?'

You shake your head without even a flicker of eye contact.

I change tack. 'Henry looks tired. Shall we put him to bed?'

Nothing.

At this point, I realise that language on its own is futile, which is annoying because, as I said, your cake is of the red Henry Hoover variety, and I'm convinced you're going to love it. But you won't give in to reason, so I pick you up and explain that you have a cake in the kitchen.

'Naaaa. Dadda. NAAAA!'

I move quickly, taking three extra-long strides to carry you into the kitchen while lifting you upright like Rafiki does when he presents baby Simba to the African plain inhabitants in *The Lion King*. My aim, of course, is to direct your attention away from your plastic Hoover toy and over to your edible Hoover cake so that your rage levels reduce and everyone can continue having a lovely time.

A second passes. Then another, and then …

'Ooofer,' you say, pointing to your cake.

Thank God.

We sing 'Happy Birthday' while you yank Henry's icing-covered hose, dislodging it from the cake before Mummy can get a picture. No matter, we carry out on-site repairs, take the photo and then let your grabby little hands get on with vandalising Henry. You've only had cake a handful of times in your life, but you know exactly what it is. You pick up a piece bigger than my fist and give me a look as if to say, 'Can I, Dad?'

'Yes, you can, son.'

Next, we move on to what I fully expect to be the shittest part of your party: pass the parcel. It's a fun little game in the same way that hidden bank charges and stubbed toes are fun!

Despite this book being a brand-new parenting adventure, it was only five days ago – in *Toddler Inc.* – that I revealed a comprehensive list of debate-winning arguments as to why pass the parcel is the worst example of forced, manufactured fun in the universe. In short, all participants know it's a fix. The person in charge believes they're hilarious, using three rolls of Sellotape to make each layer unbreachable. Then there is the social anxiety, all because each round-winner struggles to tear the next layer of wrapping paper off, meaning every participant and onlooker (yes, adults as well) hurls impatient, judgmental scowls in their direction. And to top it off, the winner always gets a shit prize. It's never an iPad. It's usually something marginally better than a Christmas cracker gift.

Though, truth be told, I can't remember the last time I physically endured this type of torture, so I'm curious to see if it still matches up to the low opinions that I have of it.

'Didn't you have a childhood?' Taci says (pronounced 'tah-see').

'Yes, I did. That's how I know this is a shit game.'

Mummy steps up as the host. *Thank God.* This is her moment, Arlo. Her childcare experience means that she is more than qualified to guide this situation to a smooth and enjoyable conclusion. She will shine, soar and excel. Everyone in attendance will marvel at her intuition and her ability to control a group of the uncontrollable. Her first decision is to promote me. 'Right, you're DJ. If you stand out in the kitchen and shut the door, we can make it fair for the child—'

'Ohhh,' say all the parents at once, their collective 'ohs' accompanied by some collective head shaking. Evidently, they've been to more two-year-olds' parties than we have.

Maybe Mummy isn't set to soar, Arlo. *And I thought children were fickle.*

'What?' Mummy asks.

'How is he going to keep track of who's won?' Taci says.

I'm not fussed about the whole 'everyone's a winner' philosophy, because it's bullshit and teaches kids nothing, but I also have something to add. 'Can I throw my hat in the ring? As father of the boy whose birthday we're celebrating, it would be kinda cool, if it's not too much to ask, for me to have the opportunity to see him participate.'

Mummy scowls. 'Fine! You can DJ in here.'

I start the music, but by the third beat of 'The Wheels on the Bus', I've got Taci and Rebecca (our midwife friend; you call her Auntie Raa-Raa) barking commands at me from the sidelines. 'Remember, pause the music when only one set of hands is on the present,' Taci says.

'Oh, and make sure each kid gets a turn,' Rebecca adds.

Shit. How many layers are there? I mouth the question to Mummy. She mouths back: 'Ten.' I quickly count the participants. *Nine – phew.* My heart rate is 90 bpm.

I'm playing the music through my phone hooked up via Bluetooth to a speaker. But the speaker is in the next room, and when I pause the music at precisely the right time, there's a minor audio delay, resulting in two sets of toddler-sized hands on the present instead of one. Both children look at me: the Caesar; the fate-decider. Parents scowl and shake their heads: *fucking amateur.*

'It's not my fault. There's a sound delay,' I protest, feeling my heart rate jump to 120 bpm.

After Mummy conducts an investigation, comparing the two sets of hands grasping the present, she announces the winner of the first round. It's Flint, one of Taci's kids. He removes the layer of wrapping paper and discovers a pack of chocolate buttons. And now, Flint is squeezing the bag while pulling a face – something isn't right. It's Taci's turn for investigative duties. 'These buttons are melted. Where did you leave the parcel?'

'Ah ... On top of the microwave,' Mummy answers.

Does anyone else think we're nailing pass the parcel, Arlo?

The game progresses with me continually fucking up every facet of my DJing responsibilities. It's not just the pausing of the music, which I still can't seem to master. I'm also criticised by parents for poor song choice, for not paying attention to who's won a round and for letting the music play for too long, or not long enough. I protest, explaining that it's hard to concentrate or, heck, even hear the music over people repeatedly telling me I'm doing such a shit job. But my arguments are trampled on by more head shaking. They look like a bunch of Newton's cradles.

One of the older girls in attendance, a four-year-old, looks upon the scene dumbfounded, recognising the whole thing for what it is: a sham. As for the rest of the toddlers, you're all savage, sugar-high, unstable atoms, ready to explode.

But the biggest farce is that you, Arlo, get bored with the game before we're even halfway through. You make your excuses and take your leave, along with Henry, of course, though I note that you're quickly intercepted by Nana See-See, who, thinking she can't be seen, ushers a piece of cake into your mouth. This is the fifth time in as many minutes that she's done this.

Eventually, the pass-the-parcel torture concludes, and my heart begins the long descent back down to a non-life-threatening rate.

'I stand by what I said. Pass the parcel is the shittest children's party game ever invented,' I say to Taci.

We've made it back home. It's been a difficult end to the day because you're now one exhausted little boy, but you're not too tired for a final tantrum. This one is over our decision not to let you take Henry to bed. But after we promise you that he will be here in the morning, you relent and allow us to read you a bedtime story.

I can't believe you're two. Everything about your life has been a wild ride for me, and that's only going to increase. I wonder what life has in store for us this year. I know we've got potty-training and your eventual transition to a big-boy bed on the cards, but most of all, I'm curious to see how your language develops. If all goes well, we should be having full-blown conversations together by the time you reach three.

As we go into our third year together, I offer you no assurances that I won't make mistakes and that I won't get things wrong. Yes, I have parenting experience, but that was with a little boy who is not the same one I'm looking at right now. For the last two years, on your birthday, including on the day you were born, I've told you to rest up because you have a long year ahead. Something tells me that Mummy and I should do the same.

Happy birthday, buddy. I love you.

Sleep well.

Holiday
Saturday, 20 November 2021

When you were Dory[1], I carried out a thought exercise, speculating on the rules governing instances

---

[1] Dory was Arlo's pre-birth name, which I covered in my first book, *Dear Dory: Journal of a Soon-to-be First-time Dad.*

of both parents going away together without their children. Since becoming your daddy, I've not had the chance to put that theory into practice, because of Covid-19.

But now we can, and that's what we're doing.

I've previously been skiing, but that doesn't count, because Mummy didn't come with me. She was with you. And Mummy and I have been away together once before, for her birthday this past summer. But that was in the UK – in the Peak District, only an hour up the road.

Today, we're leaving you with your nanas, who'll be sharing childcare duties while I take Mummy to Finland to see if we can catch a glimpse of the Northern Lights.

Another lesson I learnt last year was that packing to go away in the presence of a toddler was like trying to chop down an oak tree with a used condom. Luckily, we've got our newly inducted third parent – Henry Hoover – who's willing to babysit you for an hour.

Please don't hate us for going on holiday; I know we're going to Lapland to see Santa ... Shit, I didn't tell you that, did I? Arlo, we're going to Lapland to visit Santa. OK, so at first glance, we're selfish parents, going off to see the big jolly guy without taking our only child, but hear me out. Rovaniemi (where we'll be staying) is bitterly cold this time of year. It will likely be the coldest environment we've ever travelled to, and if we took you with us, we wouldn't be able to do much, apart from not letting you go outside.

We'd all be confined to the hotel, so what would be the point?

Finally, it's my and Mummy's seventh anniversary. We've not been on holiday together since before you were born – we need and deserve this!

Final, final point – we got you a kick-ass scooter for your birthday, so if you think about it, you owe us this ... right?

We're not worried about you missing us. We learnt that lesson the hard way when we went to the Peak District. Upon our return, you performed a dispassionate and quite frankly indifferent welcome for us when we reunited. We've also packed your calendar with stuff to do, so you're a busy young man and in no danger of being bored. Nana Hoover will stay at our house for a couple of days and will probably encourage you to trash everything in sight, just for a spot of fun. Nana See-See will collect you Monday afternoon, feed you leftover birthday cake and perform drop-off and pickup duties at nursery on Tuesday and Wednesday. When you wake up on Thursday morning, it will be Mummy and I who will greet you. It would be lovely if you could at least pretend you're pleased to see us.

After we've packed, it's time for us to say goodbye. 'Arlo, can Daddy have the biggest cuddle ever?'

You nod your head and comply, and then you repeat the action with Mummy. Despite all of my justifications, I'm nervous about leaving you behind. Of course, I don't tell Mummy this, especially as she hasn't stopped announcing how much she can't bear to be parted from her only child – to the extent that I'm now thinking of leaving her behind as well.

We say our goodbyes and march out the door before it becomes too difficult. In the car, Mummy is like a statue.

'Are you going to be OK?' I ask.

'Yeah, I just need a second.'

Five minutes later, we're on the road, and Nana Hoover sends us what I fully expect to be the first of many videos. This one alleviates our guilt; it's of you playing with your cars. Once again, I ask you not to hate us for going away.

Flying, And Find My iPhone
Sunday, 21 November 2021

We're staying at an airport hotel because of the unsavoury flight-departure time. Our alarm goes off at 3 a.m., and Mummy's first action – ahead of breathing – is to load up your monitor, which she accesses through an app on her phone. 'He's not wearing a vest. He's too cold!'

'He's fine,' I say.

'How do you know?'

'Because he's flat out asleep and not awake shivering.'

We dress, grab our luggage and walk over to the airport. The pre-parenthood Mummy and I would never have booked a hotel the night before. Instead, we would have driven through the night and saved on hotel costs. But when you're a parent, you learn to cherish sleep above everything short of your kids reaching a precious milestone – and even then, it's a toss-up. Now, I'm struggling to reconcile why, in my mid-thirties, I've only just learnt to adjust my behaviour.

Say what you will about Brexit (I voted to stay), but at least we now collect passport stamps when travelling in Europe. I'd like to see any adult look me in the eye and tell me they're not fussed about that.

The next few hours pass uneventfully, and we soon find ourselves taking our seats at the back of the plane, where one of my justifications for leaving you at home is validated. Many children are on the flight, and they're all a lot older than you. They're excited but well behaved. I can hear them talking to their parents about Santa, asking if they're really going to visit him at his real, actual house, where he really, really, actually lives. It's a magical scene.

'What if we die?' says Mummy, who, if you couldn't tell, is brimming with Christmas spirit and excitement about our holiday.

'We won't die.'

'But what if we do? What if the plane crashes?' she says without tapering off a few decibels of her talking volume.

'Shhh, inside-plane voice,' I say, casting glances at nearby passengers, hoping none of them are battling any flying phobias.

'What if we die?' she whispers.

'Well, then we die, and there's not an awful lot we can do about it.'

'But what about Arlo?'

'We know exactly what would happen. I took care of our wills before he was born. He will be well cared for.'

'But we won't be there to see him grow up.'

'What possible response are you expecting from me right now? Look, we're not going to die, and if we do, then we won't have any control over it. But we've taken care of the things we *can* control. We have life insurance, our wills are in order, and he has an auntie and two grandmothers who would ensure he's OK.'

'OK. I just don't like us both being on a flight together.'

I'm about to tell her to shut up when I wonder, just for a split, split second, if we should have each taken separate flights as an insurance policy. But then I scratch the thought away and cast a scowl at Mummy for killing the mood.

'This is your captain speaking. The "fasten seat belt" sign is now on, and we are preparing for take-off.'

You'll be pleased to know that we didn't die. However, let's not pop the champagne cork just yet, because Rovaniemi is as suspected: BLOODY FREEZING! I thought I was prepared. I'm used to skiing in the Alps in winter, but this is something else. It's midday, and because of where we are in the world, the sun hangs low in the sky, veiled by a thin sheet of cloud cover that gives the life-sustaining orb an opaque, milky polished-glass look. The temperature is already minus five. We take a taxi to our hotel, wrap up in as many layers as possible and head back out into the cold to the aptly named Santa Village.

The village is quiet. The winter season only kicked off yesterday, and, of course, many people are understandably reluctant to travel because of the virus. But I don't think anyone is missing out, because the place is, sadly, one giant tourist trap. We're struggling to find options for food, but we're plenty spoilt for gift shops.

We arrive at Santa's 'real, actual house' and get to spend five minutes with the main man. His English, filtered through a Nordic accent, gives heightened authority to the proposition that the man we're speaking to is indeed the real Santa. I look around the room; he has letters from children stuck to the walls.

'Children from over one hundred and fifty countries write to me, and I have over fifty thousand more of their letters in my office.'

'You keep them all?' I ask.

'Every single one.'

How wonderful. And so many countries commemorating Christmas. I had no idea the festive period was celebrated so widely across the planet. There's something incredibly unifying knowing that it is.

There's a strict no-camera policy in Santa's house. Instead, the 'elves' are here to cater for your photography needs personally and then sell you a copy for the same amount of money it costs to buy a spaceship. But rules are made to be broken, especially ones concerning photography, and especially by your mother. Your first swimming experience (covered in *Dear Arlo*) is evidence of that. Mummy sneaked her phone into the baby pool and was told off by the manager – but only *after* she'd taken the pictures she wanted. And so, Mummy sneaks behind a display shelf of soft-toy reindeers, and she films a few seconds of Santa in action, conversing with another family. The video is for Haylee, who has reminded Mummy on many occasions that she wants to see footage of the real Santa and that she will be most upset if we don't provide her with some.

Next, we find the one open restaurant and order food. Being inside warm and not rushing around affords us an opportunity to video-call you. We're a couple of hours ahead, so you won't have gone down for your nap yet.

Ring, ring.

No answer …

'I'm going to try again. I bet your mum has her phone on silent,' Mummy says to me.

'Probably,' I agree.

Ring, ring.

Again, no answer …

'Why is she not answering?' Mummy says with ruffled feathers.

'Are you expecting a helpful response from me?'

Twenty minutes pass. Mummy tries again.

Still no answer …

I'm now a little fidgety myself. I know we can't fuck off out of the country and expect an immediate response to every message and phone call, but we did confess our anxieties on leaving, and we were assured that we would be kept up to date.

'Oh, I know, I'll check the Find My iPhone app as I have your mum's phone linked.'

Her app check confirms that you guys are at home, or at least Nana Hoover's phone is. Hopefully, you're not on your way to the hospital.

'If her phone is at home, then surely she would have checked it by now,' she says.

I don't respond, but the same thought crosses my mind. We're in a tricky spot: we're fortunate enough to have a support network that has allowed us to go away, and knowing that my mum raised me as a single parent means I'll never take that for granted, but at the same time – *Mum, pick up the fucking phone!*

Just then, Mummy's phone lights up – *Ring, ring. Thank fuck for that!*

'Hello,' Mummy says.

'Hi, sorry, we went out for a walk, and I left my phone at home. I'm really sorry.'

This was always the most likely scenario, but it's tough to remain rational when we've flown abroad without you for the first time. But now we know you're OK, we can get back to relaxing and enjoying our trip, especially as you were far too busy trashing the house to talk to us.

After we eat and pay for our meal, we wander outside and over to a prearranged meeting point, ready to begin the next item on our itinerary: hunting for the Northern Lights with a photography tour operator.

It's dark. It was dark hours ago. At this time of the year, the sun rises a little after 9.30 a.m. and sets again at around 2.30 p.m. The temperature is now ten below. The minibus arrives to collect us. We exchange pleasantries with the other tourists and set off in search of the elusive green aura.

When it comes to travelling, I'm happy to hold my hands up and say I'm like a spoilt kid at Christmas: I always want more – no matter how many incredible places I visit and experiences I collect. I shouldn't, but I do. And one of the most sought-after experiences on my wish list is a glimpse of the Northern Lights.

We drive to two locations. No lights.

Next, we park up on the edge of a frozen lake that's collected a thin layer of snowfall. Silver-white light emanating from an almost full moon reflects off the surface. The skies are clear; the thin veil of cloud from earlier has long gone. There is a small congregation of stars spread out across this tiny patch of cosmos that we're observing as eager onlookers – anticipators – hoping to share in the beauty of the spectacle we're all so desperate to see.

Come on. Come on. Show your se—

'Look!' says the guide, pointing.

But pointing isn't required.

Tranquil green mist tears a seam through the sky, arcing, almost like a rainbow but with a less defined curvature. At the end of the curve, the green mist spreads, diluted by the night sky, like unsettled dust particles, as if a godlike being held the lights in the palm of their hand and then dispersed them with an almighty puff of air.

The sight is beautiful and awe-inspiring. Another once-in-a-lifetime, emotionally rewarding experience collected. This is why I love to travel.

I wonder what I'll collect next.

Batteries And Apple Bobbing
Monday, 22 November 2021

We've received the following updates from Nana Hoover about your well-being today:

- Henry is on his third set of batteries. He's averaging a pack a day.
- Henry now has an eyepatch on the same eye you wear yours.
- You do not miss us at all.

We video-call you, and this time Nana answers immediately. It seems we've caught you at lunchtime – well, sort of. Nana Hoover is allowing you to go bobbing for apples, but with a few modifications: there are no apples or water, just a bowl full of ratatouille and couscous. Nana's justification for allowing you to eat your dinner like a dog is that the other day you said 'shit', and we all laughed. Naturally, this prompted you to repeat the word.

And then again.

And again.

And then a few more times for good measure.

What that has to do with eating habits, I'll never know, but it would seem Nana has identified a legal loophole in the parenthood manual that says something to the effect of: 'Mum and Dad did something they shouldn't, so that means Nana can do, and has done, the same.'

Oh, and another thing. I've lost count of how many messages we've had from friends and family asking us how much Arlo is enjoying his trip to Lapland.

Awkward …

Holidays Should Mirror A Toddler's Schedule
Tuesday, 23 November 2021

'You've designed our holiday around a toddler's schedule,' says Mummy, who I think is impressed with how I've cross-pollinated our parental and travel experiences.

'How so?'

'You always say that the secret to navigating a day with a toddler is to have one main activity in the morning and then one in the afternoon.'

She's right, Arlo, I do say that. Time passes quickly in parenting, like flour falling from a sieve whose holes are too big. Even if all you have to do that day is get dressed, leave the house and walk to the shops, it's a full-scale operation. Three hours feel like three minutes, and life is always stressful when you're continually battling a clock that is consistently outmatching you. But having one activity to focus on in the morning and another in the afternoon provides anchor points throughout your day, keeping you grounded and hopefully reducing stress levels.

I'm not saying there's no stress, because stress is one of the many shadows sewn into the parenting gig, along with tiredness, hair loss and an absence of sanity. Still, less stress is much more tolerable than lots of stress, and my secret to less stress is to have two activities spread out, with a nap thrown in in the middle. It's simple toddler management ... No, it's simple *one-toddler* management. God help parents who have more than one small human in their care, although I'm sure in that instance, 'God' comes in the shape of a bottle of gin that's steadily topped up by a parent's constant flow of alcohol-contaminated tears. Whatever works for them, Arlo. You won't find me passing judgment.

Staying with the toddler theme, yesterday, Mummy and I didn't have time for an afternoon nap, and we were exhausted and a bit grumpy. Today, however, we've had some time in between activities to nap, shower and otherwise relax. Now we're energised and looking forward to our afternoon activity – which is more of an evening activity, but you take my point.

Finally, to round off toddler comparisons, the tour company we're using has been lending us their all-in-one snowsuits to help us defend against the cold. Mummy especially, because of her petite frame, looks like a toddler in an all-in-one Babygro. But, they're warm and snug, so despite our ridiculous appearances, there are no complaints.

There we have it: fun, naps and warm, comfortable clothing. Oh, to be a toddler!

Lessons Learnt From Holiday
Wednesday, 24 November 2021

Having the opportunity to get away means I've finally been able to put my theory of parents going on holiday without their children into practice, and, harnessing lessons I've learnt from this trip, I can now complete the reflection exercise.

My belief that parents need time to themselves, including the odd holiday, remains unchanged. And I will encourage other parents to come around to my way of thinking (if they haven't already). But there's a caveat: they need to go away without falling victim to guilt and self-loathing all because they've prioritised themselves over their children (for once).

Understand, Arlo, you are and will always be the biggest priority in my life, but I can't be the father I want to be if I don't give care and attention to all aspects of my identity. If I succeed in doing that, and I do so free of guilt, then I stand a chance of becoming the best version of myself – a version, or state, that's emotionally fulfilled. And it's a state that you have the potential to absorb too through osmosis. On the flip side, parents who don't achieve this risk their children absorbing unfulfilled emotional states from them, which is tragic. For them and the human race.

November

If I'm fulfilled in every aspect of my life, then, in turn, I can provide you with the necessary energy and tools for you to grow up and become the best possible version of yourself – fulfilled, motivated and thirsty for adventure.

In some respects, I like to think I've begun my tenure as a grandfather already because by embodying an example – or framework – that I believe is right, I'm able to teach you to do the same while, of course, respecting your individuality. This framework is then set up to be passed down from generation to generation.

That might sound like cheap manipulation tactics to justify a child-free holiday, but I assure you it's not, and I often bang on about this stuff because I believe the majority of parents ignore what should not be ignored. And while I take the point that many parents may not be lucky enough to have access to the kind of support network that our family has, many do. But they cannot get over that hurdle of self-manufactured parental guilt that distorts a parent's understanding of how much care and attention they should be diverting to themselves.

I've missed you every day I've been away. But the sheer joy of having the experiences I've had overruled the periods of being a dad longing for his son. We've had an incredible few days. I went into detail about the Northern Lights, but that doesn't begin to capture what we've experienced. We visited a private husky farm and went sledging on a frozen lake; we went ice swimming; we trekked in a nearby national park where they had frozen waterfalls – all truly spellbinding stuff. In the years to come, I'll always be able to look back fondly on that trip.

Also, it doesn't feel like we've taken the piss with childcare. Both of your nanas were able to chip in, and everyone had a wonderful time with you. Throw in a couple of days at nursery on top, and it's worked out very well for everyone.

Finally, and this one is bittersweet: you didn't miss us. Apparently, you asked after us the odd time, but you didn't get upset. You behaved beautifully for both of your nanas, and you went into nursery fine. A bit of me is gutted about that. As a family, we're very affectionate. Plus, we've had the whole pandemic business that's meant you spent most of your first year of life with just Mummy and me. For you to cope as well as you have done without us is, I'll admit, a little sore to weather. But, of course, the alternative scenario is that you missed us like crazy, and knowing that would have put a dampener on our trip that might have been too hard to shrug away. So, of the two, I'd rather you didn't miss us than did. But also, fuck you.

Does this mean Mummy and I will be going away again without you? Yes, absolutely. We spoke about it at length on the plane journey home. Mummy said she doesn't think she could cope with going away any longer than we did, and I agree – we've been away for four full days. And she doesn't want to make this a monthly habit, but one or two times a year will be OK.

To cap off this reflection exercise, I also mentioned in *Dear Dory* that we'd bring you back a fridge magnet any time we went away. I've made good on that promise and then some. Not only do you have a fridge magnet, you also have a postcard en route from Santa's post office and a reindeer soft toy. You're most welcome!

I have bloody missed you!

Punishment
Thursday, 25 November 2021

6.30 a.m. 'Nana, Nana!'

Mummy and I leap out of bed and bound across to the other side of the house in response to you calling out. *I wonder if you're as thrilled to see us as we are to see you.*

The sight of our smiling, loving faces triggers a response: first, a look of shock, then one of disdain and finally one of despair. I can't tell which arrived first – you screaming for Nana or you bursting into tears, but it would seem you're not quite as thrilled to see us as we are to see you.

You're in a horrible mood with us, and it doesn't let up all morning. Tantrums occur every other minute.

Mummy tells me this is you punishing us for going away.

I don't understand. You hadn't shown us any interest on the phone. Did I misinterpret that? Had you been upset with us all week? And is that why we had little in the way of enthusiasm from you during our video calls?

Confirmation that this is holiday-related behaviour arrives shortly afterwards, when Mummy tells you that you're getting in the car to drive to Nana See-See's. You immediately run over to me, wrap both arms around my waist and begin crying, 'Dadda, Dadda.'

I've fucked up.

I've really fucked up.

Despite my reflection and rumination about our trip away being a success, I've failed to realise that this *has* affected you. And I feel awful.

'Hey, buddy, it's OK.'

'No, Dadda,' you say, still clinging to me.

'Can I talk to you for a second?'

'Yeah.'

'Listen to me. You're only going to Nana See-See's for a little bit while Daddy goes to work, and then you're coming back home, where I'll be waiting. I promise I'm not going anywhere. I'm going to stay at the house. You're only going for a little bit, and then you're coming back.'

I accompany my explanation with a lot of arm waving and body language to land the message that I'm not selfishly fucking off on another holiday.

And the message does land because you untangle your arms from me and allow Mummy to put your shoes, coat and hat on. You leave the house without further protest.

This behaviour has shaken me. I check the accommodation emails from the weekend Mummy and I spent in the Peak District for her birthday last

November

year – the same weekend when you had no issues with us being away – to see if we were away for two or three nights.

It was two.

Still, though, what gives? Is this separation anxiety? I thought that was a baby phase. I thought we had left that behind long ago.

I guess not.

It's bedtime, and we're battling another frustration resulting from us having gone away. This one is over your blanket. Usually, you select what side you want, then Mummy lays it out like a rug, and we sit on it for story time. But it would seem you and Nana Hoover have changed things up a bit because you're trying to explain the new amendment to the routine, and Mummy and I aren't exactly *getting* it.

'I think he wants us all to get under it,' says Mummy – who is usually bang on with her translations. But not this time. We ask you to show us, use different words and then repeat both the words and the actions. But we're still not getting it.

Hmmm, what now? Oh, I know. 'I need my phone.'

Ring, ring. 'Good evening, Mother – I need your help with something.'

Nana Hoover fills in the gaps in our knowledge. What we should have been doing is sitting against the wall, placing your cover over our legs, but with our toes poking out the bottom so that we can perform the toe-wiggle dance.

How the fudgicles did we not get that?

Drunk Mummy
Friday, 26 November 2021

It's 3.30 a.m., and Mummy has just stumbled through the door, having had a night out with one of the NCT[2] mums. A drunk Mummy means I'm forced to play the Drunk Mummy board game, one that relies on patience, strategy and tenacity. I'm definitely not in the mood for board games, but then, who is at 3.30 a.m.? I wish there was an option to opt out, but there isn't. So, I begin mentally cycling through a list of priorities ahead of meeting my opponent: territory, communication, eye contact and hydration.

The game is set.

The board is our bed and the objective is sleep.

Soon after, I hear her approach.

Let's begin.

Territory: if I remain too close to the outside on my side of the bed, she'll come in for a cuddle, restricting my freedom and pinning me in place. She's like a sea lion on land, undulating her body, shifting sideways until she obtains skin contact before falling asleep.

---

2 National Childbirth Trust – a charity that supports parents through birth and early childhood. We're friends with other parents from the course we were on before Arlo was born.

The science is baffling, I know, but a drunk Mummy is somehow three times heavier than a non-drunk Mummy, and I simply don't have the strength for a move-drunk-Mummy-over-to-her-fucking-side-of-the-bed manoeuvre. So, I quickly shuffle to the middle of the bed, ensuring I have plenty of room to retreat when she does inevitably fall asleep.

She opens the bedroom door. 'Oh, zchello, baby.'

Communication: this is a tricky one. If I don't respond, then she treats this as hostile rudeness on my part and will no doubt begin shaking me – something that would in no way benefit my life. But neither can I respond like it's the first time I'm seeing one of my besties in over a year. No, the trick is to garble some sort of acknowledgement back, slurring my words so that she can't possibly understand anything coming out of my mouth.

'Babyyyyy?'

'Ershes ahsdh yawn yawn yawn.'

'Oh, you're not really awake, are you? That makes me very sad. I want to talk.'

'YAWN.'

Eye contact: even though I've played my communication part expertly, Mummy will still suspect a ruse, assuming that this is a game I've been waiting up all night to participate in. She scans my face like it's a word-search puzzle with only one more word left to find – one she suspects is lying underneath one of my eyelids, eyelids that I can promise you are shut, firmly, to the point where I'm now in quite a bit of pain.

This sounds easy, but it's not. Mummy is more silent than silence – stiller than a statue and more patient than a loving parent. I'm desperate to see if she's still out there waiting to pounce. This is psychological warfare, a battle of wills: predator versus prey. I mustn't give in. And I don't.

Eventually, she abandons her campaign, gets undressed and notices something on her bedside table.

'Oh,' she says.

Hydration: as a precaution, I prepared a glass of water for Mummy before I came up to bed. I did this for two reasons. First, it's a nice thing to do. She always does this for me, and she's quick to point out when the deed is not reciprocated. Second, Mummy having a lubricated throat reduces the chances of her breathing sounding like a dragon inhaling a large draught of air before burning down a village full of farmers, and then exhaling like … you guessed it: a dragon burning down a village full of farmers.

Night night, Arlo. I guess I'll see you in a couple of hours – maybe even three if I'm lucky.

A Prelude To Potty-Training
Sunday, 28 November 2021

Though it's not something we've tried to initiate, potty-training is fast approaching. A combination of you watching Mummy or me or your cousin Haylee, who is potty-trained, on the toilet has fostered curiosity and a desire to have a go yourself.

November

At first, you wanted to sit on the toilet with the aid of a potty seat just for the sake of sitting. But that quickly became part of your evening routine, and you've since performed a few wees on the toilet. The three of us are incredibly proud when you do this. Another charming element of the weeing-on-the-toilet activity is, when you finish up, I remind you to 'shake'. But despite me showing you how you do this, instead of shaking your willy, you shake your hand. But it's a shake of the hand that's very different from, say, waving. It's its own thing, a signature choreographed handshake – which I find charming, and I'm in no rush to correct.

That covers wee-wee. What about poo-poo?

So far, it's not happened, but I am trying to teach you. I do this by squatting down in front of you when you're on the toilet, pressing my hands together as if praying, and then I lean forward and release an exaggerated straining sound. You mirror my actions. I'm not sure if you understand what I'm trying to teach you or if you're just playing along because it's a fun bit of silliness (I suspect it's both). You follow my movements with interest like a student does when their teacher imparts wise words – or actions. It's a slightly surreal scene and might sound ridiculous the way I'm describing it to you, but it's oddly intimate, and to be honest, it's a phase I'll look back on fondly. At least this element of it; I appreciate we've not begun 'proper' potty-training yet.

And that brings us nicely on to what's happening right now. It's evening, and Nana Hoover is here. You make the following pronouncements. One: you don't want to wear your nappy. Two: you need a poo-poo.

Interesting. This could be your first code brown on the toilet.

Mummy rids you of your nappy and says, 'Remember, as soon as you feel it coming, run to the toilet, and you can do poo-poo, OK?'

'Yeah.'

We sit back and let you crack on with life. The objective here is to create an environment where it's not apparent that three adults aren't brimming with excitable energy, all because you *might* do your first poo on a toilet. We don't want to put you under pressure.

Fifteen minutes pass. Mummy and Nana are in the kitchen, and you and I are in the living room playing with your cars.

'Dadda. Poo-poo.'

Oh my fucking God – it's happening. OK, OK, OK. Let's everyone just calm down and not overreact.

'You need a poo-poo?' I say.

'Yeah.'

'Do you want to sit on the toilet?'

'Yeah.'

'OK, go on then, walk over.'

But you're hesitant. I expected you to bound over, full of confidence. But you haven't. Something is wrong, but I'm not sure— *Oh fuck!* 'Arlo, have you started doing your poo-poo already?'

'Yeah.' You look and sound guilty.

'That's OK, buddy, we can clear it up if it goes on the floor. It's no problem.'

I skirt around the large toy-car-park apparatus that's between us. A quick inspection reveals you have indeed begun your business.

Fuck, fuck, what do I do? What would Mummy do?

Thud – I'll let you deduce what that was.

'Erm, can I have some assistance, please?'

Mummy enters the room. She takes one look at the floor and springs into action. Within the space of a microsecond, she's carried you over to the toilet, placed you on it and made it back to the living room with tissue to clear away the mess.

Now, three adults are loitering nearby, waiting to see what happens while you remain sitting on the toilet.

After a minute or so ...

Plop.

'Good boy, Arlo,' say the three adults in unison.

Yes! Yes, yes, yes, yes, yes. You did it! You did your first poo on the toilet. Admittedly, it was half a poo – the second half. But no one here is going to take anything away from you. We all clap and cheer and congratulate a young man who's reached a huge toddler milestone.

Your first poo in a toilet!

Well done, buddy – I'm so super proud of you.

December

parent prayer
noun

A solemn plea for help from God or any other godlike being who moonlights as a parent sympathiser.

> Unknown: thought to have originated from a father of twelve kids

Elf On The Shelf Revisited
Wednesday, 1 December 2021

Allow me to recap a conversation from a few nights ago.

'Are you sure you want to do this?' I asked.

'Yes,' Mummy said.

'And you understand that, once we open this can of worms, the worms will never be able to go back in said can and that the worms will routinely position themselves to spell out the word "REGRET".'

'Hmmm. Now I'm doubting myself. OK, let's leave it until next year,' she said.

'Are you sure?'

'I'm sure.'

And that was the end of that. Or so I thought.

But it would seem Mummy has had a change of heart because the postman has just swung by, and I'm now holding a box with a transparent front panel. Within it, clear as North Pole daylight, is an elf sitting on a shelf.

What do I even do with this?

If you haven't guessed, I'm holding the required hardware for us to observe a tradition based on the book *The Elf on the Shelf*, something that's taken the UK by storm over the last decade or so. I don't know much about it, but I'm not entirely in the dark. For instance, I know that the *rules* say that no one can touch the elf, otherwise it loses its magic; I know the elf will appear, like a Christmas edition of *Toy Story*, in a new location every day; and I know parents' therapy bills go up by about ten orders of magnitude. You cannot go scrolling through any social-media platform in December and not learn this, even if you have no kids.

But, unlike a newborn baby, the elf comes with an instruction manual. Actually, it's more of a beautifully illustrated book. Having just this second finished reading it, I'm pleased to report I'm now clued up on what's expected.

The elf is here to keep an eye on you, and he – it is a he – will report back to Santa each night. Every day, the elf will be in a new location for you to find. And we're encouraged to give the elf a name – his temporary name is Scout.

Personally, I think we're a year too early for Elf on the Shelf. But we have your cousin Haylee to consider. She'll be all over it, and she'll likely ask you about your elf, so we might as well get some practice in for her sake.

December

At 6.45 p.m., Mummy returns home. You're currently naked and hiding behind a cushion. After 'surprising' Mummy, you return to your television programme. You're wrecked and more than ready for bed, so we need to get this elf business started.

'Oh, Arlo, what's that?' I say, feigning surprise and pointing to the shelf.

'Oh. What's that?' you say.

'I think that's an elf who's come to see you.'

I grab the storybook that came with the elf, the one with the instructions, and I begin casually flicking through the pages with some solemn, curiosity-filled facial expressions – overacting to the point where the frown lines on my head are like battlefield trenches.

'Arlo, look what Daddy's got,' Mummy says.

You're not interested. You've returned to the television.

She tries again. 'Arlo, television time is finished now. Would you like to press the button to turn it off?'

'ArrhhhhhHHHH.' You accompany your screaming with a bit of fist-pounding on the sofa.

'Do you not want to hear all about the elf?' I ask.

'AHHHHHHH.'

I guess not. 'OK then, what about if—'

Thud. That's you hurling Louie, your soft-toy BFF, on the floor.

Am I to assume that we've concluded our first Elf on the Shelf experience?

Yes. Yes, I am.

Horizons, Advent Calendars And A Mega Strop
Thursday, 2 December 2021

The top of our stairs has become a distant horizon, one that moves further away the closer I get, like a riddle from Greek mythology made real. And any progress I do make towards the unreachable line in the sky is filled with pain. Why? Because I'm second in a queue of people trying to get to the top. The person in front of me is you. And you're by no means in a hurry. The time elapsing between each step is so great that my muscles have seized up – I'm like a robot who's been left out in the rain to rust.

Please hurry the fuck up, Arlo.
'Dadda, Ooofer.'
'Yes, I know you've got your Hoover, but you trying to carry it and climb the stairs at the same time is butchering my sanity. Do you think Daddy could take charge of Hoover-carrying duties, at least until we get to the top?'

You shake your head while pointing to yourself, saying, 'Ah, ah, ah' – which is you attempting to say your own name.

Christ, kill me now – we're not even halfway up yet.
'Come on, Arlo, keep on moving.'
'OK.'
'OK? That's funny because you acknowledge that you'll continue moving, but then you stop moving altogether. And now you're vacuuming.'
'Yeah. Ooofer.'

December

I'm in a tricky situation. The only reason I've allowed you to bring good ol' Henry along for the stair ascent is to limit the chances of a tantrum. You see, I need to get a cute video of you opening your advent calendar for Nana Hoover, a calendar that happens to be hanging in the hallway upstairs. She made it for you last year. It's handcrafted and quite the sight: one metre square in size, boasting twenty-five numbered pockets and a centrepiece image of Santa flying through the sky on his sleigh. She's filled each pocket with a unique gift (I'm afraid none of them contains sugar). We couldn't open number one yesterday, because by the time you got back yesterday … well, you know how The Elf on the Shelf went.

After the lifespans of three gods elapse, we make it to the top of the stairs. Mummy begins to explain the concept of an advent calendar but quickly changes her strategy when she sees your attention move back to Henry.

'Arlo, there are presents in here.'

Bingo!

Your attention snaps back. Mummy points to the first pocket while telling you to look inside. You're engaged, you're smiling, and the camera is rolling. For your first advent gift, you pull out a dinosaur sticker. You carry out a micro-inspection, decide the sticker's not all that and shove it in my hand while returning your gaze to the next pocket.

Gift number two fares better. It's a model of a small lion. You give us your best impression of a roar. But before we can invent a narrative to begin an imaginative-play activity, you lunge for the remaining twenty-three pockets, keen to excavate more Christmas treasure.

'No, Arlo, that's all for today. We'll do another one tomorrow. Shall we play with your lion?'

Scenes. Absolute scenes.

First, you throw yourself on the floor and roll around like a football player gunning for a penalty. Then you slap your mother, which results in me taking Henry Hoover away and explaining that if you can't use kind hands, you can't play with Henry.

Your response is swift.

'AHHHHHH!'

You are a flurry of wrath and destruction – you slam two swinging arms into your nearby tool station, grabbing fistfuls of small parts and throwing them as far as angry two-year-old arms can manage.

First the elf and now the advent calendar.

I remember our first Christmas when you were a newborn. Mummy turned to me and said, 'I can't wait to build our own Christmas traditions with Arlo.'

I wonder what she's thinking now.

Christmas-Tree Assembly
Friday, 3 December 2021

It's time to erect our artificial Christmas tree. Naturally, Mummy is in charge.

'The bigger pieces go on the bottom, and then they get smaller the further up you get,' she says to me.

Arlo, is she for real? 'Oh, I see, so basically, you take all the bigger parts, and you place them on the bottom, and then you whack the smallest piece on the top.'

'Why have you started being a prick already?'

'I'm sorry, but on this occasion, it's you who's the prick.'

'Why?'

'Because I know what a fucking Christmas tree looks like – next you're telling me that shoes go on your feet.'

'I was just saying.'

'I know, but now you've said, we can proceed to the next stage of this exciting little endeavour.'

She ignores my existence and starts taking out the pieces and organising them into piles. They're colour-coded, so it's quick work.

'I think you should be in charge of unfolding all the branches, and then if you pass them to me, I'll do them again, but properly, before attaching them to the tree. Make sense?'

'Total sense.' *Total nonsense.*

'Good.'

I prohibit myself from verbally dropping any sarcastic remarks, though the same cannot be said for what's happening in the privacy of my mind. Weirdly enough, holding back on sardonic pronouncements has the surprising effect of lifting my spirits. I'm not sure why, but I suspect it's because I'm proud of myself for showing such restraint. *Evidently, fatherhood has matured me.*

The tree is finally *properly* assembled.

The lights are next. Mummy begins dangling them in a spiralling formation. Once her work is complete, she takes a step back to review her efforts. I can tell from her expression that she's not happy. And I'm confident I know why.

'We don't need more lights,' I say.

'We do ... Wait, how did you know I was thinking about lights?'

'Because we've been together for seven years.'

'Yes, but—'

'We don't need any more lights. We haven't even decorated it yet.'

'Hmmm. Well, I'll be reviewing the situation once the decorations are up.'

I can't wait. Fortunately, we've run out of time for today. Mummy is busy all afternoon, and I need to get back to work. Come to think of it, she's going out boozing tomorrow, so she'll be too hungover on Sunday, and we probably won't get round to concluding this bullshit until Monday. I guess I'll check back in with you then, Arlo.

My Dadda!
Saturday, 4 December 2021

Seeing as Mummy is out on the lash tonight, I figured we'd go away and stay at my mate Ian's house. Ian has two kids. One of them, Eddie, is only a few months older than you, and he has lots of age-appropriate toys that I'm sure he's excited to share with you. Also, by staying away, I'm afforded the bonus of not having to play Drunk Mummy.

We get to Ian's and have an enjoyable and relatively tantrum-free afternoon, though you did kick off at me on our way to the park. You held me personally accountable for the trains not appearing in your field of vision regularly enough. I'm not kidding; the pattern that you followed was thus: you'd see a train and yell 'Choo-choo!' before waving at it as it raced by. Then, you'd give me a shove while whining – toddler-speak for 'Daddy, make more trains appear'. But as far as toddler antics go, that's nothing. I only mention it here because it's amusing that you somehow expect me to be in control of the train-departure schedule.

It's now early evening, and you and Eddie are eating at the table. I'm sitting nearby. Also present are Tom and Evie. Tom is married to Ian's sister-in-law, and Evie is their ten-week-old daughter. They live nearby, and they've come over to say hello.

'Fancy a cuddle?' Tom asks me.

'Damn right I do.'

He gently places Evie in my arms, and my mind retrieves records of what you were like at ten weeks old. *How were you this small?*

You observe the scene for a split second in silence. But then ... rage ... jealousy ... and more rage.

'Dadda. Dadda. DADDA!'

You're vigorously shaking your head, using one arm to push yourself out of your high chair and the other to bang the table.

'DADDA!'

Never have I seen you react in this manner. You are furious that another small human who isn't you is occupying my attention.

'Arlo, calm down. Daddy is only having a cuddle with Evie. It's OK.'

'ARRGGGHHHHH!'

I have no choice but to hand the quiet, peaceful, sleeping baby back to Tom before she becomes none of those things, and I turn my attention to you, my green-mist-sprouting, envious, angry little man.

'What's harder, the newborn stage or the toddler stage?' asks Tom.

'Do you really need to ask?'

Washing Hands
Sunday, 5 December 2021

Do you want to hear my new least favourite dadding chore? I know the clue is in the title, but I will tell you again to underscore how little I enjoy it. My new least favourite chore is washing your hands.

It begins with a battle over the positioning of your stall, or 'step' as we call it. You like to be the one to decide its location, but you always push it tight up against the wall. We have a floating sink in our downstairs toilet, so positioning the step *underneath* it means you're not standing vertically – you're slanted at about seventy-five degrees, which, take it from me, is a less than ideal geographic location. But you skirt the risk of falling backwards by holding on to the lip of the sink using the same two hands that we need to wash.

I explain that you need to put your hands under the water, and accomplishing that objective involves bringing the step towards us a touch. You respond with grunts and non-verbal noise, which I presume is an invitation for me to go fuck myself.

Eventually, I use one foot to drag the step back so that you're no longer mimicking the Leaning Tower of Pisa. You're now ready to put your hands in the sink while I turn the taps on. The taps themselves are beyond your reach, which happens to be the only saving grace of this whole affair.

Next, we have a tug-of-war-like battle over your sleeves: me trying to roll them up, and you trying to roll them down. Eventually, I succeed, but that's probably the wrong verb to use as you have a habit of resting your forearms on the sink, and I'm apparently incapable of rolling your sleeves up far enough to prevent them from becoming soggy.

Then we have a 'conversation' about the temperature. You're surprisingly meticulous about this, refusing to contact the water for any length of time beyond a septillionth of a second unless the thermal reading is to your liking.

And then there's the water itself. You're fascinated with a little thing called 'pressure'. You might not be able to reach the taps yet, but you sure as hell can reach the spout. You lift your hand and impede the exit with a fleshy barrier – forcing the pressurised water to seek another means of escape, which it finds via the narrow gap between your hand and the spout, blasting a 360-degree horizontal curved sheet of water that makes contact with the back walls, my T-shirt, your face and your sleeves: a double kick in the nuts because it makes all prior measures I took to keep your sleeves dry redundant, even though those actions also amounted to failure.

My next move is to turn the tap off, and your next move is to scream at me.

And there you have it. My new least favourite dadding chore.

Decorating The Christmas Tree
Monday, 6 December 2021

You're in bed fast asleep and Mummy has recovered from her work Christmas do, which means we can finish decorating the tree. I expect it to be as much fun as running out of petrol in the middle of the night on a quiet country road with poor phone coverage. I've selected a Christmas playlist to summon some much-needed festive spirit into the atmosphere.

'You're in charge of putting the baubles on,' Mummy says.

'Are you sure?'

'I am.'

I sense a trap. 'OK, and what are the rules one must follow if they're the Head of Bauble Placement?'

'You just have to ensure that they're evenly distributed.'

The trap is sprung. And it is a trap, Arlo, because even if I got my tape measure, protractor and scientific calculator out and somehow computed with mathematical precision where to place every bauble, I'd still get it wrong. So, I mentally say, *Fuck it, let's just get this over with.*

I make it to my fourth or fifth bauble-hanging before Mummy steps in to *assist* by snatching one out of my hand and placing it *correctly*.

'Can I ask a question?'

'Of course.'

'This even-distribution thing you're gunning for, does that apply to the side of the tree that we'll be pushing tight up against the wall and that no one will ever see?'

'Why wouldn't it?'

'I know – so silly of me – I just wanted to double-check.'

Mummy's movements are comical to watch, and I'm having a hard time stifling giggles. She's slowly orbiting the tree like it's Planet Earth and she's the moon. Her eyes have narrowed, and there's an accompanying low-sitting frown. Every so often, she'll select a location for a bauble that's in her hand, or reposition one of the ones I've hung. I can hear her muttering to herself, 'This section needs more white ... This needs improving.'

It's funny, but now it's less funny because I can feel her burning, disapproving-of-my-choices eyes boring into the centre of my brain.

'Can you stop doing that?' I say.

'Doing what?'

'You asked me to hang these wood-slice decorations.'

'Your point being?'

'My point being that there are eight of them. I've hung six, and I've just watched you reposition four of them.'

'Well, you're not distributing them—'

'Right, fuck it. You finish the tree – I'm going to bed.'

And you know what, Arlo, that's precisely what I did. *Stupid fucking Christmas-tree decorations.*

'Fuck'

Tuesday, 7 December 2021

'Dadda!'

I respond to your call even though you should be asleep.

As far as bedtime goes these days, if you call one of us in after we say goodnight, we go in, lay you back down without saying a word and then leave. We can expect to do this about half a dozen times if it's a bad night. We *never* verbally engage, so as to limit the chance of you displaying more silliness.

But recently, you've begun to employ dynamic strategies to force more after-bed interactions with us. One of these is to ask for a soft toy, a fairly smart move on your part because a soft toy is quickly thrown into your cot in silence without us defaulting to saying the word 'no', which would breach our 'do not engage' rule.

I enter your room, lay you back down and make to leave. 'Poo-poo,' you say.

This is another tactic you've been employing. Again, smart, because we have no choice other than to get you out and change you. Sometimes you fib, but we still have to check, so you are guaranteed some level of successful interaction, fib or no fib.

A quick sniff test confirms you're not lying. Never mind. I'll change you, but we will not be conversing.

'Dadda, where's Nana See-See? Dadda, where's Mamma? Dadda, where's Nana See-See?'

It's hard, but I don't make eye contact, and I'm somehow managing to keep a straight face, though the corners of my mouth want desperately to go against gravity and rise.

'Dadda, where's Mamma? Dadda, where's Lisa? Dadda, where's Nana Ooofer?'

I fly through the nappy change and apply cream, but I struggle to put the damn lid on. Actually, let's pause for a beat so I can get something off my chest: what the fuck is up with stupid fucking nappy-rash creams and their stupid fucking screw-top lids that are fucking impossible to line up? They're so user-unfriendly. I've struggled with them since you were a newborn. Applying cream without getting it everywhere can be challenging enough, but no parent needs a quick challenge from *The Crystal Maze* thrown in on top.

Back to the present – I still can't get the lid on! I mumble the softest and lowest mumble of all time – it's actually more of a whisper: 'Fuck's sake.' It was so quiet that it was more of a thought.

And yet …

'Dadda, fuck! Fuck! Fuck! Dadda, fuck!'

I bury my face on the floor so you can't see me laughing, but you've identified some sort of social cue because now you're laughing as well.

'Fuck. Dadda, fuck.'

Eventually, I get the lid on, re-dress you and put you back to bed, all without saying a single word, but I can no longer control the muscles in my face, which are turned up into a grin. There's also some light sniggering as well. As I walk out of the room, you utter another 'fuck' for good measure.

Carers' Day
Wednesday, 8 December 2021

Yesterday, you woke up with two swollen eyes – you looked like you'd been punched. You were also in a cantankerous mood, and you didn't go to nursery. Today, your condition hasn't improved. After calling the NHS 111 number, we're advised to take you to the hospital. We all go, but, because of Covid-19, we're told that one parent will have to leave. The NHS still has a one-parent-only policy.

'Me or you?' I say to Mummy.

'You go. I'm not leaving him. I'll call work and tell them I'm not coming in.'

Here's the thing about you being ill. If Mummy stays off work, she doesn't get paid. If I stay off work, I get paid. However, Mummy refuses to leave you when you're not right, and I'm not about to interfere with her maternal impulses, because parenting toddlers is hard enough, but parenting unwell, angry and aggressive toddlers sucks balls. So, I guess the question I'm posing to myself is this: is a day of Mummy's wages worth not having to parent under unfavourable conditions?

Hell, yeah!

A Pre-Bed Snack
Thursday, 9 December 2021

'Arlo, listen to Daddy.'

'OK,' you say through a big grin.

'We don't eat the soap, do we?'

You shake your head while still grinning.

'Right, go ahead and wash your hands.'

You comply for less than a microsecond before trying to stick the bar in your mouth, managing to make tongue contact before I can confiscate it.

'Arlo! Don't eat the soap.'

'OK.' Again, you say this while smiling, which tells me you have no plans to do as you're told this evening, something that's confirmed as soon as I release my grip.

'Arlo ... Actually, knock yourself out. It won't taste very nice, but I'll let you learn that for yourself.'

You pause what you're doing and give me a look, like you're a poker player trying to read an opponent. You suspect a ruse, and you're evaluating your next move carefully. After a few beats, you again bring the soap bar towards your mouth and start licking it like an ice lolly.

'Is that yummy?'

'Hmmm, yum.'

Rebellious little fucker. I let you crack on because, at this point, all my chips are in the pot, and intervening would amount to me folding. You're still licking the soap, and you're still smiling at me while, of course, maintaining eye contact. Not once do the muscles in your face rearrange themselves in a way that tells me you find the taste of soap disgusting. And now the end of the bar has disappeared inside your mouth, and your teeth have begun shearing a piece of it off – a piece you fully intend to swallow.

Fine! You win.

I step in and retrieve the bar of soap that now possesses some deeply entrenched tooth marks. Normally you'd throw a tantrum, but you don't. You're still smiling, and I know why. Because even though you've just turned two, the scene that took place only moments ago was a battle of minds between father and son. You're confident you've won, and I'm not about to argue. Point to Arlo.

Colouring In
Friday, 10 December 2021

Another morning, another request by you for a father-and-son colouring-in session. We like to do our colouring-in on the dining room bench because it's low down enough for you to reach. I get everything ready, starting with the positioning of your plastic mat, which sits underneath the paper. The mat prevents you from performing enthusiastic wide-berth back-and-forth arm motions, moving the in-use colouring pen off the paper and on to the dining-room bench – like a set of windscreen wipers. By the way, the bench – it wasn't cheap. Next, I gather up the pens and paper. Finally, I move the armchair that's situated close to the bench further back because when I use the term 'wide-berth back-and-forth arm motions', it extends beyond the possibility of you drawing on the bench. Sometimes, you sweep your arm in a 200-degree arc, causing you to contact the back of the armchair with whatever pen you're holding. The armchair also wasn't cheap.

We're now ready to take up position and let our imaginations run wild ... sort of.

'Dadda, rrrr Ooofer.'

'Red Hoover, again! Can't Daddy draw something else for a change?'

'No. Rrrr Ooofer.'

Fine! You always insist I draw a red Hoover. The other day, I defied instruction and sketched a Christmas tree. You were outraged. I'm too scared to risk a similar reaction today, so I submit to the knowledge that I'll be drawing more red Hoovers, thus allowing the familiar steps of this little dance routine to ensue.

What dance routine would that be? Let me explain.

I'll start by drawing the Hoover outline. Then I'll move on to shading. I'll have barely begun this when you arrive unannounced over on my side of the page, with the intention of *helping*. Ninety per cent of the time, my personality loves this – *really loves this* – because we're bonding. But there's an 8 per cent part of me that wishes you'd at least use the same colour. After all, if you order me to draw a red Hoover and then sabotage it with a blue pen, you're setting me up to fail big time.

And then we come to the barely-worth-shouting-about 2 per cent. You can't yet colour in the lines, and, as monstrously unforgivable as this is, it's a little bit annoying – 2 per cent annoying, in fact. I know; I'm a terrible human, but here we are.

This wouldn't be a problem if you allowed me to draw something else for a change, but you insist on constraining my creativity with a set of shackles, so I've decided to unleash my 2 per cent piece of resentment on you.

Also, can you please replace the lid once you've finished with a pen?

999 Call
Saturday, 11 December 2021

I've had to call the police because some thieving twat has just jacked our neighbour Andreas' car. The story is terrifying. Andreas loaded it up and returned to the house to collect his daughter. She's a little younger than you. He left the keys in the ignition; his back was turned for a handful of seconds at most. But in that short time, an opportunist walked by, saw the car and decided to steal it.

Andreas saw the thief, and gave chase, predicting that he would drive down our curving road before turning left at the junction and heading back up in our direction. If he turned right, he'd find his way on to a busy street that's always congested – and where it's easier to attract attention.

Andreas predicted correctly. He headed the thief off on the next road for a stand-off. I can only assume that adrenalin was driving what was such a poor decision because there is no way that a man-versus-car match-up will see the man come out on top. Apparently – and I learnt this after the incident – Andreas threw himself into the side of the car and tried to smash the window. Unfortunately, the only thing he achieved was glancing contact with the speeding car – *his* car – and he was knocked to the ground while the thief got away. Luckily, Andreas wasn't seriously injured.

There are a couple of things that I can't shake. If Andreas had first put his daughter in the car, would the thief have still done what he did? Second, I only knew to dial 999 because Mummy was leaving the house at the same time with you, and she saw part of what happened. She'd done the same thing as Andreas: she loaded up the car then came to get you from inside our house. The car was parked right outside (Andreas' car was across the street), and the keys weren't in the ignition, but play that scenario out a thousand times, and I can't help but ask if we would always have been so lucky.

Because Andreas left the keys in the ignition, his insurance will likely be invalid. What a shitty thing to be dealing with at the best of times, let alone this close to Christmas.

As for the scumbag thief, I hope something horrible befalls him. Bastard.

'NEE-NEE, Dadda!'
Tuesday, 14 December 2021

It's 6.30 a.m., and we've already had our first disagreement of the day. When I put the television on, I asked you what you wanted to watch. You said 'nee-nee', which is your way of referring to any emergency vehicle that has a siren. But I didn't know what show you meant by 'nee-nee', because that's a pretty broad reference. And despite me making some fine logic-based guesses, you started getting pissed off at my continued incompetence, yelling 'NEE-NEE, DADDA!'

As it turns out, you meant *Fireman Sam.*

Now, anyone reading this would probably raise their eyebrows at how I didn't figure out the obvious connection. But hear me out.

First, one of your favourite *Bing* episodes is about a fire engine. Your favourite show at the moment is *Cocomelon*, which is a show composed entirely of toddler-friendly music videos of nursery rhymes. There are a lot of episodes, and many of them contain emergency response vehicles. Plus, it's difficult to keep up with your favourites, as they change daily. My final point is that you've only watched *Fireman Sam* about three times in your life.

So, no! When you get pissed off with me for not immediately understanding what you happened to mean this particular morning when you demanded 'nee-nee', you can do one. Stupid *Fireman Sam*.

Oh, and get this: when I had figured it out, we got through less than thirty seconds of an episode before you demanded *Cocomelon*.

In other news, Mummy feels like shit; she's holed up in bed and has had to take a Covid-19 PCR test.

Not Again!
Wednesday, 15 December 2021

A couple of weeks ago, scientists identified a new Covid-19 variant. It's called Omicron, and its discovery immediately caused the planet to return to panic stations. Omicron features a long list of mutations – more than previous strains – and it's unclear how effective the vaccine is against it. But I think I have a rough idea because – guess what? Mummy has Covid-19. Again! I assume it's this new variant.

According to the government, today heralds a new highest number of cases for the UK. The total is just shy of eighty thousand. I guess Mummy is one of them. Hopefully, you and I won't join the statistic, though I don't see how we can avoid it. I've taken as many precautions as possible, but it's not pessimistic to say that Santa might be bringing us Covid-19 for Christmas. As a matter of fact, I woke up this morning feeling a little under the weather myself, but

I quickly came to after having a coffee and when you stopped shouting in my face for a cracker.

I've consigned Mummy to our bedroom. She is only to leave when she wants to use the bathroom. I've also performed a full top-to-bottom sweep of the house, attacking the place with Dettol, paying particular attention to door handles, light switches and anything else that we touch regularly, meaning I had to spend a whole five minutes with your Henry Hoover toy. No need to get jealous. I then added another layer to my already comprehensive Dettol fumigation programme, this time with spray. I've shrouded each room in mist. The house now looks like I've left a bunch of dry-ice machines plugged in.

The scientific community has advised that a third vaccination – a booster jab – *could* help combat Omicron, although, as I said, it's a new variant, and scientists need more time to study it and assess whether the vaccination programme remains effective. I don't sit in the anti-vaccination camp; I've already had my shots and I'm happy to have my booster jab. Except I can't, because the NHS website keeps crashing on me. This is a widespread issue in the UK.

Mummy is beyond gutted about her present situation. We're due to have our annual photo with Santa at our favourite soft-play park tomorrow. She was buzzing. But now she can't go. I know it's just a photo and the priority is our health, but part of Mummy's DNA includes biological protocols that put her love for Christmas above anything else, aside from you perhaps. Definitely above me.

However, I have a plan.

It will sound like a shit plan, but in years to come, I think we'll all be grateful for my shit plan. Basically, I'll test myself and you in the morning, and if we're clear, then we will go and see Santa, but we'll bring the iPad with us. Come picture time, I'll pull up a still photo of Mummy and hold it up so that we get our family portrait. The more I think about it, the more I think it's less of a shit plan and more of a mighty awesome one. I have no reason to believe it won't be anything other than a resounding success.

Santa's A Misogynist
Thursday, 16 December 2021

Mummy remains out of action, though she feels much better. You and I are still showing no signs of being ill. We've each taken a test, and they're negative, so we're off to see Santa with Auntie Lisa and Haylee.

We park up, sign in and wend our way to the upstairs of the soft-play adventure park, until we come to the entrance to Santa's grotto. However, Santa is busy, so we're told to go and play for half an hour and come back later. We're given cards that show the various activities that we can partake in; each one requires a stamp. We'll need these cards to gain entry to Santa's grotto on our return.

The first thing we do is paint a Christmas decoration. Last year, you chose (or Mummy chose; I forget) a reindeer. This year, I suggest a star, but you opt for a Christmas pudding. Once you have unleashed your artistic talents upon the white-clay canvas, we go and play.

At our postponed time, we head back to Santa's grotto. Lisa has to take Haylee to the toilet, so you and I go in alone. No one asks to see my card to stamp it.

The owners at this place go all out every year to set-dress the grotto in an impressive manner. I'm taking in the views when an elf maiden (I'm sure she's the owner) approaches and invites us to go and see Santa.

Enter chaos and a lot of stress.

The first stress-inducing variable is my plan to involve Mummy as much as possible. This starts with me video-calling her; I'm trying to direct the camera so she can see you, and I'm also trying to get something out of the experience for myself, watching your eyes take it all in.

You take one look at Santa and then dash off to the side to explore a pile of fake presents. I say goodbye to Mummy and put the phone on the floor because I'm trying to pull an iPad out of your changing bag while exchanging pleasantries with Santa and the photographer, and begging you not to destroy the fake presents that are only there for appearance's sake.

'Hoover.'

'No, there's no Hoover in there, but come and talk to Santa and tell him all about your obsession with Hoovers.'

'Yeah, tell Santa, Arlo,' says Mummy, who's still with us despite me supposedly hanging up on her, which I clearly didn't do. And now Auntie Lisa's calling me, while I'm still struggling with the iPad.

December

You're now standing on a bench. Lisa has hung up and immediately rung back. I've finally wrestled the iPad from its location and made it to the bench alongside you to try and coax you into sitting next to me so we can have that nice family photo. Santa is sitting two metres behind because he still needs to socially distance.

'Are you ready for your photo?' says the photographer.

'Just about. Can you try and get the iPad in? My partner is ill and couldn't make it today, and she's gutted.'

'That doesn't sound good,' Santa says.

'I've got Covid, Santa,' shouts Mummy.

'Well, I hope you recover quickly, otherwise who's going to cook the Christmas dinner?'

It's at this point that several things happen: the photographer begins snapping photos; Auntie Lisa tries to call for what is the third or fourth time with me having no choice but to ignore her – again; and finally, I come to the tragic realisation that Santa is a misogynist.

The photographer finishes, and I turn and thank Santa, noticing that he's a different Santa from the one here in the previous two years. I'm momentarily saddened because the previous Santa was about 106 years old, and I'm wondering if he's even alive.

We leave the grotto, and I call Lisa back. She couldn't get in, because I had the cards, but they still haven't been checking, so now she's made it in and it's fine.

The last sixty seconds have been incredibly stressful for me, Arlo, and my mood doesn't improve when we go to view the photos. Most are out of focus, and the iPad was way too bright, so the camera flash overexposed the screen, and you can barely make Mummy out. Why the photographer didn't tell me to lower the brightness, I'll never know.

Let's end by recapping our annual Christmas photos, shall we? 2019: no Covid, and you were a newborn. We have a perfect family photo of you having a cuddle with Santa. 2020: Covid meant us having to socially distance, and your lack of company beyond me and Mummy meant you freaked out big time in the grotto; the best shot is of you in complete and utter distress while Mummy and I are smiling like sadists. 2021: you and I in shot, smiling but slightly out of focus, with me holding up an iPad showing an image less like a photo of Mummy and more like the supernova of a dying star. I wonder what next year will bring.

Place Your Bets
Friday, 17 December 2021

I feel awful, but Mummy feels better, so she's tagged me out. I spent the morning in bed, and then I drove up to take an on-site PCR test. I didn't bother taking you, because if Mummy and I have Covid-19 and you're displaying symptoms, then we'll go out on a limb and assume you have it too.

Surprising No One
Saturday, 18 December 2021

I woke up to a message from the NHS saying I've also got Covid-19 for the second time.

Here are some of my isolation highlights from today:

1. You putting a paint-covered hand into your mouth and telling me it tasted 'dirty';
2. You trying to stick both your fingers and the end of a phone charger into a plug socket;
3. You sticking the wrong end of the snot-sucker in your mouth;
4. You eating a modest amount of Savlon cream.

I'm so glad we've postponed the Elf on the Shelf for another year.

December Monthly Review
Sunday, 19 December 2021

You have become fiercely independent. Any attempt to help you accomplish anything is often met with ferocious and strong-willed resistance. This can be observed every night when, as part of your bedtime routine, we put your Henry Hoover toy away at the top of the basement stairs. Trouble is, there is hardly any floor space, and you have difficulty stacking Henry and his accessories in a way that enables me to close the door. If I shift the extension rods (which are connected to the hose) even a millimetre, you first Hulk-rage, and then drag Henry back out again to restart the excruciating process from the top. I've used one example, but you're like that with almost everything.

Tantrums appear without warning and are often triggered by the unknown. And oh boy, are they dramatic. You dance around whatever room you're in with both arms held up before dropping your body to the floor and thrashing out your legs. But as quick as they come, they vanish, usually on the heels of a question that's asked as a means of distracting you.

You might recall that, in the run-up to your second birthday, your speech development slowed. Well, it's like someone flicked a switch on your birthday because we've noticed a huge improvement – to the point where I can no longer keep track of new words[3]. You're confident to give almost any word, and some phrases, a go. My favourites include 'torture', a word Nana See-See uses to describe you; 'crack', your preferred word to describe a trump; and 'Oh, Christ', which Mummy often says to you in an Irish accent when you have a wobble or stumble. You find the phrase amusing. What's strange, though, is that you refuse to say both your own name and Louie's (your soft-toy BFF).

There is a lot more faffing around on your part before bedtime. It was becoming a stressful part of my day (again), but we've solved that problem by taking you up to bed a lot earlier. You still go down at the same time, usually around 6.45 p.m., but going upstairs early at 6.15 p.m. allows you time to clean your teeth, act up, sit on the toilet, act up again, sit through three bedtime stories with a lot of interruptions and negotiate how many soft-toy companions you're allowed to take into bed with you, companions that are then removed as soon as you fall asleep.

You wanting to sit on the toilet happens several times a day. You've still yet to drop another number two, but you can squeeze out a wee no problem. As I mentioned before, we're in no rush to officially declare we're starting potty-training but we will of course

---

[3] A word of caution: Arlo's speech becomes very advanced during the course of this book, so I remind you of one of the golden rules of parenthood: don't compare your children with others! It's a depressing road to walk down, and there's no need. All children develop at their own pace. What makes our species beautiful is that we are all unique.

encourage and support your choice to sit on the toilet whenever you want. Often, you only want to sit on the toilet so I can flush it, something you like to watch.

Imagination is another area where we've seen changes, especially during story time. When we read *The Very Hungry Caterpillar*, we have to allow time for you to pretend to eat all the foods, along with feeding me and Mummy whatever we request. You have another book, one about farm animals. You insist we flip between the page showing the cow and the pages featuring all the other animals. This is because you pretend first to milk the cow and then to feed the other animals in the book. Watching this brings a lot of joy.

At the end of *Toddler Inc.*, I explained how you'd taken to favouring me over Mummy. While this is still broadly true, it's only the mornings when you really kick off at her, especially if she's the one to get you from your cot. But we avoid the issue with the unspoken agreement that, at present, I'm the one who will collect you, because no one wants a battle at 6.20 a.m. each morning. I can sort of relate to how Mummy feels. When Nana Hoover comes over, my rank is immediately reduced. The position of 'favourite' goes to Nana, remaining in place until she leaves.

Us all having Covid-19 again is not fun. Mummy is out of isolation on Wednesday, and our period ends on Christmas Day, which, when you think about it, is lucky really. We've got my nan and grandad coming up to stay (GG and GG Hazel). We were set to spend some time with them before Christmas, as well as during and after it, but we've had to adapt our plans slightly.

While being stuck in isolation is tough going, it's easier than it was the last time we all had the virus because you are a very entertaining and funny individual.

Our third year of parenting adventures is now well and truly under way!

Adventures In Isolation
Tuesday, 21 December 2021

First, as per the prerequisites of a successful bath-time operation, you piss in the bath. Then, continuing to follow said prerequisites, I tell you not to drink the bathwater, even though you've begun chugging it down with the aid of your electric-pink silicon jug. After that's over and done with, you fill the jug back up and offer it to Mummy, with possibly the biggest grin I've seen you pull yet.

'No, Mummy does not want to drink your weed-in bathwater.'

'Dadda?' you say, now offering me the jug.

'I'm good thanks, buddy.'

Next, you use an old make-up brush of Mummy's to 'paint' my face with your recently consumed beverage of weed-in bathwater.

Finally, to cap off another successful and fuzzy-feeling-inducing bath-time operation, you splash me in the face a dozen or so times, blaming the whole thing on Master Yoda. Master Yoda appears on your wellies and nowhere else. You don't possess any other sort of Yoda toy, so how you think you can allocate any blame to him and get away with it is beyond me. At least when you blame your soft toys, there's something to point at.

It would seem I've asked Santa for all the fun this year, and evidently, I've been a very good boy! By the way, you appear fully recovered.

More Adventures In Isolation
Wednesday, 22 December 2021

First, let's take a moment:

A Dad's Prayer

I am a father, who has been beaten,
soul hollowed by my toddler,
thy enthusiasm gone;
my fill of fun well and truly done,
on Earth as it is in Heaven.
Give me a day, a day to stay in bed,
and forgive all the tears that fall from my face,
as I forgive Arlo for his excruciating presence.
Lead me not in his direction, but deliver me far
away from him, as far away as possible. Like, really
far away, God – basically, pick a distance, then
double it eight times.

Amen.

I kid you not, Arlo, about ten minutes after I prayed, Auntie Lisa sent a message to Mummy, telling her that Boris and his pals down at Westminster have changed the isolation rules from ten days to seven days. Which means you and I can leave today. As long as we each take two separate Covid-19 lateral flow tests and they're all negative, freedom for us both has arrived early.

This really is bloody good news. For one, I'm also feeling better, and I want to leave the house. I've got cabin fever, and I've been weighing up the pros and cons of deep-throating a cheese grater. For another, GG and GG Hazel (your great-grandparents) are on their way up, and I didn't think we'd be able to see them until Christmas Day.

All of us, including Mummy, have done two tests each, and we're all negative. Please, Covid-19, you've really outstayed your welcome now. Piss off!

Kitchen Assembly
Thursday, 23 December 2021

We're at Nana See-See's house for Haylee's third-birthday party. Nana Hoover, GG and GG Hazel have come with us. You are insisting that everyone dance the hokey-cokey, dragging all of your grandparents and great-grandparents up to participate. Mummy and I stand watching, sandwiched between those that came before us and the young man that came after. I'm reminded of just how many people you have that are besotted by you. You are wonderfully fortunate. Try and remember that, if you can.

After the party, we drive the oldies back (they're staying at Nana Hoover's), and then back to our house so I can put you to bed. I've left Mummy behind because there wasn't enough room in the car, and she wanted to stay and help clean up anyway. She promises that she won't be long and says that she wants to build your Christmas present with me.

After I get you down for bed, I pour myself a glass of wine and watch something on Netflix while I wait for Mummy, who has yet to materialise, despite several messages telling me she 'won't be long', which we all know is a Latin phrase meaning 'I'm having a *few* drinks'.

Fuck it, looks like I'm building this thing – it's a kitchen – by myself. *Right, let's see what we have here – whoa! That's a lot of pieces.* Arlo, assembly will take a great deal of concentration. It has a dozen different types of screws. Everything is coded, but a lot of the screws are similar-looking – hence the need for concentration. Fortunately, I'm alone, which means …

I gently step into a zone of immersion and intense focus, becoming one with the task at hand. I am centred. Grounded. Ready to create.

Let's begin.

Three A4 screws ... Aha, here they are. So, I use those to attach part H to part G, and then I can add—

'Babyyyyyy?'

Fuck! Red alert. It's the Matriarch, Arlo. And I'd bet a considerable portion of my inconsiderable wealth that she is not wholly compos mentis.

'Baby?' she says again, appearing in the doorway. 'Oh, there you are. You've already started. Would you like me to help you?'

'I think I'm actually good. I'm almost done. Why don't you—'

'I'll go and get my PJs on and come and give you a hand.'

Please don't.

'One mooooment.'

Christ. Mummy changes and arrives back on the scene, lumbering across my temporary workspace like a drugged-up giraffe stumbling around a hobbit's bathroom, kicking three of the kitchen pieces away from the very specific and neatly arranged spot where I had placed them. Then she snatches the instructions from me and begins taking over as foreman of the operation.

'Well, that's not even a letter in the English alphabet, so that's a little bit stupid, isn't it?'

'Why don't you turn them the right way up?'

'Oh yeah. Ha ha, silly Mamma.'

'Look, I know you want to help, but you were supposed to be back ages ago, and instead you elected to get drunk, which I have no problem with, but I do have a problem with you supposedly helping me.'

Bringing her voice to barely a whisper, she says, 'I will be so, so quiet, and so, so still and be the bestest helper ever. Test me right now, which piece do you need me to hand to you?'

'That one,' I say while pointing and trying not to laugh so as not to encourage her.

CRACK.

'Oopsie, I dropped it. But it's just a little oopsie. Here you go,' she says, picking the piece back up and handing it to me. 'I'll do the drill—'

'NO! I mean, no. I'll be handling the drill.'

'Oh, OK. Are you sure? I can do it.'

'No, baby. Do you want me tell you what you're in charge of?'

'I would very much like that. What can I do to help you?'

'You're to sit very still, hand me only the pieces that I repeatedly point to and not get in my way, because this is quite a complicated bit of kit to put together, and I need to concentrate.'

'You got it. You won't even know I'm here.'

'Thank you.' I turn my attention back to the instruction manual. *Right, where was I? Ah, yeah. A4 screws, and then I need part—*

'I-see-what-we-need-to-do.' She snatches the instructions again, hands me a piece we don't need and continues barking orders. 'We need to put this piece here,' she says, stabbing at where she thinks our attention needs to be. 'Can you see? Can you see it, baby?'

'That's not quite right.'

'Yes it is. How is it not?'

'Because you're reading step one of the instructions while holding the piece for step twelve. Also, I've already completed the first six steps, so that's probably how I'm able to say you've got it wrong.'

'Oh … Well, why don't … erm, hang on … hang on just a minute … one more sec … I'VE GOT IT, BABY!'

'Brilliant – hang on, have you just dropped one?'

'I may have done a tiny little crack.'

Christmas Eve
Friday, 24 December 2021

I need a carrot. *Gotta be one in the fridge.* (Insert image of man opening fridge.) *Huh, no carrot? What about the tall cupboard?* (Insert image of man opening tall cupboard.) *Where has she put the bloody carrots?* Aha! It's got to be the pan drawer, Arlo, right? (Insert image of man opening pan drawer.) Wrong – it's empty.

Ring, ring.

'Perfect timing. I'm having trouble locating a carrot,' I say to Mummy.

'Oh, I didn't get any this year. I didn't think we needed them.'

'Didn't need them? What on earth are poor Rudolph and Co. supposed to do for nutritional replenishment?'

'Oh, don't worry, I've told Arlo we'll give Rudolph an apple.'

'Well, you can go ahead and tell Arlo that you were mistaken and that I'm off to Mum's to find a carrot.'

'OK, baby, we'll meet you there.'

Why is a carrot important? I can't explain why, it just is. Maybe it's because I've observed the leave-stuff-out-for-Santa-and-Rudolph tradition for the last two years, even though in the first year you were a newborn. In both years, a carrot has been on the menu, and I guess I've grown attached to having control of what I leave out for Santa at least until you're old enough to use your own voice and not have the Matriarch manipulate you with her hogwash about apples – an apple isn't even part of the same food group as a carrot.

And it's not just any carrot I want; I want the best-looking carrot money can buy. This carrot needs to be a thing of beauty to make up for the abhorrent abomination that was last year's monstrosity. I don't want this carrot to have any kinks, crevices, twists or knots. No, I've got my heart set on a carrot that has the appearance of an orange icicle.

An hour later, I get to Nana Hoover's house to find you, Mummy, Nana, GG and GG Hazel.

'Mother, I need a carrot.'

'I don't have any, but apparently you're going to use an apple ... though I can see from your face that's not at all what you intended.'

'It's not. I need a carrot, and we need to put an end to this horrible rumour about apples.'

'Well, I don't have one. I'm sorry.'

Fucking useless! I'm going to have to go—

Ring, ring.

'Hi, Mamma Bear,' says Mummy.

Yes! Nana See-See will definitely have a carrot, especially as her name used to be Granny Feeder. I begin hopping up and down, drawing attention to myself from the other side of the room.

'We'll be over in ... hang on a sec, Mum.' She turns to me. 'What is it?'

'Ask your mum if she has a carrot I can have.'

'Mum, do you have a carrot? ... Yes, you can have a carrot.'

And Bingo was his name-o. Excellent.

Another hour later and Nana See-See has hand-selected three carrots for me to choose from. None of them quite fits the dream I had of a shiny orange icicle, but there's certainly one handsome carrot among the lot of them, and that's the one I pick.

Finally, we get home and prepare our offerings. This is very special. It's like I said: I've been doing this for the past two years, but it's been me on my own. This year, you're old enough to get involved. You help with all the arrangements, choosing ice cubes for Santa's Baileys that isn't Baileys – it's the cheaper alternative that you get in Aldi for half the price. Sorry, Santa. Then you carry the plate of mince pies and the lone handsome carrot over to the table next to the chimney. Even the plate itself is special because it's a *Thomas the Tank Engine* plate I had when I was a child that GG and GG Hazel sent up earlier in the year. This is a bloody good dadding moment.

Not long after, we take you up to bed.

'Arlo, do you know who will be coming to visit us tonight?' I say.

'Santa.'

'That's right.'

Like I said, bloody good dadding.

Once you go to sleep, we get all the presents out and place them around the tree. Unlike the whole carrot-and-cheap-Baileys-alternative thing, this *is* the first time we've been able to do this because, historically, we've always been at Nana and Grandad See-See's house for presents. I feel like this year really marks the start of our own Christmas traditions.

You know what? Fuck it. There's enough room on the plate for an apple after all.

Christmas Day
Saturday, 25 December 2021

I begin my Christmas morning with a telling-off from you because I am the only member of our household who isn't wearing matching pyjamas. Once the situation has been rectified, we head downstairs with Mummy, who's full of excitement and anticipation. However, both of those emotions are partially diluted as you take one look under the Christmas tree and ask for your Henry Hoover toy. But then you change your mind. Instead, you go and inspect the offering we made to Santa.

The *four* mince pies are gone as well as the knock-off Baileys, which may or may not have been refilled.

The handsome carrot is less handsome owing to a third of it having been bitten off, and the remaining half of the apple is even less handsome than the two thirds of the once-handsome carrot.

The next thing you do – which reveals so much about who you are now – is to grab the nearest present and give it to me. Then you try and give the next one to Mummy.

Last year, opening presents was a chaotic and frenzied affair, because there were too many people, and it was difficult to keep track of what was going on. Focusing on you was all but impossible because of how much noisy activity surrounded us.

This year, it's the opposite. The environment is calm, lightly populated and without distractions. You've now well and truly mastered unwrapping, and so it's honestly as perfect as it gets for me. I mentioned yesterday that, this year, it feels like we can begin building our Christmas traditions, and I think we've found the winning formula, at least as far as mornings are concerned.

You got a kitchen set, kitchen accessories, a den-building kit and a small wooden gym set that came with weights. You were not even remotely fussed about the weights, though you did swipe the protein-shaker bottle and add it to your kitchen.

Nana See-See video-calls. You can tell this morning has been tough on her. 'This is the first Christmas in thirty-nine years that I've not had to put presents under the tree in the morning, or seen you and Lisa, apart from when you were travelling.'

'I know, Mum, but we'll be over later,' Mummy says.

Thirty-nine years? That's a long time, Arlo. I feel bad for Nana See-See as it was my suggestion to have Christmas morning at our house, just the three of us. But I don't feel guilty. I understand that this is one of those bittersweet moments, and I guess that, one day, you too will call us up and explain that you won't be coming home for Christmas for whatever reason. These are real birds-leaving-the-nest moments, even if your birds have grown up and got families of their own.

At 10 a.m. we have visitors. GG, GG Hazel and Nana Hoover are here for breakfast and more presents. You continue to remain in a happy, playful and buoyant mood and the morning proceeds without a single tantrum.

After naptime, we drive to Nana See-See's house for dinner – which is ten-out-of-ten-fill-your-pants-up-with-a-lot-of-excitement good. Then we have more presents.

You really have to hand it to Nana See-See. Not only has she had to adjust to a new Christmas Day format, but she's also done something else that she's never done before, which is practise restraint on the number of gifts she got you and Haylee. She's only got you a few presents each, which is a massive deal for someone of her generous personality and tendency to switch her ears off when she's told she always buys too much. Your main toy is a wooden fire station that takes me an age to assemble.

I loved Christmas as a kid, but as I grew up, I stopped enjoying it. Then I met your mother, and through her, I began enjoying it again. This year, I've travelled back to my childhood because I now *love* Christmas again. You have been such bloody good fun. Your tantrum-free clean sheet continues all day. I think you might kick off when Mummy announces to you that she will not be driving all the way home just to get your Hoover, but you react indifferently. You also go down to bed with zero complaints or post-lights-out shenanigans.

Merry Christmas, buddy; this really is just the beginning.

Boxing Day: Lessons Learnt
Sunday, 26 December 2021

We've spent the day at home playing with your new toys. Nana Hoover, GG and GG Hazel have been here all day and we also had Auntie Lisa, Haylee, Nana and Grandad See-See swing buy for a couple of hours. Much like yesterday, it's been bloody perfect.

There's a lot to take away from this Christmas, all of it positive. The Christmas Day format is something I foresee we'll maintain for the next few years: the three of us in the morning, then my side of the family over for brunch, and over to Mummy's side for the afternoon. That way, we spend quality time with everyone without it being too loud and chaotic.

Building your presents before Christmas Day was a smart recommendation by Mummy, and we'll continue to mirror that approach for future festive seasons. As soon as you realised you had a kitchen, you fully immersed yourself in it for at least an hour, which is a huge block of time for a two-year-old on any day, let alone on Christmas Day.

We didn't rush presents. If you wanted to play with the thing you opened, we let you. Then, once you were bored, we asked you if you wanted to open something else. Sometimes you did, and other times you wanted to play with another toy. All of this was fine, and it helped keep the tempo down and prevent you from getting overwhelmed.

Back to family: one of the reasons I wanted to be at home this year was so that Nana Hoover could get time with you. I stopped loving Christmas as an older child and started hating it because of – and this is in no way her fault – Nana Hoover. Past experiences hadn't really given her any cause to get excited over Christmas, and, over the years, that rubbed off on me. It's why I never spent much time with her during the holidays. She always opted to work. I believe that she felt she was doing everyone else a favour by taking herself out of the equation of how we split our time, and not expecting me to travel back down to Kent when I could spend the time with people who enjoy Christmas. And while she's never once been asked to make that sort of compromise, it's nice that she feels like she doesn't have to any more. This is mostly down to you. She's moved up to Northampton to spend more time with her family, and you're here. Naturally, she wants to hang out with her only grandchild on Christmas Day.

It's the same with GG and GG Hazel. It's been decades since I last spent Christmas with them. It's possible they would have come up if you weren't around, but your presence well and truly sealed their fate because they have loved hanging out with you. It was very special seeing my grandad interact with you. You found it most amusing when he blew his nose, and you would say 'Ohhh, GG!' every time he pretended to do something silly. That's something I'll remember forever.

Ageing
Monday, 27 December 2021

In *Dear Arlo* I spoke about GG, and how it was comforting to see him reach the age he's at now, seventy-nine, still being physically capable and having a sharp mind. During Christmas I had a chance to speak to him about ageing.

'The thing I've discovered about ageing is that if you focus on what you can no longer do, then you set yourself up for a pretty miserable existence because the older you get the less you can do, of course. And that never changes. But if you see your limitations as a chance for you to review what you can do and focus on that, then growing old becomes a lot more tolerable.'

It was reassuring to hear him say that, as it's an attitude I've subscribed to as well – though I'm in my mid-thirties and haven't been too hampered by any physical limitations. I think to myself that it's all very well taking that position now, but could I maintain that positive mindset when I'm having to have a catheter bag changed every other day? Not that GG has one, but you take my point. GG's attitude suggests I can; it's certainly one to aspire to.

It also reinforces the belief that I am in no way premature in designing my exercise regime to ensure I'm as physically capable as possible in my twilight years. One of the highlights from the last few days was you asking GG to sit on the floor and play with your trains with you. It took him some effort to get on and off the floor. But you know what? He bloody did it, and I have the image cemented in my mind. Of course, you'll never remember it, but take it from me – it was a special moment.

Just a couple more points about ageing, and then I'll let you get back to trashing the house. Point one: Nana See-See, I've always thought, is in remarkable physical shape. She's always on her hands and knees playing with you and Haylee. How is she able to do that? Simple: she's consistently been line dancing several times a week since her twenties. It's been a constant for the majority of her life, and her physical conditioning reflects that. So the lesson here is that you should try and maintain a healthy lifestyle. Never stop exercising.

My final point concerns appearance. Every year, I look in the mirror and I notice new grey hairs and more lines in my face. If I look at a picture from a few years ago, it's clear I was better-looking than I am now. But of course, in two or three years' time, I'll look at a picture from today and think the same thing. Like GG's point about accepting physical limitations, gradually declining looks are another thing you must learn to accept. The alternative is to spend your later years wishing you looked the way you did in your twenties – basically, a sure-fire way to live a miserable existence. So now I embrace every grey hair and every line on my face.

You might think it's premature for me to be giving you advice on ageing given that you've just turned two, but you'll catch up in no time at all. When you do, hopefully the combined wisdom from your father and your great-grandfather will help you accept those things you have no control over so that you can enjoy all physical aspects of your entire life, not just your prime years.

Now, I believe there was some talk about trashing the house.

New Year's Eve
Friday, 31 December 2021

'Top-up?' asks Sean, holding a bottle of red wine.

'Go on then.'

We're at our friends Sean and Rebecca's house with a few others to see the new year in. You and the rest of the children are all asleep. You went down with hardly any fuss – you've all behaved beautifully.

In your little-over two years of life, Mummy and I have never got drunk at the same time. But we've had such a wonderful Christmas, and we have no plans tomorrow, so neither of us bothered to ask the other who was getting up with you in the morning. We just sort of rolled with it, hence my acceptance of a top-up, which I believe is my fourth glass. I probably shouldn't have another, especially as I had a few beers as well, but if I probably shouldn't have glass number four, then I certainly shouldn't have glass number five, and if I certainly shouldn't have glass number five, then glass number six is a very silly idea indeed but not as silly as glass number seven or the glass of port but ... *Hang on, why are Sean and Mummy having a race on the kids' police bikes?*

Never mind; where was I? Ah, yes. And if the glass of poorrrrt wsa a slly ten wte untl you ere whatttt ... zzzzzzz.

January

Felicity Faffatron
noun

Someone who faffs for more than an appropriate amount of faffing time, especially when trying to leave the house with their toddler and partner.

The Parenthood Dictionary
Adventures in Dadding Edition

New Year's Day
Saturday, 1 January 2022

I have woken up in the House of Hades. No, it's worse than that. The place I'm in makes hell seem like an all-expenses-paid trip to the Maldives. My head is the recipient of drum-beating that never ceases and nails-on-chalkboard scraping. My throat feels like it's lined with sand from Mars; it's parched and cracked – scorched from the toxic fumes of my red-wine breath.

I feel sick.

So sick.

Other-worldly spirits who get their kicks from the suffering of mortals have hurled every single one of my brain cells onto torture racks and begun pulling on levers and cranking gears – maximising my pain and suffering.

God damn you, red wine! You ruthless bastard. Thou hast defeated me; I am thy vanquished enemy.

I want to cry real tears.

When will this end?

Oh God, I'm a parent; I have to do dadding today. How is that possible? The thought prompts a shudder that sends the final vestiges of last night's port vapour up my windpipe far enough to engage my taste buds. *I think I'm going to be sick.*

We're staying in Sean and Auntie Rebecca's spare room. You're asleep in a travel cot, but you're stirring. *Please stay asleep. Please stay asleep. I'm begging you – please stay asleep.*

Your eyelids snap open. 'Dadda.'

Damn! 'Morning, buddy, shall we go downstairs?'

'Yeah.'

I leave Mummy sleeping and get you out, and we begin our slow, and in my case agonising, descent down the stairs. I beg the universe to grant me one small mercy and spare Mummy this horrible, hellish hangover so she can take over parenting as soon as she wakes.

She appears ten minutes later. 'Oh dear, Arlo, Daddy doesn't look like he's living his best life, does he?' Mummy says.

Thank Christ, she's up. 'How do you feel?' I ask, crossing my fingers and toes even though it hurts to do so.

'I'm actually all right.'

'Really? Thank fu— I mean, that's good to know.'

'Wait, where are you going?'

'To go and be sick.'

As it's the new year, I was planning to share with you some insights about things I do or think about that I wish I had begun earlier in life. But sharing wisdom is the last thing on my mind, especially as I'm sitting on the floor cuddling the toilet and throwing up all of last night's bad decisions.

Happy New Year, son.

New Year's Resolutions
Sunday, 2 January 2022

I was never one for New Year's resolutions. I could never get behind the narrative. You shouldn't need to wait until the new year to make changes to your life. To me, it seems that most people commit to a New Year's resolution because society demands it. And to resist the mandates of society is to single yourself out as an oddball. So, we fall in line and imitate what everyone else is doing. Because it's the done thing. Because how can we not?

That upsets me.

I wonder how many people have vowed to learn a new language this year. And out of all those people, how many have a reason for doing so outside of saying, 'It's kinda cool, and I need something to commit to, so why not a new language?' Real change comes from within, not from blindly following social trends and out-of-date plot beats.

However, I've rethought my position – sort of. I *do* believe in fresh starts and resets. And the new year *is* a great time to reset. But so is a new month, a new week or a new day. To implement a goal or resolution effectively – at any time of the year – you have to do two things.

First, you need to select things you *want* to work on. If you don't, the change you seek to make will fail. Going back to languages, let's say you plan to backpack around South America for six months. In that scenario, maybe learning Spanish or Portuguese is precisely the goal you want to set yourself. But spend time figuring out what you want and why you want it. Then get to work.

Second, you have to set yourself up for success. If you want to lose weight, you shouldn't pay to join a gym that takes you twenty minutes to drive to, where parking is a nightmare and the equipment is always in use. Instead, leave your kit out the night before, and exercise at home first thing in the morning. Understand that while willpower and discipline are powerful allies, they fatigue quickly and are not dependable for long-term solutions. But if you create an environment of favourable conditions, you reduce your reliance on them. Soon, a new habit is formed, and your behaviour slides from conscious action to unconscious action – it becomes automatic. Discipline and willpower are no longer required.

I follow the same process for planning the year ahead as I do for each week. I sit down with my journal, review what worked and what didn't and then iterate. I do this each month and each year, and I've found it very effective. Maybe it will work for you.

I didn't intend to mention my complaints about New Year's resolutions. I bring it up now because of the timing and because I have what I believe to be a better and more effective approach that you might use for yourself one day.

What I actually wanted to talk to you about is a list of practices that I deeply value and wish I'd begun earlier in life. It's a short list, but it's one I have thought a lot about since you were born. In fact, with it being a new decade, I had planned to talk to you about this at the start of 2020. But guess what? You were a newborn baby, and I didn't get a chance to do a lot of deep reflection that year, because I was too tired, smitten and anxious, and I was busy learning skills in a brand-new industry: parenthood.

Now that I've traversed the newborn-baby phase and recovered from my outrageous hangover, I'm in a position to return to the subject. Remember, these are things I value in my life today that I wish I had begun earlier.

Number one is journaling. I only started doing this when I turned thirty, but the practice has transformed my life. Through journaling, I have carved out an unexpected career as a writer, made better and smarter decisions and consistently adopted good habits. I use journaling to record ideas and note down quotations, life lessons and areas to explore and research.

If I'm feeling emotionally bogged down and triggered, my journal becomes a proxy for my subconscious mind, and my pen becomes a scalpel. I use those combined tools to perform brain surgery, exploring the reasons for my psychological burdens so that I might offload them or develop a list of actions I can take to resolve them.

I believe the secret to maintaining a meaningful and purpose-filled life is daily reflection and constant introspection. My journal is my therapist, available to me twenty-four hours a day, three hundred and sixty-five days a year. And the best bit? My therapist doesn't charge me a penny!

Next, travel. Don't worry, Mummy and I will kick-start what I envision as your passion for travelling. If we are products of our environment, then I am committed to littering yours with passport stamps. And then it will be up to you. Conversely, I love being a happily settled family man, but, like fatherhood, travelling is fused to my identity.

Learn financial literacy. I wish I had realised the importance of investing in and building assets and letting them grow over time. Incorporated into your financial literacy should be the practice of saving as much money as possible, and this should be a bigger priority than owning the latest smartphone. With financial literacy, you can work towards owning the most precious resource in the world: time. You'll have as much of it as can be had, and it will be yours to spend however you want. While I'm not there yet, I'm working towards it, and I'm confident I'd be there already if I'd been more financially literate in my teens and twenties. Again, I will help you with this.

The final item on my list regards non-fiction. I know I covered this point in *Dear Dory*, so I won't go back over the same ground now, but you'll soon learn there is a difference between education and learning. The current British education system is flawed, often discouraging young people from seeking knowledge. On the other hand, learning is a paradise, a wonderland you can visit to explore its endless nooks and crannies, its maze of twists and turns, its warren of rabbit holes. Use learning as a mechanism to fulfil all of your curiosities and foster new ones. Treat it like an IV drip, and hook it up to your veins. A passion for learning will ensure you level up, becoming a happier, kinder and more open person. And when I say non-fiction, I'm not saying you should confine yourself to reading physical non-fiction books (though that's my preference); also listen to audiobooks, watch documentaries, seek out mentors – find whatever medium you respond to best, and then start fostering the need to ask questions of yourself and of the world you inhabit. The answers are out there, I promise you.

That's the end of my list. To recap: journal, travel, learn to be financially literate and consume non-fiction. Hopefully, this will help you. If it does, promise me you'll help others along the way and share your knowledge. Your enthusiasm for your passions gives off a tangible aura, an ambience that some people will find enticing should you be willing to share it with them. If you do, you might inspire them.

Nursery
Tuesday, 4 January 2022

It's 8 a.m., and we're standing by the front door. Mummy is getting you ready to leave the house.

'He's nervous,' she says.

'I know. He'll be OK,' I say.

Come to think of it, we're all nervous. You're nervous because you're starting another new nursery, and Mummy and I are nervous because you're nervous, and we're second-guessing our decision to move you to a *third* new setting in under a year.

So why have we done this?

Childcare.

You go to nursery on Tuesdays and Wednesdays. Until today, Nana See-See collected you at 3 p.m. when you finished. But Nana See-See also cares for Haylee on Mondays and Tuesdays, picks her up with you on a Wednesday *and* collects her again from nursery on Thursdays and Fridays. In short, that's a lot of nana-ing, and she's struggling with such a heavy childcare commitment. It's not hard to see why.

After suspecting she was feeling this way, Mummy and Auntie Lisa sat her down and got her to open up. It took some doing. Nana See-See was reluctant to admit it to herself and others. But, eventually, she confessed she was finding it all a bit tough – leaving us with something to think about.

What if we put you in for an extra two hours, and I came and collected you after work? No. I would need the car, and Mummy uses it. Then there is the cost impact. Also, I work from home now, but eventually, I'll be asked to return to the office, at which point pickups might become a challenge.

The other option was to move you to Mummy's place. Car challenges go away, and Mummy wouldn't have to rush around in the morning getting both you and herself ready to drop you off at one location and then drive to work at another. I rarely get involved in the mornings at the moment because I'm downstairs in the basement writing before starting my 'proper job'.

And Mummy's nursery is a wonderful environment that's very different from your previous settings. Child development is led by what each child is interested in that day. They don't have lesson plans; they wing it. If you show up one day wanting to play with dinosaurs, staff will create a dinosaur-related activity. I LOVE this. It's how I believe all learning should be done – led by curious minds.

We could have moved you here earlier, but because of Mummy's presence possibly hampering your development – something we believe was a factor in your original setting – we didn't.

But a lot has changed since then. You're older, more independent and used to mixing with staff and children. Plus, we get a great discount.

I'm sorry to do this to you again. We've had to make a decision without knowing if it's the right one. I guess we'll just have to see. Please don't hate us.

'Have the best day, buddy. Daddy will see you later on, OK?'

Mummy calls ten minutes later. 'He was fine while I was there, but he got really upset when I had to leave.'

I can tell she's crying.

'He'll be OK. I'll pick him up early, and he can play upstairs with my mum and trash the house. He was always going to have a couple of tough days, but we know what he's like – he's the most adaptable kid on the planet.'

'I know.'

I end the call with Mummy and text Nana Hoover, explaining that we may need her today. Fortunately, this was all prearranged.

But she isn't required.

Because, two hours later, I check the parent-accessible nursery app where staff post updates and observations about the children. I find a message waiting for me from one of your key workers, Jasmine:

> Arlo has had an amazing morning. He has taken a particular interest in the obstacle course, needing some reassurance at first, but then tackled independently [like a fucking boss, no doubt].

There's more:

> Arlo has been making friends too, encouraging children to go on the obstacle course and asking

January

his new friend to sit at the table, pulling her out a chair before pouring her some 'tea'.

That, right there, is a big box of reassurance packaged up and sent express delivery to the hearts and minds of both of your parents.

YES! YES! YES! Mate, you bloody little hero. I am proud, relieved, happy and ecstatic. When you consider today is your first day in a new environment – you have progressed phenomenally well. I'm so bloody proud of you. Wait, did I say that already?

I later learn that your new friend was the manager's daughter, and when you asked if she wanted tea, she replied, 'Gin?'

Nursery Day 2
Wednesday, 5 January 2022

Ring, ring.

Finally, an update. 'Hello. How's he getting on?' I say to Mummy.

'He's having a wonderful day. It doesn't bother him that I'm there at all. In fact, he was getting his nappy changed, and I walked by and he said, "Mamma, up there, work," while pointing upstairs because he knew where my room was. Then he said, "Buh-bye".'

Like yesterday, I'm buzzing with warmth and fuzziness at hearing this.

'There's just one tiny thing,' Mummy continues.
'Oh?'

'Jasmine dropped a bottle on the floor, and Arlo said, "Oh, shit."'

Ah. 'Am I to assume you're as proud of that as I am?'

'I guess I am proud of him for swearing on his second day in a new nursery.'

Damn right we are. You go and eff and jeff your way as much as you want, son. You just continue having a good time of life.

Felicity, Where Are You?
Friday, 7 January 2022

'Arlo, shout her again. Shout Felicity.'

'Felicity,' you say.

My turn: 'Felicity!'

Now your turn again: 'Felicity!'

From upstairs, we can hear some stomping, some stropping, some exasperated sighing and some more stomping.

'Is that you, Felicity?' I ask.

'Would you stop calling me that!' Mummy says.

'Felicity,' you say again, laughing.

'You can pack it in as well. Don't listen to your father!' she says, arriving in the hallway where you and I have been patiently waiting for five minutes while Mummy – sorry, Felicity Faffatron – can go about her usual routine of faffing and doing any task that runs in opposition to that of getting ready to leave the house.

'Are you ready then?'

'Yes! I'm ready. You don't have ... Crap, I've left my phone upstairs. Give me a sec.'

As soon as Mummy leaves, I turn to you, ready to cue you up for another rendition, but I needn't bother – you're already winding up:

'Felicity!'

'ARLO! Stop it!'

Ha ha ha! Serves her right for faffing, Arlo.

Choo-Choo!
Saturday, 8 January 2022

I've got a long list of writing tasks that I should be doing this morning, but I really don't fancy doing any of them. You know what? Fuck it. I'm not! Instead, I suggest to Mummy that we take you on the train for the first time. She enthusiastically agrees and invites Auntie Lisa and Haylee along for the adventure.

'Arlo,' I say.

'Yeah?'

'Can Mummy and I ask you a question?'

'Yeah.'

'Would you like to go on a choo-choo train with Auntie Lisa and Haylee?'

'YEAH! Choo-choo!'

You begin hopping up and down in excitement. I knew you'd welcome the idea, but I didn't expect such a strong reaction. 'Choo-choo,' you say again while running through the house screaming.

We get ready and drive to the station. Auntie Lisa and Haylee are already there. Haylee's excitement levels are similar to yours.

'We're going on a choo-choo train, Arlo.'

'Yeah, choo-choo!'

Mummy and Auntie Lisa engage in cyberwarfare with a more-complicated-than-it-needs-to-be ticket machine while you and Haylee run around in circles in the foreground. I'm on watch.

And now you've stopped running. You walk up to a man eating a Subway sandwich and traverse the invisible social barrier that we, humanity, like to call personal space. You're standing inches away from his face, gawping at him as he tries to enjoy his meatball baguette. I dash over, make my apologies and try to redirect you elsewhere. But you've vanished again – you're now hurtling towards WHSmith.

Upon the second – or fiftieth – recapture, I smell what I presume to be aromatic confirmation of a code brown.

'Arlo buddy, we need to change your nappy.'

Rage. Despair. More rage. And more despair. You collapse to the floor and begin hosing out a stream of tears from both eyes.

Mummy walks over, picks you up and says, 'Arlo, you can't go on the train with a pooey nappy. We need to clean you up, and then we can go on the choo-choo train.'

I volunteer to take you, but I can't. The men's changing room is in use, so it falls to Mummy while I watch Haylee.

January

Mummy returns looking like an anorexic wraith. 'I did not enjoy that experience one bit.'

Fortunately, you've reinstated your buoyant mood and returned to your favourite pastime of running and screaming. *At least you're happy.*

Auntie Lisa appears with our tickets, so we head to the platform.

You and Haylee are casting apprehension-filled glances from one side of the track to the other, looking for signs of the choo-choo train's arrival.

And then, two sets of small eyes expand to the size of large, shiny-cut diamonds, full of sparkling wonder and intrigue. The train is here. It pulls to a stop. The doors open, and passengers disembark, heralding the brief period of frantic activity that the arrival of a train in the station temporarily generates. Once those wishing to get off have done so, we're ready to board.

'Big step – one, two, three!' Mummy says, holding your hand and shepherding you safely across 'the gap'.

We find a place to sit, and for once, parenthood becomes a fraction easier than usual. There's only one narrow walkway on the train, so it's easy to box you and Haylee in by way of some sensible adult placement. That said, neither of you shows a particular desire to run up and down the train. Instead, you've each found the window. You look out at the platform as the train begins to move away.

Soon, we're free of the station, and you and Haylee become mesmerised by the world outside and by how quickly it passes before your eyes. You press your faces up against the glass, gaping at passing green fields and regiments of trees. You are as still as statues. Each adult absorbs the awe you project, never once losing sight of how important this experience is to you. *And to us.*

'Baa-baa!' you say, correctly pointing out sheep and other livestock that you're familiar with.

And to think I had planned to spend the day working. No, a trip on the choo-choo train beats wrestling with a keyboard by a conservative estimate of 3 billion per cent.

It's a short trip. But it doesn't need to be any longer. We all get exactly what we wanted from it.

Bloody good day.

Hi, My Name Is ...
Sunday, 9 January 2022

We've just finished up at the park, and we're walking back to the car to go home. I try the thing that I and the rest of your immediate family periodically do in your company.

'Arlo, what's your name? Is it ARLO?'

Nothing.

I try again. 'What's your name?'

Noth—

'ARWO!' you shout.

Oh-my-God-he-totally-said-his-name-for-the-first-time! I look to Mummy, whose face of astonishment and almost disbelief matches mine.

January

'Arlo, you said Arlo! Good boyyyyyyy,' she says.

You respond shyly like you always do when showered with too much praise and encouragement, but you're smiling. You know you've done a good thing, though I am surprised it's taken this long to happen. Nevertheless, its arrival is a glowing delight.

The thing with names is that we have no control over them. I suppose we can legally change them, but you know what I mean.

But that doesn't matter.

Because you trade a lack of control over what's written on your birth certificate for absolute control over what your name represents to you and to others. You attach ownership to your every deed and decision. Your actions, when combined, form a ledger or a blockchain, showing the world who you truly are. When people think of you, they are reminded of the things you've done. That's powerful. It's a narrative where you have complete creative oversight. There's no editor or studio head or highly paid actor with influence, no one but you calling the shots. Because no one controls who you want to be. Not even me or Mummy, though I swear to God you're no son of mine if you turn your nose up at my invitation to be a *Star Wars* fan. I'm kidding – as if that's a likely scenario.

Go out into the world and commit to acting in ways that do you, and *only* you, proud. Ignore your parents' exclamations of pride; it will only ever be your reflection that looks back at you in the mirror, so think about who you want to see.

I Have A Grand Vision!
Monday, 10 January 2022

This will be the greatest car track in the history of car tracks. I will spare no expense and give no quarter to my limitations. My creative and architectural prowess will engulf the space in which I stand, where I will build a transcendent tribute to the automobile industry. I am a storm of artistic dexterity and visual perception. I—

'No, Dadda!'

'What do you mean, "No, Dadda"? I need to put this piece of the track here to realise my vision.'

'No, Dadda,' you say again, this time shaking your head.

'Well, where should I put it then?'

'Here!' you say, indicating where you think I should lay the piece of track.

That's a terrible idea. 'Fine, but just so you know, I think you're making a Barry Blunder!'

This will be an all right(ish) car track in the history of car tracks. I have no choice but to spare many expenses, allowing Arlo to quarter my limitations at every junction. My creative and architectural prowess will barely be visible as I attempt to lay even a single piece of track – my feeble tribute to the automobile industry. I am barely a gentle breeze of artistry, and my visual perception matches that of a myopic bat. I—

'No, Dadda.'

Oh, for fuck's sake. 'What now?'

'This here,' you say, once again pulling rank and snatching another piece of track out of my hand and laying it in a place where it wasn't meant to be.

This will be the worst fucking track in the history of car tracks, and I regret getting out of bed this morning.

Violent Mummy
Tuesday, 11 January 2022

I'm in the living room with you changing your nappy.

'Ouch, Dadda,' you say while pointing to your knee.

'You've hurt your knee?'

'Yeah. Mamma,' you say, pointing over your shoulder in the direction of the kitchen. Mummy enters the room.

'Our son is accusing you of domestic violence. Did you hurt his knee in the kitchen?' I say.

'Yeah, Dadda. Mamma, ouch.'

'Don't worry, buddy. Daddy's investigating the matter as we speak. I'll quickly get to the bottom of this.'

'Arlo, don't grass me up,' Mummy says.

'So he's telling the truth?'

'Well, yeah, he banged his knee when I lifted him so he could sit on the worktop, but it was his fault.'

'Hmmm, spoken like a true user of domestic violence.'

'Yeah, Mamma.'

'Fine, he can stay with you, and you can take him to nursery then.'

'Well, hang on now, let's just everyone calm down. We don't want to be making rash decisions like that.'

'Dadda.'

'I'm sorry, son, but you heard your mother. This was an injury that you brought on yourself. Now, let's get you ready so Mummy can take you to nursery.'

Empty Threats
Friday, 14 January 2022

Mummy is trying to get herself and you ready to visit Grandad See-See. I support this activity because I'm not coming with you, meaning I'm afforded some desperately needed silence. Let's see if you can figure out why.

'Arlo, come and get dressed,' I say.

'Nope.'

'And we need to clean your teeth.'

'Nope.'

'Also, have you done a poo?'

'Nope.'

'I think you have because I can smell it.'

'Nope.'

Right, negotiations are over! I don't like resorting to physical intervention, but you've forced my hand. Naturally, you welcome my actions the same way one welcomes a spot of gout. You push, scratch, twist, yell, fight and deploy many other forms of physical and emotional non-compliance.

'Arlo, would you please keep still?'

January

'NOOOOO.'

Is today National Be a Dickhead Day? Eventually, I battle through nappy changing, teeth brushing and dressing. Then I head downstairs and ask you to follow me, an instruction which you, of course, ignore. Instead, you set up shop on the top of the landing, lying down with your feet dangling over the stairs, continuing your protest and setting your sights on ruining my morning. Mummy tries the famous distraction trick that she's so proficient in.

'Arlo, shall we go to See-See's?'

'No, Mamma.'

'Well, I'm going to go on my own then.'

'OK, byeeeee.'

Mummy looks at me and shrugs her shoulders, shakes her head and then shrugs her shoulders again. 'Well, I'm taking Henry, Louie and your dummy with me.'

'OK, bye, Mamma,' you say, successfully calling her bluff and showing no signs of budging from your current position.

If Mummy can't convince you by threatening the removal of your three most prized possessions, then we've no choice but to admit defeat.

But hell will freeze over before I submit myself to having to endure the morning alone with you, so I climb the stairs and pick you up.

'NOOOOOOO!'

'OUCH, ARLO!' That's me reacting to you back-heeling me in the bollocks.

The pain in my testicles gradually subsides, but my opinion of you does not improve. Nor does it when you throw four jigsaw puzzles up in the air and hurl your muddy shoes in the living room. Next, you do something else that makes a real bang, but I can't tell you what it is exactly, because I'm too busy filling out an online adoption application.

Nando's
Saturday, 15 January 2022

Walking through Nando's is like walking through a battlefield trapped in three time zones: The Calm, The Storm and The Aftermath. This strange, mind-bending, multidimensional reality is conjured up by the attending small humans, who insist on driving their parents through an assortment of hellish perplexities.

The Calm. Children aren't loud, animated or misbehaving. Not yet. They're quietly scribbling away at their colouring packs, which Nando's provide for them on arrival. But an absence of vocals does not equate to an absence of communication, as the children cast scowls and perform other non-verbal acts that their parents easily translate: 'What's taking so long?' 'Where's my food?' 'I ordered lemonade, but I wanted Coke!' and 'Why do they only have five stupid pencils in the pack? I need more colours.'

Parents respond quickly, silencing scowls with reassurance, dousing the flickering, nascent flames before they erupt into a fiery inferno. 'Darling, it won't be long now. They're cooking it right this second.' 'I've got Coke. Would you like a sip of mine?' and 'I know, the pencil situation is rubbish. Luckily, I brought yours from home. Would you like them?'

All noble and valiant efforts, but every one of them is destined to fail. Because next comes The Storm.

Non-verbal communication is out. Verbal communication is in. Noise spews out of the mouth of every bored and hungry child. There's shouting, yelling, crying and screaming. 'I'M HUNGRY!' 'WHERE'S MY FOOD?' 'JENNY IS OVER ON MY PART OF THE TABLE!' and 'IT'S NOT FAIR. JACK HAS BIGGER ICE CUBES THAN ME!' Or my personal favourite: 'I HATE MY LIFE, AND I WANT TO DIE!'

The carnage warrants an appropriate response from parents: regret. They regret coming to Nando's today, they regret setting the expectation that a nice family meal out was possible, and they regret having children. This brings us to ...

The Aftermath. The food eventually arrives, but it is too late. A release of too much cortisol and adrenalin has blunted taste buds and shattered moods. Mum and Dad have become hollowed, soul-torn shells of existence. There is so much mess. The kids are fighting – thrusting cutlery into bulging, red-streaked, angry sibling eyes.

But parents do nothing. They can't – they can barely marshal enough internal strength to breathe. So instead, they make promises to themselves. All of them empty. *We're never coming here again. The kids are going to bed early tonight.* And: *They're grounded for a month at least.* But one promise isn't empty: *I'm drinking a barrel of gin when I get home!*

You, Mummy and I, along with Auntie Lisa and Haylee, wend our way through the battlefield to our clean, shiny table and sit down. We order food and relax. You and Haylee are colouring, behaving beautifully.

But then ...

'Mummy, where's our food?' Haylee says. At which point, you look up and point to a waiter nearby who's holding a large bowl of chips.

'Chips? Mamma, chips? Dadda, chips? CHIPS!'

Three time zones. Each fraught with pain and suffering. Impossible to pass through without injury. The scars will be invisible. But they'll be there.

'Hi there! Welcome to Nando's. How hot would you like your sauce?'

'Lisa, Fuck'
Monday, 17 January 2022

Our support network is down by two grandmothers. This isn't great, because we rely on them for childcare on Mondays. Luckily, Auntie Lisa has the day off as she's going on holiday tomorrow. She's tagged in for a shift. Thank you, Auntie Lisa!

At 10 a.m., I get a call from her. 'Hi, I have a confession to make,' Lisa says.

'OK ...'

'I might have taught Arlo a new swear word.'
'What word—'
'Lisa, fuck!' you say. 'Lisa, fuck.'
'Oh, that word.'
'Yeah, I took the wrong junction and shouted f-u-c-k. I'm so sorry,' she says.
'I'd love to tell you that that's the first time he's said that word ... but it isn't—'
'Fuck, fuck, Lisa, fuck.'
'He's said it before, and I think he'll be saying it again.'
'Fuck, fuck, fuck,' you continue.
'Oh-thank-God-for-that. At least it's not on me,' says Auntie Lisa, relieved.

January Monthly Review
Wednesday, 19 January 2022

You ask questions all the time. You can say five, sometimes six words together, though they don't quite flow as sentences. The other day, you said, 'Mamma. Here. Sit. Arlo eat apple.' You are tons more confident saying your name now. You still pronounce it as 'Arwo', which everyone loves. You still refuse to say 'Louie'.

Your favourite question is 'What's this?' It used to be easy to answer. You would point to something like your Henry toy and ask it. One of us would then tell you or say, 'Arlo, you know what that is.' You'd then break out into a smile, as if you were having us on the whole time, and say, 'Ooofer.'

But no longer is it as easy. When you point to Henry, you point to a specific component, expecting us to somehow know a vacuum cleaner's anatomical make-up. Some of the parts I know, like the two switches: one red, one green – off and on. Fine. But you know the rectangular bit that makes contact with the floor when hoovering? I have no idea what you call that. I'm supposedly a writer, yet I can't offer any sort of adequate description for what the thing is actually called – or how to describe it. I've been calling it a 'foot piece'; a subpar description, but you caught me off guard the first time you asked me, and I panicked.

So, I downloaded the specs for the Numatic Henry HVR160 Cylinder Vacuum Cleaner, the grown-up version of your Henry toy. The part I can't describe is called a 'combination floor tool'. Suddenly, 'foot piece' doesn't seem so bad.

You recently underwent an eye check-up. It was good news. Your left eye (the weaker one) continues to improve, and you now only have to wear your eyepatch for an hour a day.

You're fussier with food. Ratatouille used to be a favourite. Mummy would serve it up with chunky pieces of aubergine and courgette. Now you regard the large vegetable pieces with a mix of disgust and suspicion before tossing them overboard from your bowl like mutineers bought to justice. But we have responded. Now, we – OK, Mummy – cuts up any food item that we think you might not eat into tiny pieces, disguising them. It works. For now.

Another nutrition-related milestone you've reached is that you no longer sit in your high chair. It's been in the cupboard gathering dust for weeks. You prefer to kneel on a 'big chair'.

Tantrums. You have this board game called Frog Frenzy – a copycat of Hungry Hippos. The objective is for your frog to gobble up more balls than your opponent's. But you fancied having a go at gobbling them yourself. We asked you not to, so you threw them. Now the balls have been confiscated, much to your vocal annoyance. Your mother and I detest Frog Frenzy.

Often you go for days without a single defiant swing of the arms. Other times, the tantrums happen more frequently. I find the ones first thing in the morning tough, like when you demand two things at once but don't want either. You bellow a war cry and often go on the attack. Don't worry; neither Mummy nor I take this personally. It might appear to be bad behaviour, but it's not. You have discovered these things called emotions, and frankly, they're bloody complicated bits of biological kit. They take a lifetime to master at just a basic level. Know that Mummy and I are incredibly proud of the young man you're becoming and we wouldn't want you any other way, even if that means suffering the odd kick in the nuts.

Potty-training is on pause. You've stopped requesting to sit on your toilet seat before bed each night. We always give you the option, but we don't push it.

Nursery is going great, though drop-offs remain unpleasant for Mummy. You're fine going into the building because Mummy takes you upstairs to her room. But when it's time to go downstairs into the toddler room, you lose it.

I'm not spared from harm either. This morning, you asked if you could play. I explained that you could, but you had to go to nursery to do so. You started crying and repeatedly begged to 'play here, Dadda'. It was agony.

But you bounce back from the tears quickly, and you have settled in remarkably well. You've formed bonds with staff: Abi, Jasmine, Sam and Jerome – whom you call 'Roam'. But Sam is your favourite. You love helping her with chores. Once we nail drop-offs, you'll be flying.

In *Toddler Inc.*, I commented on how your levels of affection had steadily grown since the summer. I'm pleased to report the trajectory has continued. When I was a boy, I used to have this thing with Nana Hoover where I would ask her for a 'hug-until-it-hurts'. Nana reminded me of this when she came for dinner recently. Now, Mummy has implemented a similar affection-based hugging protocol with you. We ask you to 'squeeze until it hurts'. And you do, squeezing us as tight as you possibly can. And it's the best; it's the antithesis to nursery drop-offs – it's an act that refuels my soul with vitality, casts down barriers, forms a sphere around my spirit and blocks out negativity, reminding me how enriched my life has been since I became your daddy.

Thanks for another happy month, son.

What's This?
Friday, 21 January 2022

'Dadda, what's this?'

'That's your Henry Hoover ... No wait, hold on.' *Breathe. Empty all thoughts – there is no spoon.*

I have now attained complete mindfulness. Distraction cannot penetrate my consciousness. I am ready to begin.

'Say that again, Arlo.'
'What's this?'
'That's the red cylinder.'
'What's this?'
'The FloMax hose.'
'What's this?'
'Crevice tool.'
'What's this?'
'Two-piece clear plastic tube set.'
'What's this?'
'Tube-set connector with bayonet locking system.'
'What's this?'
'Henry's wheels.'
'What's this?'
'Combination floor tool.'
'Oh.'

And the crowd go fucking mental! World, bathe in my undeniable, unchallengeable awesomeness.

If I ever find myself single again, then I think I know which skill I will need to put at the top of the list when writing my dating profile.

Play
Saturday, 22 January 2022

'Dadda, Arwo play?'

'Sure, you can play.'

'OK. Dadda play?'

'Of course. What shall we play?'

'Dadda, come. Arwo's house.'

You escort me to your play mat that's in our living room. On it is a large cardboard box, your 'house'. It's not big enough for me to fit in it, so we lay it on its side, put a cushion in and lie down with our heads sheltered and bodies exposed.

'Arlo, can Daddy tell you something?'

'Yeah.'

'This might be the greatest piece of architecture I've ever had the honour of residing in,' I say while marvelling at the cardboard's interior.

'Yeah, Arwo's house,' you say, proudly tapping your chest.

You might not know most of the words I've just said, but you can read my body language. You correctly deduce that I've paid your abode a mighty compliment.

But as I said, it's not big enough for daddies, so you politely ask me to leave. But it's OK because you build me a house of my own – one that looks suspiciously like the empty multipack-of-wipes box waiting by the back door, ready for the recycling bin. You've positioned our properties next to each other so that we're neighbours, facing the television. I can barely fit my head in, but that's fine.

If it's not playing houses, then it's playing with the kitchen we got you for Christmas that sits at the bottom of the stairs. You love to cook eggs, apple pies and cake, and you love it when I sit on the stair and play with you.

'Dadda, play, more?'

'Of course we can play for longer.'

'OK, Dadda. Cake?'

'I would love some cake.'

When you were a baby, I would sing a self-penned song about a horse. The song was called 'Giddy-Up, Horsey', and I would sing it while gently bouncing you up and down on my leg, winding you. That song is back, but now it's sung with you in my arms as we gallop around the house like a couple of idiots.

In *Toddler Inc.*, I had fun documenting the first time you navigated a home-created assault course. I positioned your toy rubber duck, Ducky, in 'the furthest dungeon at the Armrest Penitentiary', and I witnessed you courageously taking on the obstacles without help from me, save the odd word of encouragement.

Now, the difficulty levels have increased. For the Ducky narrative – which took place almost one year ago – we used your rainbow climbing arch and a movable slide to connect it to the sofa. Now, we use the dining-room bench, your kitchen step and a coffee table to configure a more impressive and daring arrangement.

Even how you say the word 'play' is full of charm, with your torso leaning forward and your head askance in a questioning manner – 'Dadda, play?'

As far back as *Dear Dory*, I told you how important the activity is and how as adults we lose the ability to play. We deprioritise it to make way for so many other things in life, like work. I said it would be your job to help ensure I maintain presence of mind with you. It's a task that's hardly laborious on your part because it's not that difficult to do. You are a powerful, shiny magnet that always draws my attention.

And I've underestimated how powerful the experience is, just being a dad playing silly made-up games with his son. Because, of course, they're not silly. Every second spent in our cardboard houses, every pretend sip of imaginary tea, every drama-induced foray through an assault course is laying down vital emotional bricks in your psychological foundations, strengthening the bond we share, giving you the confidence to explore your imagination in the company of others.

Never deprioritise play. Not even when you grow up and get a 'proper job'. Play every day; submit to becoming deeply involved and immersed in games, remaining present and energised, allowing creativity to override everything else. I can find no greater definition of the word 'living' than the act of playing.

I'm someone who forgot how to play. But with your tutelage, I'm remembering again – I've remembering how to fly.

'Dadda, play?'

You bet, buddy.

The Curious Case Of The Refillable Dinner Plate
Sunday, 23 January 2022

'Mamma, more?'

'Yes, you can have more carrots, but only after you've finished what's on your plate.'

You're unimpressed with Mummy's conditions, but it doesn't matter. Because, as if by magic, more have appeared. Perhaps your plate has been enchanted with refillable properties.

Your face lights up like that of a just-claimed rescue dog.

I mean, it has to be magic, right? There's simply no other explanation. They certainly haven't come from my plate as I would never undermine Mummy in front of you. And Mummy hasn't undermined herself – and they're out of your reach, so ... *I wonder.*

A few moments later, we're back where we started, with you staring at a plate devoid of carrots because you've already demolished the recently conjured-up replacements.

'Mamma, more?'

'What did I say—'

'YAY! Ta, Nana.'

Mummy and I turn our heads to locate the source of the carrot wizardry: Nana Hoover, the final participant at the dinner table – looking sheepish.

'Now, Mother, you wouldn't happen to be undermining Arlo's parents, would you?' I ask.

'He wanted more carrots,' she says, apparently settling the debate.

'Ha ha, Nana!'

You're all too aware of what's happening. You know that Nana has been naughty and that she's in trouble. But you think it's all terribly funny and seem hell-bent on continuing the farce because it means you get more carrots.

'Nana, more, please?'

'Nooooo, you keep getting me in trouble.'

'Nana, more car— Ta, Nana!'

Another look from Mummy and me and another ironclad defence from Nana: 'What am I supposed to do? He said please, and he was looking me in the eye and smiling. How can anyone say no to that?'

You throw another look at Nana, and she returns a similar one back. It's a look I know all too well because it's one I often wear when hanging out with my mates and getting up to mischief. That's what Nana Hoover is: she's your mate.

And as annoying and frustrating as being undermined is – and for any grandparent reading this book, it damn well is – I cannot deny that the bond you share with her is special. You are the best of friends. You might prefer me over Mummy sometimes, but you prefer Nana Hoover over Mummy and me every time!

Nana Hoover lives to be in the moment with you. She doesn't have to attend appointments or work through a list of household chores while looking after you at the same time. If she takes you to the trampoline park, she ensures you leave an hour before. This allows you plenty of time for your meanderings on your walk through town, time to stop and explore things that interest you. Nana never hurries.

Her loyalty to the here and now, her commitment to interacting with you every step of the way and her complete disregard for the rules – all these factors have meant you have both forged a remarkable bond.

She was like that with me when I was a child. My dad was never around, so it was just the two of us when I was growing up, but she'd always play with me. I'm not saying I was never lonely at points as an only child, but Nana Hoover was brilliant.

And that's why she is your best pal, why you love her so much and why your dinner plate is imbued with a spell that magically refills it with whatever food takes your fancy – like carrots!

The Future's Bright
Monday, 24 January 2022

A random but wonderful thought has struck me: it won't be long until we can start enjoying banana-gun fights, a childhood rite of passage and an opportunity for us to show off our bestest playground gun-firing impressions, *pew-pew pew-pew* and *huh-huh-huh-huh-huh-huh*.

I know I'm stating the obvious, but the *pew-pew* sound is from my banana laser gun, and the *huh-huh-huh* sound is from my fully automatic banoffee assault rifle.

You doubt me? Try saying these aloud.

Now What, Mister?
Tuesday, 25 January 2022

'What did he want this time?' Mummy asks.

'He wanted tucking in. Apparently, you didn't do a good—'

'Daddaaaaa,' says a voice from upstairs.

A few minutes later and I return downstairs. 'This time, he wanted a kiss.'

'Mammaaaaaaa.'

Another few minutes later and Mummy is back. 'I don't believe this – he wanted that picture of baby Jacob to take into bed with him.' Jacob is the son of Mummy's god-daughter, but Mummy's god-daughter is also Mummy's cousin, making you second cousins.

'Daddaaaaa.'

'... he made me kiss the photo of Jacob.'

'Mammaaaaa.'

'... he wanted a drink.'

'Daddaaaaa.'

'... he couldn't find Jacob, because he shoved the photo under the cover.'

'Mammaaaaa.'

'... Ewan had gone off.'

'... nothing. He wanted nothing. He just lay there staring at me.'

'... he wanted to know if Henry was sleeping in our bed tonight.'

'... he wanted to make sure we tucked Henry in properly.'

'... he told me that Jack has a drill,' Mummy says.

'Who the heck is Jack?' I ask.

'He's the builder at work making a tree house for the children.'

Arlo, we have a problem. Historically, you've always called us a few times after you go down, and we've always responded. You see this as power – something you control. And it would seem you've begun experimenting with the power you wield, learning to bend and exploit it in more creative ways.

We never engage in conversation, and we never make eye contact. But as you can see from the above examples, it doesn't matter. The hardest one is when you ask for a kiss. In what world are we saying no to that? We need a response strategy. I'm used to clocking off as soon as you go to bed, not beginning a forty-five-minute session of stair sprints. Though I'll admit, a part of me is always curious to see what excuse you give us. The more complex and bizarre, like demanding we kiss a photo we've somehow allowed you to take to bed, the more we're secretly proud of you.

And what happens when we lose the cot, and you upgrade to a big-boy bed – one without sides, bars or any other wooden impediments to stop you from escaping and wandering the halls of our house after bedtime?

I relay my uncertainty to Mummy.

'Oh yeah, that will totally happen. Aren't you looking forward to him getting into bed with us for snuggles?'

'Oh, that I don't mind. But I don't fancy the three hours between his bedtime and ours, where we're having to continuously apprehend the bastard for going on a night-time walkabout.'

'Well, you probably need to get used to that.'

'But it will just be a phase, right? A two- or three-week integration period? Like everything else?'

'Sure ...'

'Why are you saying like ... Ah, fuck!'

'What's up, pal?' Mummy says.

'I've had a million memories come flooding back in, that's all.'

'Of what?'

'Of me getting into my mum's bed as a child. And if I was old enough to remember that, then I guess it's a little bit longer than a two- or three-week integration period.'

'Now you're catching on.'

Just A Casual Father-And-Son Stroll
Wednesday, 26 January 2022

It's 5 p.m., and I've just collected you from nursery. Staff tell me you've had a wonderful day.

'Dadda, walk?'

'You can walk, buddy, sure.'

'OK, Arwo and Dadda walk.'

'That's right, but we need to cross the road, so hold my hand.'

'OK, Dadda. Dadda, look, nee-nee.'

'It's an ambulance.'

'Look, cars.'

'Do you think they're driving to their homes after a long day at work?'

'Yeah. See-See, tools.'
'Grandad See-See works with tools.'
'Ammer, saw, drill.'
'Yup, See-See knows how to use all of them.'
'Jack, drill.'
'Jack is the man building a new tree house at your nursery, isn't he?'
'Yeah, Mamma work.'
'That's right. Mummy works there.'
'Dadda, house work.'
'Correct, Daddy works at home. Can you remember what I do for work?'

You don't answer with words. Instead, you lift both hands and pretend to tap away at an imaginary keyboard.

'Yes, Daddy does typing, typing, typing.'
'Shop. Dadda and Arwo?'
'We can stop by the shop if you want. What would you like to buy?'
'Nanas.'
'Sure, we can grab some bananas.'
'YAY! NANAS.'

Nursery drop-offs might be hard, but pickups are bloody great. Especially when snacks are involved.

A Day In The Life Of Arlo: Ooofers
Thursday, 27 January 2022

Louie, something wonderful has happened; I must tell you about it. My parents took me out in the big blue car. They told me I was going on an adventure. But I refrained from indulging in too much excitement because they always say it's an adventure, even if we're off to the shops to buy bread, though admittedly, I was wearing my dragon onesie and Gruffalo slippers - perfect attire for adventuring.

And it was a good job because it *was* an adventure. The ultimate adventure. The greatest adventure of them all.

Louie, I am here to tell you that the rumours are true: heaven exists, and it is filled with splendour. Allow me to recount the tale as I experienced it.

First, I will correct a misunderstanding: heaven is not called heaven, at least not any more. It may have been called that at some point in the past, but today, heaven goes by the name of Currys. It has a purple banner above its doors - you know how much I love the colour purple. As one would expect, the glass gates are fuelled by magic, parting of their own accord whenever they sense someone close.

As you enter, you're greeted by halls that stretch beyond the horizon and heights that stand taller than the roof of the sky, exceeding the limits of my sight, penetrating deep into the cosmos. And the stars, which naturally make up the main source of light here, shine bright, filling every corner with a luminance that's both warm and welcoming.

Lining the halls are shelves of every gadget and gizmo you can imagine: devices that go *beep*, instruments that go *whoosh*, and appliances that move with such grace, such calm composure, it's as if their movements have been engineered to replicate those of a top-of-her-game ballerina.

I ran, and I ran, and I ran through those halls, darting this way and that. My parents chased me, imploring me to slow down the whole time, but I couldn't do it, Louie. My actions were no longer mine to control.

But then I did slow down. I stopped. Because I saw it.

The crown jewel.

The flagship feature.

The showpiece ... no, the centrepiece ... no, the masterpiece.

Louie, Currys has an *entire* section devoted to Ooofers! As I stood there, I could feel every one of my neurons pulsating, every cell in my body thrumming, all in response to this astonishing and unrivalled beauty. There weren't just lots of Ooofers, there were all of the Ooofers. Every single one. They had Sharks, Dysons, Vaxes and this weird model called 'Hoover'. They had big ones, small ones and sizes in between. There were different shapes and different colours - it was perfect.

January

But then it got even more perfect.

As I turned a corner ... I beheld ... a wall of boxed-up red Henry Ooofers.

I didn't know Henrys came in walls. Awe struck me like lightning. Wonder whipped through my bones. Monstrous waves of marvelling astonishment crashed into my soul as my shiny eyes realised the truth before me.

My parents were gracious enough to let me spend some time handling some of the Ooofers, understanding the subtle differences in their capabilities, and learning why some price tags' numbers were considerably higher than others. It was glorious.

When it came time to leave, I was reluctant - I didn't want this experience to end. But I had my moment, and I left the encounter knowing that the rumours were true - that heaven exists. And I tell you, Louie, it lives up to the hype.

Consequences
Friday, 28 January 2022

'You know this has to happen, don't you?'

Through a smile, you say, 'No, Dadda.'

'I'm sorry, son, but this is the only way. Maybe next time, you'll think twice before running into the kitchen for the fourth time when I tell you to stay out of it.'

'Dadda, no,' you say, complementing your still-smiling face with some wriggling as you try to loosen the grip I've got you in, but it's futile. I've got you pinned on the sofa, holding your arms above your head. You're wearing a vest, so two toddler-sized armpits are exposed and vulnerable to punishment.

'Dadda, no, Dadda.'

'You cannot escape consequences, Arlo. Now, would you please excuse me while I … *ppbbbbbbb*.' That's me blowing raspberries on your armpits. You shriek and squirm, begging me to stop. After a few seconds, I do.

'Consequences' is the name of the game we have for those times when you do something we don't want you to do, but it's not really bad, so we turn it into a game. Blowing raspberries on your body is one of those things that you sort of want me to do, but at the same time, you don't. I know this because I threatened you with consequences if you kept running into the kitchen and you did it anyway.

Spoiler: this is one occasion where I love it when you do the opposite of what I tell you.

February

oniomania
noun

The habit of buying shit you do not need but insisting to your partner that it's an essential purchase.

The Parenthood Dictionary
Adventures in Dadding Edition

'Mummy, Help!'
Thursday, 3 February 2022

I'm relaxing in the shower, gathering my thoughts together for the rest of the week, when you barge in. Usually, you pair your intrusions with a soppy grin.

But not today.

Today, you saunter in with a blank expression like you're some sort of Vulcan. Your eyes are locked on to mine as you sidestep your way to the toilet-roll holder.

'Arlo buddy, what are you planning?'

Still ignoring me, you momentarily break eye contact to position your hand on top of the toilet-roll holder.

Uh oh. My toddler has gone. He has been replaced by a small sociopath who's about to commit a crime and take immense pleasure in doing so. 'Arlo, please think carefully about what you're about to do.'

Of course, I'm asking you to complete an exercise you've already completed because you *have* thought carefully about it, and you have decided to proceed regardless.

And so ... ever so slowly ... while still maintaining eye contact ... you begin to unravel the toilet roll. The physics of the action, combined with the geographical positioning of our toilet-roll holder, means the tissue is unravelling into our toilet.

'Arlo, stop that right now!'

You don't stop.

And now the unravelled toilet roll occupies a third of the toilet.

'Arlo, I mean it, stop doing that!'

And now two thirds.

Fuck. I need to get out of the shower. No, wait. 'Mummy, help!'

'I can hear you. I'm coming.' Within seconds she's on the scene. And now, for the first time since you entered the bathroom, your blank, expressionless face breaks into a smile and then a squeal as you double down on the unravelling, building speed and momentum.

Mummy bounds over to you and grabs the offending arm, finally putting an end to your monstrosities.

You are shrieking with glee.

'Arlo, that's not good. You didn't listen to Daddy, did you?' Mummy says.

You shake your head, but you're smiling still. I look in the toilet. It's full of tissue paper.

Four flushes later and I cannot believe we've not had to call a plumber.

Threat Watch At Soft Play
Saturday, 5 February 2022

```
... SCANNING ... SCANNING ... SCANNING
COMPLETE

THREATS IDENTIFIED: 4

SUMMARY OF THREATS:

THREAT 1: YOUNG MAN - SIMILAR AGE TO
ARLO - HIGH, OFF HIS TITS ON SUGAR,
RUNNING AROUND BY THE SLIDE.

THREAT 2: YOUNG GIRL - OLDER THAN
ARLO - SIGNIFICANTLY BIGGER THAN HIM
AND MAINTAINS ZERO RESPECT FOR PERSONAL
BOUNDARIES. OBSERVE AT ALL TIMES.

THREAT 3: GIRL - SAME AGE AS ARLO.
SHE LIKES IT WHEN BAD THINGS HAPPEN
TO ANIMALS, AND WHEN THINGS BURN.
PARENTS DIVORCED BEFORE SHE TURNED TWO.
SHE EXPLOITS THEIR FAILED-RELATIONSHIP
GUILT TO A FAULT. SHE IS A SPOILT,
MANIPULATIVE BULLY WHO HAS NO REGARD
FOR OTHERS. A ROGUE. IF REQUIRED,
PREPARE TO NEUTRALISE THREAT AT PACE.
```

```
THREAT 4: LARGE ADULT MALE. DOES NOT
BELONG. HE LOOKS TO BE BALDING AND
UNFUNNY AS FUCK—

RESCANNING ... STANDBY ... STANDBY ...
STAND—

THREAT 4 REVISED AND DOWNGRADED TO
NEUTRAL. REASON FOR CHANGE: SCANNER WAS
LOOKING AT A MIRROR.
```

Oniomania
Friday, 11 February 2022

The postman has delivered a ... Actually, I have no idea what it is. It's been vacuum-packed, and it looks like a piece of fabric with feathers stuck to it. 'What on earth have you bought?' I ask Mummy.

'Oh, wait until you see this bad boy. You're gonna love it.'

Mummy removes the outer packaging and holds the product up for inspection. I still have no idea what it is, but I can see that what I mistook for feathers is, in fact, a black piece of fleece-backed fabric with poppers.

'What is it?'

'It's a buggy muff.'

'I'm sorry, a baggy muff?'

'No, idiot, a b-u-g-g-y muff. You attach it to the buggy, and it stops your hands from getting cold. Genius, right?'

I am stunned – a large block of confusion: bewildered and baffled and utterly speechless.

'What? Don't you like it? Say something.'

'It's not that … How much did you pay for it?'

'Tenner. Fucking bargain, if you ask me.'

'I wish you had told me about your cold hands earlier. I could have saved you some cash.'

'How so?'

'Well, I read about these new products that all the kids are using to help with cold hands.'

'Really? Tell me about them.'

'They're called gloves.'

'Ha ha, silly. But you don't always remember to bring gloves out, do you? A buggy muff solves that because it's always attached to the buggy.'

She's got me there, Arlo …

Carson's Birthday
Saturday, 12 February 2022

We've gone to Sean and Rebecca's house to celebrate their son Carson's second birthday. You've been looking forward to it all day for two reasons. One, you have a soft spot for Rebecca, or 'Auntie Ra-Ra' as she's known. Second, you've already installed the following equation into your operating system:

$$Birthday\ party = Cake$$

We arrive, but despite spending a fair amount of time here, it takes you a while to warm up to your surroundings. There are adults and children you don't know, and even those you know are mixed in with a bigger-than-you're-used-to-sized crowd. We believe your wariness towards groups is a result of your Covid-19-to-present upbringing.

Speaking of Covid-19, Rebecca is doing her bit to reduce the chances of the virus spreading, which a medium-sized gathering is likely to encourage. She does this by writing the names of guests on glasses, ensuring no accidental cross-contamination.

I notice this, and then a moment later, my eyes wander over to the food table where four small humans – including you – are fingering, mishandling and committing abuse to the platters of food, ensuring that Rebecca's attempts to practise safe standards are futile.

You're dipping a nacho into a pot of sour-cream-and-chive dip, then sucking the dip off and dipping the same nacho back into the pot again. Next, you lance two fingers through a piece of quiche. Finally, you take a big bite of sausage, decide you don't like it and begin spitting it out. I make it over just in time to capture the remains in the palm of my hand as they fall from your mouth.

The theme of the party is diggers and dinosaurs. There's a sandpit where kids can play with construction vehicles to dig up fossils. There's also a handmade plaster-of-Paris volcano surrounded by green slime.

And now, a scary and ferocious-looking T. rex has arrived on the scene, one that looks suspiciously like

Sean in an inflatable T. rex costume. Most of the kids jump up and down in excitement, but some do not. Fear grabs hold of one toddler, a young lady. She shouts for her mummy.

But the bigger kids are not afraid. Not one bit. They're looking at the dinosaur and assessing his weaknesses, searching for areas that are ripe for attack. Once they complete their assessment, they move in like a pack of velociraptors, commencing a violent and coordinated assault. They do their best karate kicks and their most powerful punches.

The T. rex is overwhelmed. He goes on the defensive, lifting his pathetic, weedy, short little arms, but it's useless. Next, he spins around, leveraging his oversized inflated tail to force his opponents into a retreat. But in the chaos and confusion of flailing limbs and excitable energy, one of the young velociraptors stumbles back before tripping, landing in the green-slime-filled tray at the base of the volcano.

'Whaaaaaa,' the young dino-tot says.

No one knows how it happened. For my part, I'm pretty sure it wasn't the T. rex's fault, but it doesn't matter, because no one is about to blame anyone else. And now the T. rex's father has arrived and put the T. rex in a headlock. He drags him to the ground, where the raptors strike, mauling the fallen apex predator, shrieking in a gleeful frenzy.

The adults have no choice but to intercede. They drag the T. rex away and book him in for an emergency appointment with the vet. Moments later,

Sean arrives, looking like he's just been mobbed, which, of course, he has.

Now it's time for another party game: whack the piñata.

Enter Ewan.

Ewan is Rebecca's nephew. He's eight, and he's been bred for one purpose and one purpose only: to destroy the piñata. His whole life has been leading up to this moment. I've watched him train all afternoon. To the casual observer, you'd think he was enjoying himself like all kids do at parties. But I see what others do not. He isn't smashing back handfuls of sweets just because they're sweets; he's onboarding energy. He's not running up and down the house screaming; he's warming up – channelling his inner rage.

And now he is ready to fulfil his destiny.

Rebecca climbs onto the kitchen worktop and dangles the piñata, a teal-coloured baby T. rex with orange spikes on its back, from a fishing-rod-like device. The kids gather around her, excited.

Ewan blocks them all out. His mind is still. He's not competing with any of them, only with the limits of his own strength.

'Right, who wants a go first?' says Rebecca.

The kids scream. But not Ewan. Instead, he marches up to Rebecca and holds out his hand. His silent cunning is rewarded as Rebecca hands him the whacking stick.

Parents, including me, make daring moves into the circle to pull back our respective toddlers and preschoolers because we've all seen the rage that swells in Ewan's eyes.

He steps up, narrows his focus and scans Rebecca's movements, noticing the gentle sway of the piñata and the subtle rise and fall of Rebecca's wrist as she tries to keep it steady.

'Take two hits, and then let someone else have a go,' she says.

Ewan pulls back, charging all his energy, all his power. And then he strikes.

WHACK.

It's a tremendous effort. But it's barely dented the baby T. rex, which is apparently a lot tougher than it looks.

Ewan is flabbergasted. He administered a level-ten power-crusher move that would have vanquished most foes.

But the piñata is not most foes.

'Try again, Ewan,' Rebecca says.

He does. This time, he contorts his face in a hardened-clay-like shape of wrath, charging his inner strength once more.

WHACK!

The sound is deafening. The blast wave nearly knocks us all off our feet.

But ... the piñata still stands.

'OK, Ewan, let someone else have a go.'

The dejected young man has no choice but to hand over the whacking stick to the next in line. He steps back and begins reviewing what went wrong with his technique.

The other kids, including you, have a go. You give it everything you've got, but your barely-over-two-year-old arms just don't have the strength to take on a baby-T. rex piñata.

Soon, the whacking stick makes its way back to Ewan.

Once again, the crowd casts a wide berth, giving Ewan the space he needs to project all aggression at his opponent. His mummy, Rebecca's sister Gail, shouts encouragingly from the sidelines, 'Come on, Ewan, you can do it.'

'ARRHHH!' shouts Ewan as he unleashes a level-twelve life-obliterating kneecap-smasher move that ripples the very fabric of time.

Nothing. Another small dent at most.

He charges again. 'ARRHHH!'

WHACK.

Once more, nothing.

'OK, Ewan, let—'

'ARRHHH!' *Whack, thump, whomp, wallop.*

He pours his rage, his high blood-sugar level and his fury into a melee attack, deploying everything in his arsenal – all his offensive knowledge that he acquired from studying cartoons and sparring with his younger brother. He tries different angles, different swings and different arcs. He twirls – dodging this way and then that, but he finds only failure in his efforts.

He is beaten. His shoulders slump as he accepts that he will not be acquainted with destiny today.

But he's not alone; no one can best it. And a quick glance at Rebecca tells me her shoulders are burning from having to hold up the dangling piñata for so long. Luckily, Sean's dad is back to save the day. He takes point and eventually breaches the hull of the vicious reptile, spilling its innards: Mars bars, Twixes, Milky Ways.

The velociraptors move in, scouring and scavenging the battlefield for spoils. Ewan acquires the lion's share – small solace in the face of failure but solace, nonetheless.

Maybe next year, Ewan – keep training.

Playing In The Park
Sunday, 13 February 2022

We're on our way to the park. It's just you and me. Who knows what adventures await us?

The Great Train Robbery
'Dadda, sit on gween one.'
'OK, but are you sure you'll be OK driving the train by yourself?'
'Yeah, Arwo drive train, Dadda.'
'Fine. I'll sit back here and watch out for threats. You just need to keep us moving at full speed for a few hours until we cross the border into a place … where law enforcement can't follow us.'
'Quick, Dadda, come here.'
'I'm coming, buddy.' I edge along the outside of the carriage until I come alongside you in the driver's compartment. Then I slide in to take the seat next to you. 'Is everything OK? Have you spotted something?'

'Yeah, I have. White bird. Look, Dadda,' you say while pointing to a 'white bird'.

On The Trail Of The Runaway White Bird

'Arlo, I don't know if we'll ever find the white bird again. It's proving elusive.'

'Dadda, there,' you say, pointing.

'Good God, you've done it. You've located the missing white bird after all those months of searching. Steady now, we dare not spook it. Otherwise, it will take off, and we may never chance upon it again. Remember what I taught you. Crouch low, and follow with soft feet.'

You adopt the position, becoming the embodiment of your training, slowly stalking your prey. You crouch lower still and make ready to pounce. But then you suddenly stand up and point into the distance. 'Look, Dadda, ship.'

The Ocean Voyage

'These be rough seas, Captain Arlo. Rough seas indeed. I fear the rigging will not hold,' I say while purposely swaying the park apparatus, which is built to sway. But it would seem the swaying is too sway-ey.

'Dadda, off!'

'But Captain, I'll surely be swept up in the ferocious waves and drown. How will you manage the ship without your first mate?'

'Dadda, off Arwo's ship.'

'FINE!'

February

The Special Banana Shop

'Good afternoon, young sir. Is this your shop?'

'Yep, Arwo's shop, Dadda.'

'Well then, let me start by congratulating you on such a fine establishment. You must be very proud.'

'Yeah.'

'And what do you have for sale today in this magnificent shop of yours?'

'App-pulls.'

'Apples, you say? In that case, I'll take a nice bag of delicious apples.'

'Here you go.'

'Thank you kindly, and here's some money.'

'Ta.'

'I'm also after some books. Do you have any for sale?'

'Yes, I do. Here you go.' You hand me an imaginary stack of books, a stack I gladly accept; I marvel at some of the titles.

'Some of these have been on my list for a very long time. Thank you.'

'Nanas?'

'You don't sell bananas, do you?'

'Yeah. Nanas in Arwo's shop. Pink nanas.'

I indulge in a powerful gasp of awe. 'You won't believe this, but I love pink bananas even more than I love apples and books. I will take as many as I can carry.'

'More app-pulls?'

'Well, I thought we would go home and see Nana Hoover.'

'Nana Ooofer? At our house?'

'Yeah. Do you want to go and see her?'

'Yeah. Bye, park. Bye.' You wave to the park as we leave, and then we go in search of the car.

All in all, a bloody fun trip to the park.

Jack and Gillian
Tuesday, 15 February 2022

The commentators, Jack and Gillian, wait with the venue's spectators in quiet anticipation as the next rider and his horse stand by gate A, ready to begin their dressage routine.

'All quiet now,' says Gillian. 'Everyone is excited to see the next contestant. He's not been on the circuit for very long, this next rider, has he?'

'That's right, Gillian,' says Jack. 'The rider's name is Mr Arlo, and he is riding Arlo's Daddy, offspring of the great Nana Hoover. Mr Arlo has owned Arlo's Daddy for a little over two years. I was surprised he didn't ride Nana Hoover for this event because she's a famously submissive horse, submitting to any demands Mr Arlo makes.'

'Agreed, but I wouldn't rule out Arlo's Daddy just yet. He too has been known to be a massive pushover at times,' Gillian says.

'Absolutely. Let's see what they can accomplish together.'

'He's not the most attractive horse I've ever seen.'

'No, he's not. Let's hope the judges don't hold that against them. All right, here we go ... and they're off.

First is the sofa ascent. There you see it. Arlo's Daddy has crouched low enough for Mr Arlo to clamber on – how's the lift …? It's good, it's very good, and now Arlo's Daddy is cantering from the sofa over to the stairs, issuing the mandatory horse noises. Judges score the impression based on auditory similarity, body-language enthusiasm and how much the rider smiles. And now Arlo's Daddy is instructing Mr Arlo to hold on. He reminds him of that a second time. Will he remember the third, fourth and fifth warnings for Arlo …? Yes, he does, and bloody hell, Gillian, he's even managed a sixth warning. That will impress the judges.'

'Now "the rise of the stairs",' says Gillian, taking the commentary reins. 'Up they go, expertly handled by Mr Arlo. Not only is he holding on, but he's lowered his head down to reduce resistance. Now the landing, and it's the money shot – first, a big double "neigh" jump, followed by a gallop into the master bedroom, where we can expect to see Arlo's Daddy making his way to the far side of the bed – and he does. Now for the "bend-down drop", where both horse and rider get as low to the ground as possible, beginning the final challenge of the routine, the "hide-from-Mummy".'

'And here she comes,' says Jack, 'Arlo's mummy, systematically searching every corner, every space and every crevice for Mr Arlo and Arlo's Daddy … uh-oh, Mr Arlo needs to be careful here. He can't laugh too loudly. If Arlo's mummy is alerted too soon, the judges will dock points. And now Mr Arlo, making yet another performance error, has dismounted Arlo's Daddy and he's standing up in plain view. If she looks in his direction, it's all over. But somehow, she's looking in every direction apart from where Mr Arlo is standing.'

Gillian is positively stunned. 'In all my years of commentary, I have never seen anything like this. He's going to do it.'

'Gillian, I think you're right, and now Arlo's mummy turns the final corner just as Mr Arlo shouts "boo".'

'Jack, it's a perfect surprise. Arlo's mummy had no idea. Just check out the look on her face – pure shock! And now Mr Arlo and Arlo's Daddy are performing a celebratory lap of the floor again. They know they've done enough for a podium position, and it's going to be gold. The crowd is rightly standing up to applaud the wonderful team of Mr Arlo and Arlo's Daddy. Wow – what a night!'

Boxes
Wednesday, 16 February 2022

'How long are you planning on keeping these boxes in the house?' Mummy says.

'Look, I'm willing to have an adult conversation with you but only if you use the correct terminology. First, they're not boxes. They're houses,' I say.

'OK, how long are you planning to keep these "houses" in our actual house?'

'Between forever and a very long time.'

'I'm going to throw them out.'

'You most certainly will not, you witch. How are we to build a mighty fortress without the raw materials? That's like expecting you to cook a pasta dish after I've thrown out all the pasta.'

'Fine.'

'Fine with the houses remaining? Or fine – you accept the challenge to cook a pasta dish without any pasta?'

'Keep the houses.'

A few hours later, I receive a notification from Amazon telling me that a book about things constructed out of cardboard is on its way. Which is awesome, except I didn't buy it. 'Did you buy a book on building things out of cardboard?' I ask Mummy.

'I sure did.'

'You wonderful creature. What's caused the sudden change of heart?'

'I figured that this mighty fortress of yours won't be very mighty if you're the foreman, so I've ordered the book for ideas, and I'm replacing you with me as the person in charge.'

'That's brilliant.'

'I'm glad you think so.'

'But …'

'Go on.'

'Well, you know how I like it when you're in charge of craft-related affairs. I'm all fingers and thumbs and F-bombs – you're much better suited to the role. But I do have a very specific design in mind, one that I'm convinced would allow the completed construction of the fortress to qualify as "mighty".'

'I will hear you out.'

Yes! This means I'm still in charge. 'Thank you. And another thing – you're not the only one who's had dealings with Amazon today. I spoke to a lovely chap there who told me I don't have to bother with the return-label process for the storage box I was planning to send back.'

'What's that got to do with cardboard fortresses?'

'You mean *mighty* cardboard fortresses. Well, you see, the reason I was sending it back was that it was damaged, but the chap told me to dispose of it rather than send it back, and if I don't have to use the packaging it came in—'

'Then we have one more cardboard box to add to our collection.'

'You got it, baby!'

'Wonderful!'

'Oh, and just one more thing. I've reordered the storage box again. It should be here tomorrow—'

'So another cardboard box. For fuck's sake! Are you done?'

'I am. Wait, I'm not. I have just one final thing to say, and then I'll leave you alone.'

'OK …'

'Can we have pasta for tea tonight?'

'No, Mummy!'
Thursday, 17 February 2022

It starts when Mummy tries to insert herself into the game we're playing. We have three large cardboard boxes (the ones I recently campaigned to keep in the house). They've been your favourite thing to play with all week. One 'house' is for Arlo, one is for me, and one is for Henry Hoover.

Mummy wanders over. I explain that I would like to share my house with her, but you quickly mount an appeal urging me to reconsider and firing off hostile body language at the woman who gave birth to you.

She tries to win you over by suggesting a bold development project: stacking one house on top of another. 'Look, Arlo,' Mummy says, 'I've built you a block of flats.'

'No, Mummy!'

The project is put on hold indefinitely.

Next, Mummy pretends to chase Henry and eat him. Your reaction is admiringly protective ... of your vacuum cleaner. You charge into Mummy with a body slam, repelling her intention to eat Henry, and then you run to your red comrade and wrap your body around him. 'No, Mummy!'

Mummy redirects her nutritional intentions towards something else. Cake – your favourite! 'Arlo, can you make Mummy some cake?'

'OK.'

Having finally accepted Mummy into the dynamic, you wander over to your toy kitchen and gather everything you need.

'Can Mummy have the purple cake, please?' she says.

'Mummy, no, go away, upstairs, take a nap.'

Wow.

I'd like to think that you wanted Mummy to go upstairs to bed because that's where she's been all day – oh, did I forget to mention that she's ill and hasn't been to work, and this is the first time today she's made it downstairs. But, in truth, you don't want her to play.

'Can't Mummy stay downstairs and play?'

'No, Mummy. Away. Dadda, tea?'

Brutal! Absolutely brutal. Poor Mummy.

Mummy has researched the whole preferred-parent thing. Unsurprisingly, the behaviour is common. Children will often reject a parent or caregiver when they feel secure. You hear of this when parents return home from being away and discover that their children behaved beautifully for their grandparents, only to transform into mega-twats when reunited.

A phrase like 'No, Mummy. Away' isn't a statement of dislike or permanent rejection, it's a temporary position based on the current activity the child is absorbed in.

Mummy and I each have something to take away. Mummy must work on not taking this personally or at least letting you see her take it personally, and I need to be clear when I can't be your playmate. Neither task is easy. I find it hard to say no to you.

Don't feel bad about this. The memoirs I write are a chance for us to record our experiences as they happen with no embellishment. This is part of our combined journey as a family. It's all part of the process, and that's nothing to feel ashamed about. We're all learning together.

Stairs
Friday, 18 February 2022

Please don't fall, Arlo, please don't fall, Arlo, please don't fall, Arlo.

'Like that, Dadda?'

'That's right, mate, but don't look at me. Look up at Mummy.'

'OK,' you say, swinging your head around to face Mummy at the top of the stairs.

'That's right, baby boy, just keep crawling up and don't stop,' she says.

Let me bring you up to speed: you're on the stairs, alone. We're teaching you to climb them by yourself, entrusting you with a new piece of freedom you didn't have yesterday. It's a real bird-leaving-the-nest moment. But when birds leave the nest for the first time to take flight, they don't always succeed. Some succumb to gravity and fall to the floor, a risk

I'm all too aware of as I watch you climb without the stabilisers or crash mat provided by a parent behind you.

Our stairs are narrow; they've claimed scalps in the past, including yours when you fell down them last year owing to some confusion between Nana Hoover and Mummy. Luckily, you walked away from the experience with barely a scratch. You fell because you stopped climbing and stood up to look behind you – the same thing you've just done when pausing to check with me that you were doing it right.

Why now? Because you're older and more capable. And, much as it pains me to admit it, you need to master getting up and down by yourself. And Mummy and I need to find the courage to back away and give you the freedom to try and, if fate calls for it, to learn from your mistakes.

But you reach the top and, as instructed by Mummy, crawl a few feet forward before standing up.

Success! 'Good boy, that was excellent, and really good listening,' Mummy says, giving you the praise you deserve.

Now it's time to come down.

'This side, Dadda?'

'That's right, mate. Sit close to the wall, and then hold the railing.'

'OK.'

'Take it one step at a time, and concentrate on where you're putting your feet.'

'OK, Dadda.'

That's right, son, plant your feet, take it slowly, and don't get distracted by the television. That's another step – you're almost halfway down. I'm purposely standing back. I calculate whether I could reach the bottom in time to catch you should you fall. I'm not optimistic. Still, I take stock of what toys are in front of me, planning a route should I need to make a dash for it. *Only a few more steps left.*

'Dadda, Arwo do big hop?'

'You can do a big hop on the last step.'

You enthusiastically cover the few stairs while holding on to the railing, keeping yourself steady and stable. When you reach the last stair, you squat and 'hop' on to the floor.

'I did it, Dadda!'

'You sure did, buddy. You did an excellent job. Give me a high five.'

Clap.

'Now, remember, you can go up and down the stairs by yourself, but what must you remember to do?'

'Get Mamma or Dadda.'

'That's right. Just tell one of us so we know where you are.'

'OK. Dadda. Where's Flop?' Flop is one of your soft-toy companions from *Bing*.

'I think you left him upstairs. Would you like me ... I mean, would you like to go and get him by yourself?'

'Yes, I would. Ta, Dadda.'

'Go on then. Up you go.'

All birds leave the nest eventually.

February Monthly Review
Saturday, 19 February 2022

You say 'Dadda', 'Daddy' and, much to my dismay, 'Tom' interchangeably. Tragically, I believe 'Dadda' will soon leave us forever. I know it's just a word, but I've grown incredibly attached to you saying it, and I'll miss it when it's gone.

You've developed a phobia of public toilets. You freak out as soon as we try and lay you down on a changing table; you get so upset that you start shaking. We've had to start laying you down in your buggy to change you. It's awkward, but it stops you from blowing emotional gaskets. On Mondays, both Nanas takes you and Haylee to a local playgroup in an old church. It's freezing! Nana Hoover believes the cold is responsible for your latest aversion. It's hard for me to reconcile myself to the notion that this is possibly the first time you've experienced real trauma. And, despite Nana's best guess, we can't say for sure where it originated.

We've had a couple of birthdays this month, meaning you had access to food items that rarely appear on the menu. I've already mentioned the party-equals-cake equation. Another one you've dreamt up is pub or restaurant dinner equals chips. And if you have chips, then you obviously must have tomato ketchup to dip them in.

I hate it! But as I've said before, I always knew we'd have to succumb to social pressures. Otherwise, you're the only kid in a group who's not allowed to eat the thing that everyone else is eating. That's cruel. But at the same time, I'm mindful of how easy it is to let standards slip. Nana See-See doesn't help. She makes an effort, but it was only yesterday I had to remind her that if she wants to give you ice lollies, then can she please make them herself out of fruit and natural yoghurt. That said, I concede the point that it's difficult to challenge norms. Also, I'd never be stupid enough to piss one of our childcare providers off – that's the equivalent of self-harm.

Language development continues travelling up that steep trajectory. It's an absolute delight to observe. My favourite new phrases are 'Yeah, baby', 'Not impressed' and 'Goodness gracious me'. You're now in a space somewhere between saying one-word responses and questions and having full-blown conversations.

I remind myself that it won't be long until you'll leave this phase behind and that we need to pay close attention to it. Soon, you won't say 'mash chay-choo'; you'll say 'mashed potato'. 'Cat-pilar' will become 'caterpillar', and 'Henmy' will be 'Henry'. It's already begun. You never could say 'red'. You'd say 'rrr' instead. But no longer; now you say 'red' with perfect enunciation.

A final point on language: I'm pleased to report you've not sworn this month.

Whenever we go to a place where there are toys, like a gift shop, you pick something up and ask if it's 'Arwo's'. It takes considerable discipline from both parents to ask you to return it. It's hard because you're not bratty about it at all. You ask softly, with bright, wide eyes. But it's important that you don't always associate going somewhere with you automatically getting a toy.

Playing remains a dream for all of us. You know that Mummy works in childcare, but I'm not sure if I ever told you that Nana Hoover used to work in childcare as well. One of her jobs was to help parents who struggled with the concept of imaginary play with their children. She says parents would find it embarrassing. I cannot wrap my head around that one. Playing imaginary games is the best.

Sharing is an issue, as I assume it is for most two-year-olds. For the past three Fridays, we've had a young man named Flint over to play. He's six months older than you. He's been hanging out with us while his mummy, your mummy's friend Taci, recovers from surgery. He's a sweet kid. He loves diggers and cars. But you get very possessive of your toys when he comes over to play. I get it; it's tough. I have early memories from my childhood of not wanting to share my things. But you are beginning to grasp the concept. The other day, you brought my foam roller over to me and said, 'Dadda, share this with Arwo?'

Excluding Thursday's hiccup, you've been warmer towards Mummy. This is perfectly summed up when we walk down the street and you choose to hold both of our hands. The image captures everything I wanted out of parenthood – the three of us, a team, finding our way forward together, taking one step at a time. Each of us learning, helping one another and practising forgiveness when we go the wrong way or when we accidentally step on each other's toes.

That's what we've been doing. And we can't be doing a bad job, because you remain, 99 per cent of the time, a happy, playful, caring, imaginative little boy who loves to get up to mischief.

Final update. And this one is huge: I've dismantled your cot. You're now in possession of your very own big-boy bed. It's been a surreal and emotionally charged afternoon assembling it. Bits were missing. You were trying to 'help'. Mummy downloaded the wrong instruction manual. I've done very well not to swear (too much). But that's all behind us now, just as long as we remember to close the stair gate at night!

At the start of the year, I speculated on the big milestones you'd cross. I came up with three: potty-training, big-boy bed and language development. It's three months to the day since I told you that. Already, your language is soaring. Now you've made the leap from cot to big-boy bed, leaving potty-training as the final major milestone until – *fuck* – until you start school!

Thank you for another month of the parenthood gig, and sleep well in your new big-boy bed.

Apple Pie
Sunday, 20 February 2022

We've just finished dinner. You, Mummy and Nana Hoover are sitting around the table while I prepare dessert in the kitchen. We're having your new favourite, apple pie, which has become a Sunday-afternoon tradition. Grandad See-See works away in Yorkshire during the week, and he brings us one home on a Friday. We allow you to have a small bit on a Sunday, while I eat the rest the following week. Yes, this is a nutrition double standard, but it's not about to change – just be thankful we're becoming less uptight with food.

I return from the kitchen and pass the dessert-filled bowls round. Then I take my seat and watch the most extraordinary events unfold.

First, you carry out a portion inspection featuring zigzagging glances at all the bowls on the table. You can tell something is not quite right, but you don't yet possess the communication skills to say, 'Dad, you prick, why is my slice smaller than everyone else's?' Soon, the glancing becomes frowning. We all know precisely what you're thinking, and we struggle to contain our smiles.

And now a new expression: not one that speaks to the injustice of the situation – no, this one is more calculating. You're formulating a response. It's a fascinating moment to witness. *What are you planning?*

After a few seconds, your face transforms again as calculation gives way to curiosity and wonder. You turn to your mother, tilt your head in that adorable posture that no one can refuse and calmly ask, 'Mummy, Arwo have some of your apple pie?'

Mummy has to turn her head away so you can't see her laughing. Sensing you have the advantage, you press her again. 'Mummy, Arwo have some of your apple pie? Please, Mummy?'

You've done it. She gives you some of hers while your piece remains completely untouched.

'Ta, Mummy.'

'You're welcome.'

Three seconds later ...

'Mummy, Arwo have some of your apple pie? Please, Mummy?'

'Arlo's got his own apple pie. Why don't you eat yours?' she says.

You take a second and retreat into your mind, once again formulating a response. This is a game of chess. A few moments later, you play your next move. 'Arwo's too hot. Some of your apple pie, Mummy. Please?'

You've got her again. She cannot refuse you. That's now two bites you've secured without touching yours. You are an expert tactician.

But she refuses the third request. 'Arlo, you have your own piece. If it's too hot, then blow on it.'

Your response is all but instantaneous. You turn to your bowl and quickly blow it before turning back to Mummy. 'Arwo's apple pie, too hot. Arwo have some of your apple pie, Mummy?'

Unbelievable!

The three of us are now stifling giggles and handing you 10/10 scorecards for your performance. For the billionth time since becoming a parent, I have been surprised by your intelligence and capability. Children are fascinating creatures.

But it seems you've run out of moves because Mummy rejects your fourth request, though we've heard it all before. 'Arlo, you've had enough of Mummy's now. Keep blowing on yours until it cools down.'

'Please, Mummy.' Every single molecule of your biological make-up has been told to work in whatever way it can to make you look as cute as possible.

'Well ...' says Mummy, already faltering, 'if you eat yours, you can have more of mine.'

Mummy then gives Nana and me a triumphant nod suggesting she's won. I presume that *she* presumes your piece is still too hot, and that she will have eaten hers by the time yours has cooled down.

But she's wrong because ...

'Arlo, stop eating so quickly!' Mummy says.

Nana Hoover and I can no longer contain our laughter. We are all watching you wolf down your hot food like a starved animal who's chanced upon leftovers; you cannot possibly be enjoying it.

And yet, thirty seconds later, you place your spoon down delicately in your empty bowl, turn to your mother and casually ask, 'Mummy, Arwo have some more of your apple pie?'

Fucking priceless!

Spotify
Tuesday, 22 February 2022

I'm in an abusive relationship with Spotify. It's both toxic and volatile. And hard as it is to admit – I'm the abusive one.

Let me explain.

Spotify does everything in its power – its literal algorithmic CPU power – to please me. It starts by listening. How many relationship complaints are down to the other person not listening? Through my music choices and my curation habits, Spotify listens to everything I tell it, and then it uses that information to offer suggestions about what else I might like to hear – basically adding value to my life.

And how do I respond? By getting angry. I'm not in the least bit on board with its endorsement of a Mexican rendition of 'Hop Little Bunnies'. On the contrary, I find no song on earth more grating. But Spotify doesn't understand, because I keep playing nursery rhymes. Its job is to respond to the information I'm giving it, even though I can promise you that I'd rather drink a toenail smoothie than listen to nursery rhymes.

Talk about sending mixed messages.

Poor Spotify. On paper, it's doing everything it should do when in a long-term relationship. It's trying to mix things up to keep life interesting – growing with me. And yet, I tell it every day to go and fuck itself and to shove its 'Hokey Cokey' recommendation up its arse, along with 'Mary Had a Little Lamb' and

'Itsy Bitsy Spider', none of which qualify as musically pleasant experiences.

To cap it off, I commit the worst relationship-abuse misdeed: I blame it all on Spotify, telling them that it's all their fault and that they're making me angry.

Since coming to terms with the malignancy of my actions, I've made some improvements. From now on, if nursery rhymes are to be played, then they go through Mummy's account.

Sorry, Spotify. Hopefully things will soon improve. But seriously, stop playing 'Baby Shark'.

Arlo's Daddy Versus Arlo
Wednesday, 23 February 2022

'All rise for His Honour Judge Chumley Sebastian Warner the Third,' says whoever's job it is to announce such things in court – the clerk?

Whack, whack.

'Order, order in the court,' Judge Chumley says, banging his hammer as he takes his seat. With his out-of-control, untameable sideburns, the judge looks like a man who turned eighty, eighty years ago.

The defendant in the dock, Arlo, has been accused of ripping open several teabags for no reason other than sheer bantz. Arlo's daddy leads the prosecution, while Arlo's mummy stands in his defence.

This is a slightly unusual proceeding because both the defence and the prosecution also happen to be key witnesses. To properly adjudicate the matter,

Judge Chumley has called both Arlo's mummy and Arlo's daddy to the witness stand so that he can begin a line of questioning.

The jury, people of a mix of ages, ethnicities and backgrounds, sit in the jury box twiddling their thumbs and wondering how soon they can break for lunch, what's for lunch and how generous the portion sizes will be.

'Now,' begins Judge Chumley, directing his gaze to Arlo's daddy, 'you believe Arlo is guilty of criminal damage to several Taylors Yorkshire teabags, do you not?'

'I do, Your Honour.'

'And the defence, Arlo's mummy: you don't believe a crime has been committed at all.'

'Your Honour, the young man on trial is an actual saint. He's not capable of any wrongdoing. He's simply perfect.'

'Your Honour, my learned friend here is full of shit.'

'Is that so? Go on.'

'On the morning of the incident, three people were present: Arlo, Arlo's mummy and I. Neither I nor Arlo's mummy were anywhere near the crime scene when the incident occurred, and that's despite us being wonderful parents who never leave their child unattended. Only Arlo was there, and when I walked in on him, I saw him with my own eyes ripping a teabag in half while laughing.'

The judge looks at Arlo's mummy, who begins stuttering and stumbling. 'Well ... we don't ... know that it was intentional.'

'But intention or no intention, you don't deny that there were split teabags all over the worktop.'

'Now that I think about it, I don't recall seeing anything. I think my learned friend here is the one who's full of shit.'

'Does the prosecution have any evidence, or is it simply your word against hers?'

'Your Honour, I do have evidence. I have on camera the entire episode, which includes footage of Arlo's mummy being present.'

Arlo's mummy is stunned. She turns to Arlo, panic strewn across her face. Even the jury seems mildly engaged now.

'Your Honour, OK, perhaps I do remember the split teabags, but Arlo did not commit the crime on purpose. It was an accident, you see. He likes to help me separate the teabags and put them into the tea jar. It wasn't his fault.'

'What do you say to that, Arlo's daddy?'

'I think it will be better if I just show you.'

Moments later, a large projector screen is wired up, and Arlo's daddy plays a video for the jury. It shows Arlo sitting on the kitchen worktop with ripped-teabag contents sprawled everywhere. Arlo is wearing a wide, cheeky grin that tells the viewer he is loving life.

'Arlo, what have you made here?' says Arlo's daddy on camera.

'A mess,' he says, very deliberately waving his hand in the sprawling mass of diced-up tea leaves, turning the existing mess into a bigger mess.

A colossal intake of breath sounds out across the court.

The jury is stunned.

Journalists are scribbling notes down, desperate to make the evening edition.

'Order! Order in the court,' Judge Chumley barks. 'We'll now adjourn while the jury—'

'Actually, Your Honour,' says one of the jurors, 'we've already deliberated, and we have a verdict. Arlo is as guilty as they come.'

'Noooo!' shouts Arlo's mummy. 'My angel is perfect – leave him alone, you bullies.'

Whack, whack. 'Order!'

Everyone quietens down so that the judge can deliver his verdict. Arlo looks up, a little nervous but not *that* nervous.

'Arlo, I hereby sentence you to clean up your mess, for which you will need the aid of a vacuum cl—'

'YEAH! Ooofer! Dadda, Arwo get Ooofer and help?' says Arlo, already sprinting out of court and over to the basement door of his house where the vacuum cleaner lives.

Back in court, the judge addresses the room. 'I guess that's lunch. Court is adjourned.'

Whack.

Cyril
Thursday, 24 February 2022

'I am bringing enthusiasm and an unrivalled can-do attitude to this project. What will be your contribution?' I ask Mummy.

'Cashew nuts?'

'I can work with that.'

The project in question is, of course, the construction of the mighty cardboard fortress. The book Mummy ordered last week has arrived, and I am now perusing it for inspiration to see if I can add to my already established awesome vision. After a few seconds, I admit to myself that the ideas in the book are *possibly* better than the ones I had in my head.

'This is the one,' I say.

'The castle?'

'It's a fortress, but yes.'

'It says castle in the book.'

'No, it says shut up.'

'It does not.'

'It does, right next to where it asks if you're trying to ruin this experience for me, can you see?'

'Fine, fortress. It says we need two twenty-four by twenty-four by twenty-four-inch boxes.'

'Damn it!'

'Why damn it?'

'Because we don't have those.'

'How do you know? You haven't even measured, Harry Half-a-Job.'

'You're right, but I have correctly deduced two things about the three boxes in front of us.'

'What's that then?'

'First, none of them are the same size, so I'll go ahead and take one point, and also they're not square, because, if I remember my basic maths correctly, a twenty-four by twenty-four by twenty-four-inch box is a square box – or a cube if you want to hurl the semantics card in my face.' *Another point to me.*

'We'll have to find something else then. What about this cottage?' Mummy says, having turned to a new page of the book.

I guess we could build the cottage and then make adjustments so it looks more fortress-like. 'Very well, what do we need?'

'We only need one large twenty-four by twenty-four by twenty-four-inch box,' she says.

'Damn it again.'

'Why? We can use the big one, no?'

'What is it about the concept of a square that you're not grasping?' I say.

'Fine, let's look for something else then.'

We do, but it's apparent that despite having three different-sized boxes, we need more raw materials, especially if we're to create anything large enough for you to play *in* rather than *with*.

The situation calls for decisive leadership, someone brave enough to take the reins and guide us through these rough and uncertain times. 'There's only one thing for it,' I say.

'What's that?'

'We'll need to go off-piste and freestyle it from here. Don't worry. I've got us covered.'

'Great. What's your plan?'

'Are you familiar with the film *The Human Centipede*?'

'Yes, but—'

'We're doing that. The cardboard version.'

Mummy tries to protest but I block out her noise (no mean feat) and enter my mind space. I begin mentally sketching out concepts and designs for a fabulous cardboard centipede.

'We'll position the boxes in size order and cut the flaps so we can parcel-tape them to their counterparts,' I say, more to myself.

'Wait, aren't you gonna measure ... I guess not.'

I can't hear Mummy through the torrents of creative, flowing energy spilling out from every cell in my body. I move in with a box-cutter knife to sculpt the joints. I deftly slice away with precision, making subtle improvements at every opportunity. Soon, following the deployment of my creative skill (not Mummy's – she's sitting there gawping at me like a gormless idiot), I stand back and survey the completed work for stage one. I've done a banging job.

'Right, now we can fuse the pieces. I will work inside. You will work outside. You are to hand me pieces of tape as the enclosed space is too confined for me to wield the necessary tools. Do you understand? Are you ready?'

'This is never going—'

'I said are you ready? And yes, it will.'

I lie on my back and slide into the belly of the soon-to-be-alive monster arthropod. Mummy hands me pieces of tape, but she's doing what one would call 'a complete and utter wanky job' of it. She makes me wait for long intervals between haphazard thrusts of her arm in my direction proffering an almost always too-small piece of tape. She's not concentrating at all; some pieces are stuck together before they're transferred to my more capable hands.

'Can you please give a shit about your only son?'

'Piss off, I am.'

'You're not. And I'm beginning to suspect your heart's not in this project either.'

'Oh, it is, baby, all of it. I promise you,' she says in an utterly unconvincing monotone.

'What are we going to call it?' I ask, giving her another chance to participate.

'Cyril?'

'That's actually not terrible. Cyril the Centipede it is.'

After I complete a thorough and exemplary effort on the interior attachments, I slide out to inspect Mummy's labours.

Tut, tut. She hasn't applied herself at all. There's been no consideration for the tape placement or application, as if she's been humouring me the whole time – a theory that's confirmed as she leaves the room to go and make a cup of tea.

I go about undoing and redoing everything. Once I've rescued her bullshit efforts, I sculpt a beautiful pair of antennae, draw a face and write this on the side: *Hi Arlo, my name is Cyril, and I am a cardboard centipede who wants to be your friend.*

I'm so proud of the work that I send a picture to one of my mates. He quickly replies with: *Now that is a serious caterpillar! Great job, mate.*

I don't respond. Instead, I make one minor alteration. On the side, it now says: *Hi Arlo, my name is Cyril, and I am a cardboard ~~centipede~~ caterpillar who wants to be your friend.*

Mummy returns. 'Why is Cyril now a caterpillar?'

'Erm, because ... because one of Arlo's favourite books is *The Very Hungry Caterpillar*.'

Arlo, Meet Cyril
Friday, 25 February 2022

'Arlo, is this the greatest cardboard caterpillar that you've ever been in?'

'Yes, it is, Dadda. Ta, Dadda.'

'You are most welcome, son,' I say while throwing Mummy a stern nod, which was probably more to myself than it was to Mummy because I needed your reassurance. Putting my silliness to the side for one moment – and only one moment – I admit that Cyril is no masterpiece. In fact, my cardboard-creator peers would probably label Cyril an abomination and ask me never again to refer to them as colleagues.

But it doesn't matter, because you're happy. And if you're happy, then my work here is done!

'Dadda, come in here.'
'You got it, buddy. I'm on my way.'

Medical Notes
Saturday, 26 February 2022

Patient is a two-day-old caterpillar named Cyril with severe lacerations around the mid-segment spiracles leading to a complete separation of his upper and lower sections. The incident is thought to have occurred because a small but surprisingly strong pair of two-year-old human arms wrenched Cyril apart. We need to operate immediately if we are to save Cyril's life and assuage the emotions of Cyril's attacker, who is currently screaming at his daddy to fix things. Finally, there have been reports that this is not the first time that Cyril has been ripped in half today. The surgeon on scene for the previous incident was Doctor Mummy, who performed a thorax-to-abdomen-stitch-up-with-tape-and-hope-for-the-best. I suggest we repeat the procedure.

March

bedtime
noun

The time when someone usually goes to bed – unless you're a toddler who enjoys confusing bedtime with playtime.

The Parenthood Dictionary
Adventures in Dadding Edition

Goodbye, Cyril
Friday, 4 March 2022

I walk into the following conversation:

'Arlo, what's happening to Cyril this week?' Mummy says.

'He's going away,' you answer.

'That's right, and that's OK, isn't it?'

'Yeah.'

I have no words. Only reactionary thoughts. Betrayer. Traitor. Manipulator. Back-stabber.

I won't stand for this. 'How very dare—'

'Now, now, Daddy. What did Mummy say, Arlo? We can make a new Cyril when …'

'When Dadda gets more boxes.'

'That's right, and that's the matter settled, and we don't need to complicate it, do we, Daddy?'

'Fine. You win this round.'

I slink downstairs back into the basement and begin plotting Cyril's resurrection. *His death will not be in vain.* Cyril 2.0 is coming, and he will be bigger and stronger than ever before.

I face this challenge with the will and determination to succeed … and with a heavy-duty staple gun that I've just bought from Amazon …

With my response conceived, I return upstairs.

'Here's one box we don't need to throw out,' Mummy says, indicating a small cardboard box.

'OK, what do you want it for?'

'I need to send something back,' Mummy says *very* sheepishly.

I pounce. 'Oh?'

'It's just a thing. If you must know, I'm sending the buggy muff back.'

Yes! 'Why? Is it not working out for you?'

'I maybe shouldn't have bought it, though I still think it's a good idea.'

'I agree, it's a wonderful idea if your goal is to create a shit product that wastes resources.'

'All right, you don't have to be a cunt about the whole thing.'

'You expect far too much from me. Now, shall we have a look at getting you some gloves? Have I told you about glo—'

'FUCK OFF!'

Goodnight, Arlo
Tuesday, 8 March 2022

We're failing to progress through the second of three planned bedtime stories. Why? Because you, my boy, have become a master strategist in delaying us. I don't understand how you're so proficient in a game you're new to playing – unlike your parents who have seventy-three years of combined life experience. And yet here we are, being psychologically outplayed by a two-year-old. I say that having just put the book I'm trying to read down on the floor so the three of us can dance to 'Baby Shark', an activity that no parent should be encouraging five minutes before a toddler's bedtime – one that was scheduled to begin fifteen minutes ago!

And now we're dancing to 'I Like to Move It'.

Eventually, we wrestle back control of the situation and complete the story. It's finally time for bed.

'Arwo get some friends?'

'You can take some friends with you to bed,' Mummy says while we both wait for the master performer to break out his next trick.

'They have all done poo-poo.'

And there it is.

'No, they haven't. Only ... three of your friends have done a poo-poo. Do you want Mummy, Daddy or Arlo to change them?' Mummy says.

'Arwo do it.'

'Fine. Quick sticks.'

First, you select Louie. You pretend to change him, throwing the imaginary soiled nappy out the window before putting a new one on him and then chucking him into bed. Next, you select Baby Yoda[4], who's presumably got an upset tummy because your nappy-changing turnaround time has plummeted.

'Let's speed things up, buddy,' I say.

You launch Baby Yoda into bed. Now it's the turn of one of the Boos – a Boo naturally being one of the Tombliboos from *In The Night Garden*.

Time drips slowly away as images flash through my mind: snails, sloths, ice thawing at room temperature and car journeys as a child.

You eventually complete the last nappy change and you're about to throw the Boo into bed, but then you remember you've been doing it all wrong this whole time. You shouldn't be *throwing* your friends. Instead, you should be escorting them to the footboard of your bed and assisting them in performing a 'big hop'.

And now time feels like it's reversing,

'Big hop, Boo,' you say as you throw him (or her).

'Whoa, that is a big hop,' say Mummy and I at the same time.

'No. That was only a little hop. Do it aga—'

'No, Arlo, that was a big hop, not a little hop,' Mummy says, cutting you off.

---

[4] Don't even come at me with 'that's not his name'. Obviously, I know 'Grogu' is written on his birth certificate – have you even read my author bio? Parenthood can be summed up as one lifelong string of compromises, and one of mine is having to occasionally allow Arlo's mother to rewrite *Star Wars* mythology. I will course correct when Arlo is old enough.

March

But you ignore her. You escort the Boo back around to the starting blocks. 'Big hop, Boo ... Yay! That was a big hop.'

Baby Yoda takes three attempts. Luckily, Louie only needs one, although, hang on ... you've suddenly become a statue: solid and stoic. I think you're reconsidering the distance of Louie's hop. I'm watching your face, and I can see the cogs turning as if there is an independent panel of judges in your brain debating and disagreeing with each other.

After a few moments ... 'Louie do. Little hop. Do it again, Louie.'

Mummy and I have become cartoon versions of ourselves: swollen, bloodshot eyes, thick, pulsing green veins throbbing away in time to the swing of a pendulum, while loose grey hairs drop from my skull like they're part of a suicide pact.

'Quickly then,' I say.

You hurl Louie. 'BIG HOP, LOUIE.'

Thud.

'Right, Arlo – into bed,' Mummy says.

'I need more friends.'

Oh, for fuck— 'Take three more friends, but hurry up,' I say.

You grab Bluey-D, your blue dinosaur (obviously). You're about to big-hop him in when you turn to your mother, who reads you like a children's book.

'No, Arlo, Bluey-D has absolutely not done a poo-poo. His nappy is clean.'

You've returned to that statue-like state, not moving, blinking or breathing. Until ... 'Bluey-D, need wee-wee on the potty, Mummy.'

'No, Arlo—'

Too late. You've squatted and leant Bluey-D against your drawers to do a wee-wee on an imaginary potty.

At that point, Mummy and I do the worst possible thing – we laugh. We disguise it by turning around and keeping our heads low, but you're all too familiar with this particular body-language sequence.

You've got both of us right where you want us.

You wander over and tap me on the shoulder. I grant a peripheral look to find you standing with a massive fuck-off smirk on your face. 'Dadda, more friends need wee-wee on the potty.'

We don't fight you. We couldn't anyway – we're still giggling. You line up your grey dinosaur, Roary, your stethoscope-wearing orangutan, Dr Tang, the rest of the Boos and Mr Moo Cow Chow, all ready for a wee-wee on the potty.

But you faff for so long with Bluey-D and Dr Tang that Mummy stops finding things funny. She explains that your friends are at school and in toilets housing three cubicles that can cater for their urination needs simultaneously. 'Right, all done,' she says.

I order you into bed with a slightly raised voice so the message lands that the curtains have finally come down on tonight's performance. We kiss you goodnight and walk out the door.

'Mamma.'

'What is it, Arlo?'

'I've done a poo-poo.'

When In Doubt, Live Like A Toddler
Thursday, 10 March 2022

Mummy often hijacks my attention to show me something on one of her social-media feeds. I've repeatedly told her not to do this, because what she wants to show me is something I'm almost certain I won't care about. I base this statement not on dreamt-up facts but on actual data taken from my reviewing of all the times she's hit me with a you-totally-have-to-see-this type of interruption, which I file away in one of two categories: 'worthless interruption' and 'not a worthless interruption'. The stats won't surprise you: 99 per cent of the time, the interruptions are sent to the former category.

However, tonight was one of those rare 1 per cent exceptions. She showed me a post entitled 'When in Doubt, Live Like a Toddler'. It's a list of behavioural conventions that toddlers follow automatically but forget as they grow up – for example, 'fun is always first'. I'd quote the entire list, but for the life of me, I cannot find who wrote the article originally[5] to correctly attribute it. But it got me thinking about your personality, and I was inspired to create a list of my own. Some are similar to the original list (just google 'When in Doubt, Live Like a Toddler'); others are not.

So, here goes. When in doubt, live like a toddler. Here's why:

---

5 If you know, please write to me and tell me.

1. You maintain presence of mind.
2. If you're not having your basic needs tended to, you spend your waking life committed to another basic need – the need to play.
3. You have mastered the art of saying 'no'.
4. You're proud of your achievements no matter how small, and you praise others for theirs.
5. You find joy in the smallest of things.
6. You speak from the heart, expressing the full range of your emotions even if you can't make sense of them.
7. You do whatever is necessary to achieve your goals, rarely giving up, and you recognise that an obstacle is just an obstacle and not a dead end.
8. You find it easy to forgive others.

I find it almost paradoxical that most people (myself included) forget to live life like this and only relearn it from watching their children. I'm reminded that parenthood is not one-way traffic: parent and child are both students, one learning what *is*, while the other learns what *was*.

When in doubt, live like a toddler.

Expectation Versus Reality: Co-Sleeping
Friday, 11 March 2022

Context: we're staying at Rebecca and Sean's house. Mummy has become Drunk Mummy, which means a less than desirable bed-sharing companion. Unlike on New Year's Eve, you're sleeping alone in their spare room in a double bed. You wake, and when I go in to settle you, I decide to stay in bed with you rather than return and endure Drunk Mummy.

Expectation of co-sleeping with a toddler: a harmonious state of compatibility. Father and son lie together in each other's company, finding comfort as one gently nestles his head in the neck of the other. The father wonders if there's ever been a more perfect moment.

Reality of co-sleeping with a toddler: regret. Tiredness. Constant shuffling. Agitation and astounded confusion at how a two-year-old can subconsciously track my movements and continually smash me in the face with his wayward elbows. That's despite me regularly getting out of bed and retreating to the other side.

Future recommendation: accept that sleeping with Drunk Mummy is the better of two deeply undesirable scenarios.

A Casual Saturday
Saturday, 12 March 2022

We're having a lovely day. It started with us walking into town to eat at our favourite restaurant. You measured things with your tape measure while waiting for your food and entertained the other diners in the process. After dinner, we go to the market to buy fruit, and then we go into the shopping centre, to Lush, to buy you a bath bomb.

We then leave Lush and walk around until we stumble on a temporary addition to the town, a huge *PAW Patrol* fire truck made from Lego and big enough for children to sit in. You're not yet into *PAW Patrol*, but you are into fire trucks. Naturally, we're drawn to the other families that have gathered around.

The children are eager to have a turn in the fire engine, and parents, including yours, are eager to capture photographic evidence of this experience.

But there are rules for this type of thing. Here they are:

1. Parents or grandparents must ensure their children or grandchildren wait their turn.

2. Do not photobomb another family's photo. It's rude.

3. Parents or grandparents are not to let their children or grandchildren hog the prime photo-capturing position for long. There are other families waiting, and they've all got important business to attend to.

March

4. Finally, don't be a cunt. A rule you immediately breach if you break any of the previous rules.

We've all got a stake in the game. Following the rules benefits everyone.

Enter Stupid Nana.

Stupid Nana arrives with her granddaughter a second after we do. And I know that she knows that, because she caught my warning expression: *Remember to follow the photo-in-public rules!*

But Stupid Nana elects to bypass us and the rules altogether. Instead, she drags her granddaughter over to the side of the fire engine, barking '*Ela, ela!*' at her (I presume she's Greek) and breaking rules one and two. The child currently sitting in the fire engine, the one who's just been photobombed by Stupid Nana, climbs down. Stupid Nana's granddaughter climbs up and, as aggressively directed by her grandmother, begins posing for photos.

She stands on ceremony for the first few clicks, but you can tell she just wants to play with the fucking fire engine for a bit. You know, bash a few dials and pretend to drive it – basic shit kids love to do. But Stupid Nana isn't having any of it as she circles the truck with as much poise and elegance as a piece of creaky old furniture attempting ballet for the first time.

HURRY THE FUCK UP!

Eventually, her ashamed-looking granddaughter is permitted to climb down. The two of them skulk off in a way that tells me Stupid Nana was fully aware that she broke all four rules and felt no remorse for her actions.

Such a shame. We were having a lovely family day out. I really hope she gets gout.

Ice Cream Revisited
Sunday, 13 March 2022

Another family day. This time, we drove with Nana Hoover to a beautiful village outside Northampton called Olney. We've gone our separate ways to explore the shops. Nana is with you on the street, playing with a toy she just bought you from a charity shop while Mummy and I browse in another charity shop: me for books (naturally) and Mummy for clothes.

I leave Mummy to it and return to you and Nana.
'Dadda!'
'Hi, Arlo.'
'Dadda, come with me. Ice cream.'
You grab my hand and walk me to a nearby ice-cream parlour. Then you waste no time slapping your hands and face up against the glass, staring longingly into the colourful, tasty-looking selection of ice creams on offer.

I glance at Nana Hoover – a coded message: *Have you hatched a plan to get ice cream?*

'No, I promise. He saw it and knew exactly what it was.'

For your part, you're continuing to stare. You haven't asked if you can have some, but I can see your longing-filled eyes in the reflection from the glass. As you know, we take a hard stance on nutrition, only giving in to social pressures like birthday parties. But this is one time where I think I need to bury my principles. I call Mummy and explain.

'He hasn't asked me for one, but he's looking very hopeful. I don't think I can walk away.'

'Get him one. He's behaved beautifully all weekend.'

'OK.'

I end the call and descend to your level. 'Arlo, can I talk to you?' You snap around, almost as if you were waiting for this conversation to happen.

'Yes, Dadda?'

'Would you like to have an ice cream?'

'YEAH!'

'Shall we go and get one then?'

'OK, Dadda,' you say while already walking around to the entrance. A woman holds open the door for you. There are people in the shop: a family with three teenage children. They all perform a simultaneous 'awww' as you announce your presence.

You look to me for guidance. 'When this nice lady has finished serving this other nice lady, you can tell her which ice cream you would like,' I say.

The nice lady finishes serving the other nice lady and completes the transaction. Then she turns to you and asks what you would like.

'Pink ice cream.'

'Pl—'

'Pink ice cream, please,' you say.

The family is still here watching you, still wearing that look I'm so used to seeing you bring out in others.

Nice lady hands you a strawberry ice cream and you say, 'Ta.'

We pay and leave.

This whole thing is a big deal, though you wouldn't necessarily realise it on the surface. First, our strict stance on nutrition means that you appreciate the rare time we cut you a break. You haven't taken such a simple act as me buying you ice cream for granted, and you're enjoying the experience all the more because of it. Next, when I offered to buy you one, I just asked you, plain and simple. I didn't justify my decision and tell you it's a treat, or say 'it's because you've behaved well this weekend'.

I think the language we use around food is wrong. We refer to anything unhealthy as 'treats', but this seemingly innocent language can inform and shape an individual's relationship with food – not necessarily a healthy one.

One day, you'll ask me why you can't have lots of sweets. I will tell you the truth. Sugary foods are terrible for your body, but having one every once in a while – not as a treat but as a one-off – won't harm you. This will help us maintain our approach while providing an excuse for those rare exceptions. Hopefully, you'll continue to value these experiences without taking them for granted. In return, we get something out of the experience as well, as there is nothing quite as satisfying for a parent as seeing their child in a state of happiness, even if it's one of short-lived gratification.

'Is that nice, Arlo?'

'Hmmm, yeah, it is, Dadda.'

Looks
Monday, 14 March 2022

I've been thinking about those times when you draw attention because of your looks, like yesterday in the ice cream parlour. The compliments you receive cause warm, fuzzy feelings to erupt inside me. But I've never been able to figure out if I like hearing those comments for me – because it's nice hearing remarks like that – or if it's more appreciated on your behalf. Let me explain.

Some people are born attractive (like Mummy). Others – not so much. You can't help but get visually drawn to people you find pleasing on the eye. I'm not saying looks are everything; they're not. But they are what you would call an intangible asset, and I've heard many times that it's statistically proven that looks can open more doors for you. Is that fair? No, it's not, but without getting into a discussion about cosmetic surgery, we have no control over how we look. It's just the luck of the draw.

Seeing the smiles and warm looks that other people direct at you and hearing the 'awws' and the 'ahhs' makes me wonder if similar psychology is in play. Yes, you might be far too young to be interested in dating, but the results are similar. People want to get close to you, talk to you, help you accomplish a goal like choosing a bath bomb or opening a door, or listen to you babble away, and I believe that benefits your confidence levels.

It might not be fair that good looks can open more doors for you, but many things in life that we have no control over aren't fair. If those are the conditions of the game, I'm thankful that you're on the right side of the equation. At least for now. The tide could one day turn against you. I say that because I was a first-rate eye-stinging sight as a child. Thankfully, your mother's genes look set to spare you from my fate.

Parenting Paradoxes
Wednesday, 16 March 2022

Mummy and I give you as much freedom as possible. When we're at the park, we never rush. Instead, we encourage you to explore wherever takes your fancy, whether that's a row of park benches, the bandstand or the café. We remind you how long we've got left and tell you that if you want to play on the swings, we need to head in that direction. We leave the decision to you.

Often, you want to stay and jump off benches.

'That's fine,' one of us says, 'but we won't have time to go to the park. Do you understand?'

You say you do, but, of course, when the time is up and we need to go home, you get upset because you want to go on the swings. We knew this would happen, but we let it play out anyway. Why? Because you being in control of your choices is more important to us than following strictures such as 'park must only equal swings'. Why can't park equal messing about on the benches or something else? Also, had we done the opposite and pressed to go directly to the swings, then you would have kicked off at not being able to explore elsewhere. We can't win.

When you fancy opposing us at bedtime, the entire routine can be exhausting. We're desperate for you to go to bed so we can have a break. But within minutes of you falling asleep, Mummy and I miss you.

We pour every ounce of our parenting energy into helping you grow and develop. We're incredibly proud every time you reach a new milestone or accomplish something for the first time, but we're also sad. Each day of you becoming more capable and independent is another day closer to you growing up – a day we'd gladly delay forever. But we can't. That's why being present in every moment is vital for parents and why I always bang on about it.

Having children means forgoing the freedom to do what you want when you want. You're signing up to almost permanent stress in your life owing to the demands placed on your time and energy. Sleep deprivation becomes part of your routine. Your work-life balance is bombarded with distractions that last for years. Well-being risks now carry added weight because it's not just your own well-being that you have to consider, it's that of your kids, a concern that can lead you into more stress and even less sleep.

On what planet does it sound like a good idea to get in the parenthood queue and say 'sign me up'? And yet, speaking generally and ignoring the odd exception, parents wouldn't have it any other way. The love and joy they receive from the gig outweighs and outranks everything else.

That's insane. It doesn't make any sense. But it's true.

These are all parenting paradoxes.

March Monthly Review
Saturday, 19 March 2022

My new favourite Arlo phrases are 'Calm your bones' and 'What you laughing at, Chuckles?' You still speak in a broken, staccato dialect, but what you say is mostly in complete sentences. The other day, Mummy was driving past the park when the sun was setting. You gazed out the window and said, 'Mamma, look! Park is orange-sunny-shiny,' signalling what no doubt will become my favourite phase in your language development, where you rely on your limited vocabulary to describe sights, big ideas and the world in general that's slowly making more and more sense to you each day.

You're socially more aware of what's going on. You'll be playing, and Mummy and I will be talking about you. You'll suddenly go quiet, pausing the game so you can eavesdrop.

You are starting to get to grips with labelling your emotions. You can tell us correctly when you're happy or sad, and you'll often ask me if I'm one of the two.

You grow funnier each day.

Nursery remains a fertile environment for your development. Drop-offs are fine; you wave goodbye to Mummy and then go about your day, exploring to your heart's content. I'm thankful we dared relocate you to yet another setting (remember, this is your third) as it's one that seems purpose-built for you.

It was raining heavily when I collected you on Wednesday. Jasmine brought you to the door, took one look at the weather and then asked you if you wanted her to put you in your puddle suit and wellies so we could walk home and jump in puddles. I love that approach. Incidentally, you said yes, and we had a bloody fun walk home.

Bing is back in our lives. The show has returned to the top spot. He doesn't annoy me as much as he did last year. You might recall from *Toddler Inc.* that I hated *Bing,* but you stopped watching it just before you turned two. The timing was poignant because it signalled to me that you were shedding old favourites to make way for new ones as you approached the next chapter in your life.

You've also started enjoying a show called *Small Potatoes*. It's fucking awful – I can't even be bothered to go into more detail. Hopefully, you'll lose interest in it soon.

Surprisingly, you haven't got out of bed at night once, even though your cot no longer cages you in. I thought for sure we'd be in for some bollocks on your part.

That's not to say there's been no bollocks. I recounted one such evening at the start of March, but there's been a variation of that narrative most nights. You refuse to sit still for story time. Now we ask you if you want a story or if you just want to get your soft-toy friends and put them to bed. Sadly, you often bypass story time altogether.

Speaking of nappies, you haven't shown an interest in your potty or sitting on the toilet seat since the start of the month. You also hate having your nappy changed, and you've started keeping quiet when you drop a code brown. Fortunately, other signs alert us to those.

We're not sure what to do here. You are definitely ready for potty-training, but we have a couple of holidays lined up for May – one of which is to America. I'm getting heart palpitations just thinking about how stressful that will be, and that's without the added pressure of toilet accidents occurring at 38,000 feet in the air.

Sharing remains up and down. Sometimes you're great at it. Other times you're not. As a parent, I struggle with how to land the correct message here. We encourage you to share your toys, especially ones that aren't your favourites or ones you're not currently playing with. But we also tell you that it's your choice.

The other day, Haylee was over. You were sitting up at the table eating a snack. She started playing with one of your toys, and you kicked off. We tried to calm you down, but you weren't having it. I get it. It must be confusing when we tell you that they're your toys and that you don't have to share them but then ask you to calm down when you express annoyance at someone else playing with them, even though it really is OK because you're sitting at the table eating and are not in a position to play with toys at that moment – confusing much?

We'll continue to muddle through as best we can. I believe consistent messaging is the key, but some situations are varied and subjective, making parenting and toddlering difficult.

Ending on a high note, the frequency of you telling Mummy and me that you love us has increased. And it melts our hearts. You've not yet realised how easy it would be to repurpose that statement into an effective weapon of manipulation, but it won't be long.

The Six Whys
Sunday, 20 March 2022

We're eating fajitas for dinner. Well, Mummy and I are; you've finished, and you've excused yourself from the dinner table.

'Arlo, can you sit back at the table, please?' I say.
'Why?'

'Because Mummy and Daddy are still eating.'
'Why?'
'Because we haven't finished our food.'
'Why?'
Jesus Christ. 'Because we each had more on our plate than you, and we haven't had as many snacks as you today, so we're still hungry.'
'Why?'
'Er, well, we didn't have as many snacks because you took them all, and being a parent requires an awful lot of energy – more than you can possibly comprehend, so we need more food.'
'Why?'
Because-you're-an-agitating-little-bastard-who's-driving-me-to-derangement! 'Arlo ... could you please sit at the table and wait until we've finished eating?'[6]
'OK, Dadda.'

You return. Your attention wanders to a half-eaten wrap on your plate and then to the nearby pot of sour cream. You spoon out a heap of the stuff, but instead of tipping its contents onto your wrap, you tip them into your mouth – a decision you instantly regret because you spit it all back out again, before using the spoon to spread the spat-out sour cream over your half-eaten wrap.

---

6 We quickly realised that Arlo was far too young to begin table-etiquette training and dispensed with it altogether. That said, home-made fruit ice lollies have been very effective in getting him to sit still for a while. Maybe they can help you. Just remember to use quality food-grade silicon moulds, *not* plastic ones.

But you quickly tire of this activity, giving up halfway and declaring, 'Arwo finished, Dadda. Has Dadda finished?'

'I think I have, yes. It's strange, but I've suddenly lost my appetite.'

'Why?'

Sexuality
Monday, 21 March 2022

Last week we spoke about appearance. Today, I want to touch on sexuality. 'But I'm not even three yet, Dad – surely that's too early,' I hear you say. Well, yes and no.

First, and I told you this in *Dear Dory*, neither Mummy nor I care about your sexuality. We don't care if you're homosexual or heterosexual; bisexual or bi-curious; greysexual, autosexual, pansexual, polysexual or asexual; biromantic or panromantic; autoromantic or aromantic; non-binary or gender fluid; or any of the others that I missed, so long as it's legal – stay away from those baa-baas.

I hadn't heard of many of those sexual orientations. And despite me reading a helpful article online, I've already forgotten how you define most of them. I'm sure I can re-educate myself if you come home one day and announce you're into whatever.

When Mummy comments on you being handsome, you can bet I'll add value to the comment by saying something incredibly tasteful about your bedpost, along the lines of, 'He stands a good chance of attracting many female sexual partners in life.' Such comments provoke a specific response: 'Or boys! He might be into boys – we just don't know yet!' she says.

This is when I feel the desire to hot-wire a bus and run Mummy over. Because I explain and have previously explained a thousand times that I am agreeing with her sentiment that you are indeed a handsome young man. I'm not stating what I want your sexual preference to be because I couldn't care less. But Mummy likes to pretend these conversations don't happen, climb aboard her LGBTQIA+ high horse and parrot the 'I'm an inclusive woman, and you need to be an inclusive man' line. Seriously, Arlo, she needs to shut up.

And anyway, I don't think my having to evidence my sexual progressiveness values will matter, because, based on my early observations, I believe you will grow up to be a heterosexual. Time will tell if I'm correct or not.

So what are my observations?

Let's start with Auntie Raa-Raa. You have a soft spot for her and it's easy to see why. She's pretty. As is the woman at the checkout of the local Aldi who you went uncharacteristically shy over when we were paying for our food the other day. Then there's your nursery key worker, Abi. Also pretty, and your new favourite member of staff. A coincidence? Sure, it's possible. But maybe not.

So, there you have it. Your behaviour changes when in the company of pretty females, and I believe that, even at this early stage of your life, this indicates your sexuality. I guess we'll see.

Finally, it would pain your mother and me if you ever felt ashamed of your sexuality and what we thought of it. I hope my going into detail in this chapter goes some way to breaking down any potential barriers between us in the years to come should we need to go there. All we want is for you to be yourself and be comfortable with, and proud of, who you are. Neither of us will judge, and we're willing to support you in whatever way we can.

Just remember what I said about the baa-baas – they're off limits!

Hoist The Bunting
Tuesday, 22 March 2022

You and I are at the hospital for an eye check-up with your consultant ophthalmologist. Mummy is at work. The ophthalmologist, Jenny, has just finished testing your right eye – the stronger of the two – and now she wants to test your left eye, the weaker one.

'Now, Arlo, can you look back at the screen and tell me what you can see?' Jenny says.

'Apple.'

'Good boy. And now this?'

'A cup.'

'Excellent. Next one?'

'Fishy.'

'Brilliant.'

And on it continues. You respond to everything quickly and correctly.

Now for the verdict!

'I think you can stop patching him altogether,' Jenny says.

'What ... stop? As in, stop completely?' I say, having a hard time grasping the reality of her words.

'That's right. If anything, you've been too rigorous in patching Arlo each day, and the weaker eye has become his stronger eye.'

No fucking way! Arlo, you have no idea what it's like for me to hear those words. It's hard to describe the dread that overcame Mummy and me when we were first told about your condition when you were only a few months old. At the time, they misdiagnosed you, leading us to believe you had a congenital cataract. Of course, we didn't know it was a misdiagnosis then. We were told you needed surgery immediately. If you didn't have it, you risked going blind in that eye. We were also told that our lives would involve a lot of trips to Cambridge hospital for appointments, one of which would feature a lesson in how to change your contact lens! The weight of that day still lurks in my long-term memory, the lowest moment of my and Mummy's parenthood journey.

But it didn't last.

We learnt of the misdiagnosis: surgery was off the table, and there would be no regular trips to Cambridge for appointments. You cannot imagine the weight that was lifted from me that day.

And you responded to the patching treatment brilliantly, quickly assimilating it as part of your daily routine. We started with six hours a day but gradually dropped to two. Now I'm being told we can do away with it altogether. We've gone from being told you *could* go blind in one eye to your weaker eye becoming your stronger eye.

Someone hand me a bottle of champagne, already. This is a cause for celebration! What do you reckon – shall we call Mummy?

Oh Dear!
Thursday, 24 March 2022

I'm in the house. You and Mummy are in the car, running a few errands.

Ring, ring. It's Mummy.

'Yo!' I say.

'Arlo, what do we need to tell Daddy?'

'What have you got me, son?'

You don't answer. So Mummy says, 'Daddy, we were ringing to tell you that if you use the last of the nappies in the changing bag, you need to replace them.'

Fuck! 'You know, I'm delighted you brought that up because I have a side to that story I would like to share with you.'

'I bet you have. Please, by all means, share away.'

'When I changed him earlier – when he'd done a poo that you didn't even notice—'

'Excuse—'

'It's rude to interrupt. As I was saying, I changed him, and, as you have correctly pointed out, I used the last nappy. But I set a mental reminder to restock the bag, and as God is my witness, I fully intended to do so.'

'Right …'

'Well, there you have it, you thought I was being absent-minded and that it didn't occur to me to restock the bag, but I'm telling you it did. So, I guess we're done, yes?'

'No, we're not done. You didn't fill it. Why didn't you fill it?'

'An excellent question – you're on a roll today, aren't you? I was about to restock the bag, but Arlo was kicking off because you said he couldn't take his Hoover to your mum's, which—'

'Yes?'

'Well, the reason you gave him was that it wouldn't fit in the car, which – not to point fingers – is a lie because it does. And if you hadn't lied to him, then he wouldn't have a reason to throw a strop, and I wouldn't have become distracted. As you can see, it's really your choices that led us here. If this experience has taught me anything, it's that we all need to do better. And can I say one final thing?'

'WHAT?'

'You're in the car with our son, and he's going to hear and repeat any swear words you hurl my way. But look on the bright side – we're communicating.'

March

Surprise Weekend
Friday, 25 March 2022

Last year, Mummy and a few of my mates' partners got together and organised a special Father's Day weekend. We were sent on a treasure hunt in Cambridge, which admittedly we largely sacked off in favour of the pub, but the whole weekend was bloody awesome. So awesome that we've decided to repay the favour this year for Mother's Day. We've hired a house near Horsham and told the mummies not to worry about parenting for the weekend. It's the least we can do. It even has a heated pool.

Of course, leaving her child while not worrying about leaving her child is something that Mummy is biologically incapable of doing. Since I told her about this big surprise for her – a surprise made possible by the investment of a lot of time – she's steadily been wading through the seven stages of grief. Let's run through them:

- Shock and disbelief: 'Going away? Leaving Arlo with you? But he won't have his Mummy. No, I can't be going away. Are you being serious?'
- Denial: 'There's no way I'm going away for the *whole* weekend. Certainly not.'
- Guilt: 'It's not fair if I leave him for that long. You'll have to do all the work.'
- Anger and bargaining: 'I don't have to drink that much if I don't want to, so don't

tell me to "go nuts". Can I get up early Sunday morning and drive straight home?'
- Depression: 'I'm going to miss him so much. I won't know what to do with myself.'
- Reconstruction: 'You'll send me lots of videos, won't you? And I'll be able to video-call you all the time. And I guess it's not a full weekend, because I'll be coming home early on Sunday morning. I think I can do this!'
- Acceptance: 'OK, I guess I'll go. Thank you for organising this, by the way.'

Mother's Day
Sunday, 27 March 2022

Yesterday, we went to buy flowers from the market. I said to you, 'Pick three bunches of flowers. One for Mummy, one for Nana See-See and one for Nana Hoover.' You chose from the nearest stand, which happened to be the cheapest.

When you handed them out today to their respective recipients, no one raised an eyebrow at me being a cheapskate. Why? Because I told them the truth. I said that you picked them. Suddenly, they were the most prized flowers on the planet!

You know what this means, don't you? I can now reduce my gift budget for Mummy and your grandmothers by 90 per cent, so long as I say the gifts were chosen by you. They won't care. *Ker-ching!*

A Day In The Life Of Arlo: Voices
Monday, 28 March 2022

Arlooo, can you hear me?

Oh crap, Louie, it's him again. Stop it. I'm not listening to you!

I just want to say one thing.

Fine, what is it?

You know how you're sitting next to your daddy, eating breakfast?

Yes.

And you know how part of your breakfast is blueberries?

I don't like where this is going, Louie. I wonder what he—

I want you to wipe your blueberry-covered hands all over your daddy and shriek with laughter.

No, my daddy will—

Do it. Do-it-do-it-do-it-do-it-do-it-do-it-do-it. DO IT!

Louie, he keeps pestering me. I don't think I have any other choice. *OK! Here goes.*

'Dadda.'

'Yes, Arlo.'

'Dadda, look,' I say, wiping my blueberry hands all over his T-shirt.

'Ah, Arlo. Please don't do that.'

Don't listen to him, Arlo. Listen to me, your conscience. I know what's good for you, not your stupid daddy. Besides, he's tricking you. He really wants you to do it again.

Are you sure, Mr Your Conscience?

I'm so sure. Try it again if you don't believe me.

'Dadda, look!' I say, grinning.

'Arlo, don't you dare ... Why did you do that when I asked you not to?'

Again! Do it again! Again-again-again-again-again.

'Dadda, look,' I say, again thrusting my blue and purple hands in my daddy's direction, repeatedly hitting the target, a bit like the needle in my nana's sewing machine.

'Arlo, I've asked you not to do that. Are you going to use your listening ears?'

Not on your fucking nelly, Dadda! Arlo's listening ears have gone on holiday. Arlo, give the bastard another round of blueberry-covered fingers.

'Daaaaaaddddddaaaaa,' I say.

'Arlo, don't you even think about it.'

Too late for that!

Louie, would you mind if I blamed the whole thing on you?

April

self-esteem
noun

1. A level of confidence in one's value and abilities.
2. A psychological space that children insist on targeting for attack.

The Parenthood Dictionary
Adventures in Dadding Edition

I Wish This Was April Fool's
Friday, 1 April 2022

Your new goal in life is to destroy my self-esteem.

It starts when I lie on your play mat and begin casually tapping the floor. 'No, Daddy, like Arwo,' you say, before inviting yourself to demonstrate how to correctly tap the floor in an absent-minded fashion, almost as if there were rules to follow, rules that you apparently know but I don't.

The worst thing? I bought into your bullshit and tried to follow along as you showed me the *correct way*. But clearly, I wasn't paying attention, because you kept yelling, 'No, Dadda.'

The same set of events played out almost identically when I was singing 'Happy Birthday', where my timing, pitch and tone were off.

Then I didn't tickle your tummy right. Then I didn't assemble the parts for your toy vacuum cleaner in the proper order. And my cheese-on-cracker spreading received an unsatisfactory rating. I also didn't fill up your water bottle as one should.

And let's return to the 'Happy Birthday' example because you really pissed me off with that one. We've performed 'Happy Birthday' for you on two occasions, one of which you can't remember. And you've attended a handful of birthday parties where 'Happy Birthday' was sung, but I can count them on one hand. I'm thirty-six. I've received 'Happy Birthday' performances thirty-four more times than you, and I need a lot more hands to count all the birthday parties I've attended. I guess what I'm trying to say is that you can absolutely go and fuck yourself. I can't even breathe in front of you for fear of failing to acquire your validation.

You've picked up on my prickly demeanour and frosty reception because your next move is to bake me a birthday cake: a washing-up bowl from your toy kitchen filled with a rolled-up ball of fabric. You cut me an imaginary slice, put it on a plate and offer it to me.

'Here you go, Dadda.'

'Awww, is that for me? Let me try some.'

I take an imaginary bite—

'No, Dadda, not like that. Like this.'

AND-I-TOLD-YOU-TO-GO-AND-FUCK-YOURSELF!

April

What Are You Up To, Son?
Tuesday, 12 April 2022

It's 4 p.m., and I'm in the office. I've only got one hour left of the working day, but the clock is in serious need of a high-carb meal because it's moving at the slowest of speeds.

Instead of working, I'm looking out of the window and wondering what you're up to. It's Tuesday, so you're at nursery. Are you happy? Are you content? Are you sad? Have you said any new words today? Have you been using kind hands, or have you pushed anyone? Do you miss me? Did you sleep for long enough during your afternoon nap? Have you drunk enough water? Have you spent much time outside? I bet you have. You love being outdoors. Have you painted, climbed or played with trucks? Maybe a combination of all three. Have you played with dinosaurs? Has today been a good day or a bad day? Have you laughed a lot? Have you helped anyone, be it another child or a staff member? Have you seen Mummy? Is she OK? Is she stressed? When I spoke to her at lunch, she said there were staff shortages, so I bet she's stressed. Has today been a day of discovery and development, of adventure and exploration, of utility and curiosity?

I'm wondering about a lot of things, but there's one thing I'm sure of: I can't wait to see you in a couple of hours. See you soon, son.

Communication
Saturday, 16 April 2022

Last night, you misbehaved at bedtime. This morning, your behaviour was worse; you were a monster. It got to the point where Mummy and I kept looking at each other, thinking: *Where has our Arlo gone?* And you were told off many times.

And then we realised you were sick.

The wave of parental guilt that came crashing into us was merciless. We felt awful and immediately moved to course correct with cuddles and a lot of fuss and focus.

I'm sorry, buddy. I take it for granted that you can now talk. I assumed you would tell us if you weren't feeling great, but you couldn't because you don't understand what's happening to you. What can I say? Mummy and I dropped the ball.

Approximately 100,000 years ago, humans began using these things called words. We spent time practising our words and making up new ones. Within 50,000 years, we developed languages so that we could have some proper chinwags with our mates. We used language to gossip about Carl's failed romantic endeavours and the boss's annoying habit of chewing her fingernails.

We also used language to pass on lessons we had learnt to other tribe members and our children. For example: 'Jack, don't go near that snappy lizard thing, because he will proper fuck you up, OK?'

April

'OK, Dadda,' said Jack, who later handed down that same lesson to his daughter, Jackie, but with some added parameters. He said, 'Jackie, don't go near that snappy lizard thing on your own. Instead, approach it with a bunch of your mates, surround it, and then use pointy wooden spears to stab it to death. Then cook it on a fire and eat it, but don't cook it for too long or it won't taste great. And don't forget to add salt.'

Through language, humanity created a river of knowledge. Each new generation added to the river, building upon the lessons their ancestors passed down to them. New lessons were added. Existing lessons were updated and adjusted, reacting to further information as it came in, keeping pace with an ever-changing world.

Then, a breakthrough! Some bright spark thought to write their words on their cave walls. But they quickly ran out of room, so they wrote them on paper instead (or papyrus, parchment or wax tablets).

From there, our advancements in communication and access to information multiplied: paper turned into books; the Chinese cracked woodblock printing; and Johannes Gutenberg cemented his name in the history of books by inventing the printing press in the early fifteenth century. The typewriter was invented in 1884; the first personal computer arrived in our homes in the mid-seventies; on 6 August 1991, the internet was made publicly available; and on 29 June 2007, Steve Jobs released the first iPhone.

Humanity has evolved into what it is today through a network of information sharing. That's beyond frigging awesome. And scary.

But as remarkable as our spoken and written communication is, it cannot compete with the complexity of the human mind. Words are a low-resolution filter at best.

We use them to try and describe the entirety of the human experience at any given moment, but that's impossible – we don't even possess that knowledge in the first place, so it is absurd that we're expected to then convert what we don't know into something as restrictive – relatively speaking – as words and expect other people to understand us.

Like language, the human brain evolved and developed over time. Today, it comprises a bunch of systems and departments that don't always agree with each other, making an already complicated life even more difficult.

A bit of the brain tells us when something hurts or when we're cold. Another part tells us how insanely fit Anastasia from HR is. Another part sends a message warning us how much of a prick Keith from auditing is, alerting us to act defensively around him. At the same time, we've got yet another part of the brain developing this idea for a screenplay about a clown's quest to become the greatest juggler in the world.

Now, imagine walking into a room where Anastasia's standing nearby, wearing a short skirt, but she's talking to Keith. The window is open,

April

and it's cold, and you forgot to wear a jumper, and the colleague next to you is asking if you're happy with corporate life or if there's something else you're passionate about.

Can you imagine the ensuing mental chaos in your mind? All these different thoughts will be simultaneously fighting to be heard, creating a cacophony of out-of-tune drumbeats and static clamour in your head. That's why mindfulness and meditation are all the rage now – tools to help us deal with bygone biological systems and protocols that find themselves in a world that's evolved quicker than they have.

Our brains are ridiculously complex. That's why it's impossible to comprehend how they work, especially in respect of our emotions. And if we can't fully understand the complexity of our emotions, then we sure as hell can't gather them all up and use basic language filters like happiness, sadness, fear, anger, surprise and disgust to convey our position on a given subject in any real depth. It's like trying to integrate a toothbrush with a magic spell so that we can use the toothbrush to explain the inner complexities of how the spell works. That's bonkers.

So why do we do this? The answer is simple: we don't have any other choice.

We can become better communicators, better listeners. But it's difficult to relate fully to another human being because we do not have the technology to distil the emotional experience into something we can fully grasp.

One day, this might change. One day, a chip in the brain might remove the need for any lo-fi communication channels; we'll hand out a redundancy package to the middleman and communicate directly from consciousness to consciousness.

But we're not there yet. So, for now, we'll have to make do with words and body language, things that are easy to misunderstand. Yes, you will learn more words, and through experience you will acquire more wisdom and more understanding of the world. But communication will always be chained to limitations, and it will take you a lifetime to come to terms with that.

So how do you succeed here? Easy. You practise. You practise empathy, and you practise not reacting with emotions. You accept that you may have misunderstood another person and that it's OK to admit that, to say sorry and to invite that person to try again.

Here, like this.

Arlo, I'm sorry. Mummy and I didn't realise you were ill today. I'm sorry we lost patience with you when we thought you were misbehaving. We got it wrong. It's not the first time that's happened, and it certainly won't be the last. If you're open to it, we'd love the chance to try again tomorrow. What do you say?

The English language has over 170,000 words in use. You'd think communication wouldn't be a problem. Wrong. By an unimaginably large margin.

April Monthly Review
Tuesday, 19 April 2022

Nana Hoover has moved back in with us. Long story short: I tried to remortgage her house, which I own, but hit a few hurdles. If you recall from *Dear Arlo*, I picked the keys up for Nana's place a few days before the UK's first mandatory lockdown. She had just enough time to move in, but the place was in serious need of a renovation. Nana moved back in with us once the restrictions softened, which meant we could spruce the place up. Auntie Lisa kindly fronted the bank loan to pay for the project. Once it was complete, Nana moved back, and I began the remortgage process so I could release some money and settle my debts with Auntie Lisa. However, it would seem that banks don't like relatives living in your investment property, and they weren't prepared to align themselves with my financial planning. Bastards. There are many more boring and annoying details, and the last ten days have been rather stressful, but Nana is now living with us (again) and will likely do so for the rest of the year. This arrangement has enabled me to temporarily rent Nana's house out to a family who don't share my surname, assuaging the bank's family-tie concerns and sanctioning my remortgage application.

You approve. Nana's brought her Hetty vacuum cleaner with her, which, with immediate effect, replaces your Henry as your number one toy. Your number three toy is a Henry novelty keyboard cleaner.

Because of Nana's unscheduled relocation, project Cyril 2.0 is on hold. All cardboard boxes were donated to the moving effort, but I have not forgotten. Cyril 2.0 is coming ... I just don't know when.

After months of you asking, we've decided to rethink your watching of *Peppa Pig*. Why? Initially, it was prohibited because several other parents told me that Peppa is a spoilt little brat who displays behaviours that we don't want you to pick up. Somehow, that was enough for Mummy and me to outlaw the show. But then I realised we were taking a hard line without much evidence. So, we tested the water and allowed you to watch a few episodes. I discovered that the show isn't anywhere near as bad as I was led to believe. We use Peppa's on-screen behaviour as teaching opportunities, and explore ideas such as being kind to others like poor Daddy Pig, who should by rights be seen as the show's wisest, strongest, funniest and goddam sexiest character.

Talking remains on the same sky-pointing trajectory as in the last few months. Here's a selection of sentences you've said: 'Arwo saw an orange car out of Mamma, Dadda window upstairs in the spare room.' 'Don't pause *Peppa Pig* in a couple of secs, pause in a couple hours.' And my favourite: 'Arwo got these oranges from my loft. I'm going to put this basket outside to look after Hetty Hoover and keep her safe. Here you go, Hetty. You be OK now.'

While I continue to be mesmerised by the pace of development, it's also a little scary to witness this unfolding so fast. During your monthly reviews last

April

year, I would tell you the few new words you had learnt for that month. Now you speak in complete, if still often broken, sentences, and you know that hours are longer than seconds.

You love washing up. It keeps you occupied for up to thirty minutes. You drag your step over to the sink and request bubbles, water and a few favourite kitchen utensils, and then I leave you to it. I love hearing you chat to yourself while absorbed in your business.

We've had some reports of pushing at nursery. Unfortunately, it's you who's doing the pushing. This isn't uncommon, and we're not too worried so long as it doesn't get any worse. Jasmine, says, 'He's very aware of his actions because he'll run up to whoever he's pushed afterwards and say sorry and give them a cuddle.'

I'm proud of you for saying sorry, but you must remember to only use kind hands unless you're standing up for yourself. Just don't ask me how you're supposed to tell the difference at your age.

Still no more movement on potty-training, but, as reported last month, we're not worried. We have a couple of holidays coming up, so it makes sense to get them out of the way first.

Aside from the odd afternoon nap, you've not once got out of bed, either at night or in the morning. Instead, you continue to summon us by shouting. Or, and this is new, we'll wake up to you singing 'Heads, Shoulders, Knees and Toes' or 'Happy Birthday'.

When we tuck you into bed at night, you always ask for a hug and a kiss. And you telling Mummy and me that you love us is, I'm pleased to report, a daily event.

Thanks for another month, son.

I Don't Love You
Sunday, 24 April 2022

We've spent the day in a kid-friendly theme park called Drayton Manor. One of the sections is dedicated to *Thomas the Tank Engine*; it's called Thomas Land. You've LOVED it. So have Mummy and I. You've behaved beautifully, keeping your listening ears switched on at all times as you zipped around the park like a high-on-cocaine fly around a dumpster. It's been wonderful to watch.

But it's the end of the day, and we need to transition you from 'Yay, this is awesome' to 'Ah, man, home time'. Mummy and I are always wary of transitions, particularly when going from a high to a low. We understand why you're probably about to be in a bad mood, and we're primed with appropriate levels of sympathy for when the complaints arrive.

And they do.

'Where are we going, Mummy and Daddy?'

'We're driving home now. Have you had a good day?' Mummy says.

'Are we going to Thomas Land?'

'We will go another time, but Thomas Land has closed now. All the trains are going to sleep,' I say.

'Why are we. Not going. Thomas Land?'

'I told you the trains are sleeping, but we will come and see them another time. And can Daddy tell you something?'

'Yeah?'

'Both Mummy and I are very proud of you for how well behaved you've been today, and we love you very much.'

'I don't love you, Daddy. Or Mummy.'

Ouch. That's the first time that's happened. Luckily, it's as I said, we're stocked up on sympathy to weather emotional WMDs, even if you have deployed your deadliest one.

'Well, Mummy and Daddy love you very much, even if you don't love Mummy and Daddy at the moment,' I say.

'I don't love Daddy or Mummy or Haylee or Auntie Lisa or Nana See-See or even Nana Ooofer!' you say as gravity sends you crashing down from the day's induced natural high. Your serotonin reserves were spent admiring the park's production values, but now they're depleted, and it's time to go home – life's become a bit shitty.

I remember that when I was a kid, Sunday evenings sucked balls. The weekend's activities would end, and I'd hear that dreaded sentence from Nana Hoover: 'Right, Tom, bath time – you've got school in the morning.' Fuck me, that was the lowest point of my week.

So I get it, mate, I do, and it's OK that you don't feel great about the situation. And I'll tell you something else: Mummy and I will always love you. I've told you before that you will need to have children yourself to fully understand how strong a parent's love for their children is.

'Arlo,' I say.

'Yeah.'

'When we get home, we will have time for a tiny little play, and then maybe we can watch a bit of *Peppa Pig* before bedtime. How does that sound?'

'Tiny little play with my tiny little Henry Ooofer?'

'If you like.'

'OK, Daddy.'

Breaking Point
Tuesday, 26 April 2022

'I swear to God, if I have to see another Henry or Hetty product in the house, it will break me,' says Mummy, who's just returned home to learn that Nana Hoover has ordered the base of yet another Henry from eBay (this one is yellow) to add to the collection in the garden. She plans to plant things in them.

It Has Begun
Wednesday, 27 April 2022

It's 6.30 a.m., and I've just woken up. So has Mummy. But you haven't, otherwise you would have shouted for us to come and get you. And yet, I can hear the faintest sound of activity coming from the other side of the house – tiny footsteps from a small person.

'I think Arlo is coming,' I whisper to Mummy.

'No way, really?'

'Yeah, pretend to be asleep.'

Moments later, our door opens and you shuffle in. 'Good morning, Mummy and Daddy,' you say, with a little smirk that tells us you're proud of yourself for this upgrade to your routine, one you follow up by clambering into the middle of our bed, getting under the covers and requesting *Peppa Pig*.

Everything about this ten-second experience is emotionally rewarding. It's the biggest minor milestone we're likely to see this year. It also heralds a taste of things to come because, at some point, this will happen again ... but in the middle of the night – less emotionally rewarding and more soil-your-pants terrifying.

But if this is to become our new morning routine, then it's one we welcome with open arms. 'Good morning, Mr Arlo. Did you sleep well?'

'Yes, I did, Daddy.'

The Observations Of A Fish Named Sink
Saturday, 30 April 2022

I hate all human children. They are an expression of the very worst of biology. Granted, human adults aren't much better, and it's thanks to adults I'm stuck in this fish tank here in a Chinese restaurant. It might appear big, but I assure you it's not, because it's not big enough for me to escape the confounded ignorance and stupidity of children.

Look, here come two of the things now. One's a small boy wearing glasses, and the other's a girl – older than the boy but no less annoying. Listening to their parents, I think the boy is called Arlo, and the girl is named Haylee.

Bang, bang, bang.

Yes, I can see you, fuckwits. Stop banging! Haven't you ever heard of a cunting echo? You know sound travels faster in water, right? Of course you don't. And if you did, it wouldn't matter. Such is your cluelessness.

Bang, bang, bang. 'Look, Arlo, this fish's name is Sink.'

You know, I'd almost be impressed by that name *if* she was aware of what irony was.

'Talk, fish. Talk!' she says.

I am fucking talking! It's not my fault you can't understand me. And now that foolish Arlo thing is wiping his hands and face on the glass, trailing dribble down it and grinning inanely. I estimate his IQ is lower than plankton because not only do I have no room to swim, but the one luxury of my sad little life is now impaired – the ability to gaze at humans and judge their many faults.

Now they're running around the restaurant, disturbing the other lowlifes of their kind and ignoring their parents' commands to come and sit at the table.

April

Why do children have to shriek so loudly all the time? In fact, why do they have to bother existing at all?

You know, there are these very nasty rumours that humankind evolved from fish. I'd wager not. Evolution is the process of developing, not regressing.

And now they're both back, hitting my glass, shrieking at me, demanding I do somersaults.

I hate them all.

Toddler Inc.: We're In For One Helluva Show

counter-attack
noun

The act of responding to an attack with an attack that is intended to crush opponents and deter them from ever being involved in such silliness again.

Toddler Inc. Employee Handbook
Third Edition

There were rumours. Nasty, vicious rumours. The kind that spread through the corridors of Toddler Inc. like gas from a burst pipe, stopping briefly at water coolers to pollute the ears of any none-the-wiser employees with their terrifying words. Mr Jacobs had heard them too. They were unthinkable. *Preposterous*, he thought. *Not possible.* He couldn't believe his colleagues were listening to such fanciful nonsense. *Office gossip. Nothing more.*

But the words were powerful. They whispered and they travelled and they whispered some more, undetected at first, but only at first. Soon, Mr Jacobs came to realise that every employee had heard the words: parents were getting better at parenting.

The stock price had dipped.

People were panicking, behaving in a manner that Mr Jacobs deemed unbecoming.

He needed to respond.

And he had.

The Toddler Inc. foyer had been temporarily transformed, reconfigured to host a special event. It was Mr Jacobs' idea. Having reviewed Arlo's upcoming milestone schedule, he deemed it the perfect opportunity to celebrate what he knew would be a resounding success for the company, while quashing any more talk about parents being on an even keel with their toddlers.

No expense had been spared.

He had hired a 52-foot-by-72-foot IMAX screen that was now hanging in the atrium. He'd brought in a catering company, the best in the business, to ensure guests were fed with their favourite foods and plied with their favourite drinks. The entertainment was unparalleled: circus performers, close-up magicians, comedians, music, a bucking bronco and a photo booth. He'd drawn up the guest list himself. It would be an evening to remember.

He made his way through the foyer to the entrance doors.

'You there!' he barked to a slouching young man holding a tray of welcome drinks. The man visibly stiffened up and made to instantly correct his posture. 'What's your name?'

'Tim, sir.'

'Well, Timothy, don't let me catch you making a mockery of my standards ever again. Do you understand?'

'Yes, sir. Sorry, sir.'

'Is that the 1841 Veuve Clicquot?' Mr Jacobs said, nodding to the tray of champagne-filled flute glasses.

'Yes, sir, one of the shipwreck bottles.'

'I'll take one,' he said, before swigging deeply from the glass, pausing momentarily to savour the taste and then finishing it off. 'Aha,' he said, turning his attention to the entrance once more.

The guests had arrived.

'Welcome, Pete, Andrew, Alvy, Ed, John and Brad, great to see you all,' Mr Jacobs said as they filed in.

'Evening, Mr Jacobs,' said a Toddler Inc. old-timer.

'Evening, Lee. Thank you for coming.'

'Now, about these rumours.'

'Pay no attention to that nonsense. Next, they'll be saying the planet's overheating.'

The guests were directed through to the atrium where they were permitted twenty minutes to grab a drink, make small talk and settle in.

Mr Jacobs made his way backstage to find his assistant, Michelle, waiting for him along with the rest of his entourage.

'Michelle, how long?'

'Two minutes.'

'Excellent.'

Just then the lights dimmed. From the speakers, a voice washed over the atrium floor. 'Can guests please find their seats,' said Peter, the preschooler who usually worked in the toddler-training division.

The small talk stopped. Everyone followed Peter's instructions and eagerly waited for proceedings to officially begin.

Backstage, Mr Jacobs took a deep breath. 'Michelle, can you move my eight-thirty appointment tomorrow back a few hours? I suspect I'll be feeling uncharacteristically muddled.'

'Already done.'

'Thank you. Do you think this will work?'

Michelle looked taken aback. Never in all her years serving as Mr Jacobs' assistant had she ever seen him doubt himself. 'Of course it will work, sir.'

'How do you know?'

'Because you're involved.'

One of the stage managers stepped in front of Mr Jacobs holding up a hand and counting down: four, three, two, one.

Over the speaker, Peter spoke again. 'Ladies and gentlemen, please welcome your host, Mr Jacobs!'

The guests stood and applauded as Mr Jacobs marched on stage and over to a central miked-up podium. 'Thank you. Yes, thank you. Thank you all for coming. We have a terrific evening of entertainment ahead of us.'

The crowd settled and retook their seats. Mr Jacobs waited for silence. This was a performance, one he planned to execute perfectly.

'Let me begin with the elephant.'

The audience exchanged apprehensive glances with one other.

'Yes, yes, I know. Rumours. Gossip. Scandal. Nothing more than a work of fiction designed to have us believe that toddlers have lost their momentum, that there's a stumble in their stride, that they've lost their touch. HA! A toddler who's lost their touch? Parents feeling in control? Really? Come on.'

The guests rolled their eyes despite themselves. A few even chuckled. Perhaps they'd been a bit too hasty in forming opinions.

'This is nothing more than a smear campaign to blacken the impeccable record that Toddler Inc. has maintained since the dawn of man. It is an institution that has never failed. AND IT NEVER WILL!'

Applause.

Michelle stood in the wings, more reserved but equally inspired. Tears fell from her eyes. *Bravo, sir. Bravo.*

'I could go on. But I won't. Instead ... I'll show you. Ladies and gentlemen, I give you Arlo.'

On cue, the gigantic IMAX screen came to life. It was linked to a hidden camera in Arlo's house. Arlo was of course one of Toddler Inc.'s best-known initiates. His love of vacuum cleaners was famous. Right now, he was running rings around his daddy, quite literally, while his daddy implored him to stand still so he could clean his teeth.

The audience, fully relaxed and at ease, were enjoying themselves.

'Here he is, our master manipulator, our bedtime procrastinator, pushing buttons and annihilating boundaries.'

Laughter.

Mr Jacobs used the cover of a giggling audience to quickly check the stock price on his phone. It had returned to normal. *Excellent.*

'Still believe we can't deliver? Let's see how Arlo's parents deal with back-to-back holidays, potty-training and more sugar highs than they can count!'

More applause. The guests were fired up, inspired. One stood, and then another, and another – a standing ovation filling the airwaves with cheering and reaffirmed belief.

'Thank you. Thank you. Yes, thank you. Just make sure you enjoy yourselves. After all, it's gonna be one helluva show!'

Mr Jacobs casually walked off stage, with the confidence of a man who had nailed his part, trailed by wolf whistles, red roses and even a few pairs of knickers.

'Brilliant, sir, you were truly wonderful,' gushed Michelle.

'Thank you. It did go rather well, didn't it?'

'It couldn't have gone any better.'

Mr Jacobs took out his phone and rechecked the stock price. Shares in Toddler Inc. had risen 30 per cent.

All in a day's work, he thought.

May

holiday
noun

A period of time spent on leisure, recreation and relaxation – unless you've brought your kids along, in which case it's just a normal day or a sequence of normal days, but with better weather.

The Parenthood Dictionary
Adventures in Dadding Edition

Aeroplanes: Part One
Wednesday, 4 May 2022

Knock knock.

'What ... err ... yeah?' Mummy says in a groggy, just-been-woken-up state.

'Come on! It's time to get out of bed,' hisses Nana See-See.

'O ... K.'

Our destination is Cyprus. I look at my phone. It's just after 2 a.m. The airport-transfer taxi isn't due to arrive until 3.15 a.m., so by my reckoning, Nana See-See has roused us an hour earlier than necessary. But since she and Grandad See-See are fronting the bill for this holiday, she's forgiven.

Mummy and I bring the luggage downstairs before moving into the study to have our first productive meeting of the holiday.

'Here are the two buggies we're taking,' Mummy says, pointing to the only two buggies in the room we're standing in. She points to each one twice for clarity.

'What, these two right here?'

'Yes, silly, the ones right in front of you.'

'Thank God you told me. Otherwise, I might have picked up the other two that don't exist in this room.'

The airport transfer arrives and we load up the luggage. The final things we extract from the house are you and Haylee. You both adjust surprisingly quickly to being woken up and slung into your car seats.

Mummy, Auntie Lisa, Nana See-See and I are in the back with you and Haylee. Grandad See-See sits in the front. I'm listening to him volunteer facts and figures about his working life in his distinct Irish accent to a European driver whose first language isn't English.

'I think it was junction seventy-six or seventy-seven … What's the one with the little train station as you come off and take the second exit on the roundabout?' Grandad See-See says, assuming the driver possesses similar road knowledge.

The driver shrugs.

'Anyway, we built all the steps on that train station – it was a nice little job that one. Not like most of the crap I get stuck with.'

'Dad, he can't understand you,' Mummy says.

'And if he could, he wouldn't give two shits!' adds Nana See-See.

May

We arrive at Luton Airport and begin our journey through security. It's a process I've experienced countless times, but never with one of my children.

I'm expecting stress.

But there is no stress.

Except when Mummy loses her Fitbit watch. She claims this is my fault because I was the one who retrieved her possessions from the tray that went through the scanner; it would seem it was sitting tight up against the inside edge closest to me and I failed to see it. But here's my defence: Mummy knows better than to rely on me in such scenarios. And it's actually *my* Fitbit watch. I let Mummy borrow it as a sign of my unending decency as a man, partner and father … OK, fine, I gave it to her, but my first point still stands!

Once we're through security, we find a place to have breakfast, and you and Haylee properly wake up.

You perform a few renditions of 'Bob the Builder', increasing the volume each time because Haylee says that she can't quite hear you and that you need to sing louder, even though she's sitting next to you.

Next, you both focus on the floor-to-ceiling windows beside our table. You press your hands and open mouths of wonder up against the glass, staring at the myriad of activities that you would expect to see outside an airport terminal. You each point to planes taxiing to the runway, to men and women working in hi-vis jackets and to the comings and goings of the luggage-transport vehicles.

'Look, Mummy, there's a digger over there!' you say.

'And look at all the aeroplanes, Arlo,' Haylee says.

I'd say things are going very well—

Ah, crap. 'The gate number's appeared. We're miles away,' I say.

And we don't have time for leisurely strolling. EasyJet is famous for its narrow windows of opportunity, in which passengers are expected to learn the location of their gate and then reach said gate in less time than it takes to flick a light switch. This has never been a problem for Mummy and me in the past because we're used to it, but in all our globetrotting experience, we've never once had to rush to the gate with a toddler who shares our DNA ... and who's just dropped a code brown in his nappy.

Uh-oh! We don't have time for this. But I'm not panicking. Neither is Mummy. Because we are nothing if not a team practised in the art of changing nappies. We merge our minds and become one, communicating not with words but with actions forged and refined in the fires of experience and repetition. She unravels your changing mat and lowers you down. You prepare to morph into a fiery rage, but I douse the would-be fire with a distraction – a bottle.

It works.

Mummy holds out a hand over her shoulder to me at intervals. Silently, I hand her an open packet of wipes with two partially removed for easy extraction. Then I hand her cream and a nappy bag, and I set aside a fresh nappy.

You tire of your milk, so you put the bottle down and begin thrashing your legs.

May

'No, Mummy, don't change Arwo's bum.'

I'm there. I grab your legs and hold them steady so Mummy can finish the clean-up. But then you sweep an arm, knocking over the bottle with enough force to dislodge the lid and spill the contents onto the floor and over the crisp new nappy I retrieved only a moment ago.

But it's collateral damage – nothing more. I hand Mummy a new nappy while doing my best to ignore the furious, frantic arm-flapping of Nana See-See, who's observing the scene in the same way a dog owner might react to seeing their canine companion being butchered by a psycho.

'Mum, calm down. It's OK.'

'I am calm – I'm absolutely fine … There's no problem here. I'll just …' and on she goes.

We complete the mission, pack up your bag and ask you to get back in your buggy. You refuse. We don't have time for negotiations; we're already cutting it fine to make it to the gate before it closes. So I scoop you up in my arms, and Mummy, while walking, folds up your pushchair in mid-stride. It's quite an impressive display, not to mention comical. It's like she's wrestling a mini-Transformer, forcing it into doing the very thing it was born – built? – created? – to do.

We make it to the gate on time, but we can't relax. First, there's a panic about finding face masks. Then there's confusion over our seats. And then there are concerns about the size of the queue at the gate … Scrap that. One of the crew spots us and invites us to jump to the front. He's either a parent or knows it's ill-advised to force young children to wait in line.

We board the plane and get strapped in. You're sitting next to me in the aisle seat, I'm in the middle, and an elderly Scottish chap is next to the window. Mummy is sitting on the opposite aisle seat, and the rest of our family are in the row in front.

'No, Daddy, I don't want this.'

'You must have your seat belt on until we're up in the sky.'

'Why?'

'Because ... because ... because the man driving the aeroplane needs everyone to be sitting down so he can concentrate.' *Please accept my explanation, please accept my explanation, please acce—*

'OK.'

As we prepare for take-off, I'm struck by the morbid but also comforting thought that if we crashed and died, we'd all be together, and you wouldn't be alone. This thought parallels the one Mummy had when we flew to Finland last year. Do you remember? Where she embarked on the productive little thought pattern of imagining your life as an orphan.

The plane thunders down the runway and gently lifts into the sky. We give you a dummy and tell you to suck it if your ears hurt so you can adjust to the air pressure as we ascend.

'Look, Arlo, we're in the clouds,' says Haylee.

Once we reach altitude, the seat-belt lights go off. I create a makeshift bed for you, and with your head on my lap, you fall asleep for – *wait for it* – two hours, you beautiful, special, delightful young man. Did I ever tell you that you're perfect?

Once roused from, and energised by, your nap, you quickly get to work learning about flight etiquette and seeking answers to questions such as why you shouldn't repeatedly scream 'Hello' in my face.

And then there's this:

'Don't do that, Arlo,' I say.

'Why not, Daddy?'

'You shouldn't put your hand up a woman's skirt without permission.'

'Why?'

The flight attendant and victim of your only-moments-ago attempt at sexual assault looks over, keen to see how I respond to your question. Her gaze is one of curiosity and warning – *you better not mess up this critical life lesson* – which she wears on behalf of all women.

'Why not, Dadda?' you press.

'You need to ask permission or wait to be invited. This goes for skirts or any other item of clothing, for that matter.'

'Oh, OK.'

Thank Christ. The attendant smiles, telling me I've done a sound job thinking on my feet, and then continues on her way.

But I disagree with her assessment – I haven't done a sound job, because you go for two other female flight attendants, a female passenger and a male passenger.

'Arlo, stop touching people.'

'OK, Daddy,' you say, with the resigned inflection of a small boy who's been told to turn the television off and go up to bed.

But you perk up again when you learn that you can get up and play in the aisle. You and Haylee run up and down, harrying nearby passengers as they attempt to read in peace. We get a few glares here and there, but for the most part, people enjoy watching you and Haylee playing together.

'He probably needs his nappy changing. If you scoot over to me, I can do it,' Mummy says.

'It's cool, I've got it.'

It's only a wee-wee, so I have no qualms about changing you on the seats. You lie still and offer no resistance. I'm deeply suspicious, but who am I to look a gift toddler in the mouth?

But barely twenty minutes elapse before you stop what you're doing and adopt the look I know only too well, the one reserved for periods of waste disposal, confirming my early suspicions.

'My turn?' Mummy offers.

'No, it's OK, I'll do it,' I say.

Let's pause for a second and dig into this decision: why have I volunteered for what we all know will be the lowest point of this flight and possibly my life? Curiosity is the answer. That's all. You're about to come out of nappies, and I don't know if a brother or sister resides in your future. This may be the only opportunity to test my dadding skills at 38,000 feet in the air.

I'm ready! With you in my arms, I commute to the plane's rear and patiently wait my turn to use the changing facilities.

The wait isn't long.

Once inside, however, I wish it had been, because then I would have delayed learning the harsh reality about the size of the nappy-changing space on an Airbus A321. It's tiny. No bigger than the regular aeroplane toilets, which aren't famous for open-plan living spaces. The dimensions would give a beer coaster a run for its money.

I stumble in, rotate the catch on the changing table and lower it. *How the hell is he supposed to fit on this?* I lay you down, but I have to contort your neck forty-five degrees so that the side of your head is pressed up against the wall. The table itself is as sturdy as a Hollywood marriage, jolting and shuddering as the plane reacts to conditions in the sky.

I get to work. *Ah, man.* You present me with a horrible clean-up operation: very bitty – a right bastard of a thing to clear away.

'Hurry up, Daddy.'

'I'm trying, mate.'

I move the dirty nappy to the edge of the stuttering table, with more than a third of the weight leaning over the edge. It's risky, I know, but I have no other choice; there's nowhere—

Don't you dare—

Thud.

OK, there *was* another place I could have put it: the floor. Except it never went that far because the 'thud' you heard wasn't the nappy landing on the floor. It was the nappy landing in my hand, the same hand that's apparently got precognition reflexes.

I'm overcome with a mixture of stress, fear and pride. A quick inspection reveals no signs of faecal splattering. I'm not about to take that for granted, so I set the nappy on the floor and finish the task. Then I pick you up and stagger out of the space that's one-eighth the size of a prison cell.

Impatient stares from a mother and her young daughter await us outside. Their stares say that I've taken longer than I should, that I'm a fucking amateur and that I'm not moving out of their way quickly enough.

I have just enough time to respond with a stare of my own, one that says, *Look, how about you push pause on your judgement? We can revisit your opinion once you've spent some time in that hellhole.*

As I pass them, I'm greeted by one of the flight attendants, who says, 'Next time, use the one at the other end of the plane. It has loads more room.'

We've arrived at our accommodation. We're staying in Paphos. Weathered-looking terracotta limestone tiles surround a white-rendered four-bedroom villa. There's a swimming pool with plenty of seating options and locations for sunseekers. We explore the area until Haylee accidentally on purpose locks you and herself in one of the bedrooms. Luckily, a promise of ice cream equips her with the necessary skills to open it again.

Was the journey worth it? Of course. The flight wasn't that bad at all, apart from the in-the-air code-brown nappy change – already a distant memory.

Happy holiday, son. Now, let's everyone just relax and enjoy the weather.

Ducks And Nappy Changes
Thursday, 5 May 2022

I've spent the past thirty minutes repeatedly rescuing the same duck from the swimming pool. It's a great source of amusement for the small humans we're on holiday with. I've also spent part of my day having my pretend nappy changed by the same small humans – an experience that's twelve parts weird and more parts wrong. But I'm not saying no. If I'm asked to play a game by my son and my niece, then I'm playing the damn game, no matter how bizarre the role they've cast me in is.

Restaurants
Friday, 6 May 2022

We're out walking in Paphos harbour. It's been lovely, but we're hungry and want lunch. While we're perusing restaurants, the proprietor of one of them invites himself into our personal space. He kneels to your level and says to you and no one else, 'You look hungry and thirsty. Would you like some orange juice, maybe some ice cream?'

Your eyes light up. 'Daddy, ice—'

'No, thank you!' I say to the man, whom I've silently cursed with a spell that will run his business into the ground. What an outrageous thing to do! Does his shame know no bounds? Exploiting a young child like that to manipulate our family into walking into his restaurant! I would never do that!

By the way, I would like to remind readers that *Dear Dory*, *Dear Arlo* and *Toddler Inc.* can be found at all good bookshops and that book sales mean Arlo gets to eat.

A VERY Near Miss
Sunday, 8 May 2022

First, I must apologise for being a shit dad. What's happened is that, in eleven days, you will turn two and a half, and I've not once bothered to teach you the 'Dinner, dinner, dinner, dinner, dinner, dinner, dinner, dinner, BATMAN' song.

Luckily Nana See-See is switched on enough to stop that narrative from materialising, because now you know it.

Back to our holiday: we're trampolining. You and I are on one trampoline, while Mummy and Haylee are on another. Close adult supervision is required because of the layout: two rows of six trampolines joined at the hip and head. Other participants, older kids, are running up and down, bounding between them and not adhering to any form of etiquette. I've shouted at two of them already.

But you're loving life, emitting bursts of joyful shrieks.

When we finish, we make our way to the exit to find the rest of the family. You see them and say, 'Me and my daddy bounced way high!'

You're damn right we did, son. *And not just physically, either.*

You're A Dog, Uncle Tom
Monday, 9 May 2022

'Uncle Tom, you're a dog called Bingo. Fetch this, Bingo,' says Haylee, before throwing a dolly in the pool.

'My daddy is not a dog!' Arlo declares.

The jolt of pride is fierce and electric. *My beautiful boy, he's sticking up for me. Wow, what a moment.* 'That's right, Arlo. I'm not a dog, am I?'

'No Daddy, you're a sheep.'

'Oh, I see …'

What Goes Up, Must Come …
Wednesday, 11 May 2022

The waiter, a smiling man in his fifties with heavy-set features and boasting a few meagre wisps of short-cut grey hair, absorbs himself in the task of mixing two coconut-perfumed non-alcoholic cocktails for you and Haylee.

Accompanying the smell of coconut is the promise that the newly shaken concoctions contain more sugar than is healthy for a large adult male, let alone a toddler and a preschooler.

'That is gonna send Arlo off his tits on a sugar high,' I say to the procurer of the 'holiday treat' – as if you need to ask who.

'Stop it. There's no such thing!' says Nana See-See, who's a professional ignorer of bright, large, indisputable truths that bounce up and down in front of her like a spring repeatedly coiled and released.

The still-smiling waiter presents his work to you and Haylee. I'm not sure what he's made, but you waste no time finding out how it tastes.

'Hmmm, that's nice,' you say, lurching forward for another glug.

'No such thing as a sugar rush?' I say to Nana See-See. 'Let's give it twenty minutes and see where you stand on the subject.'

It only takes ten. Your pupils don't physically dilate to the size of pennies, but the chemical reaction that's taking place inside your body is nonetheless evident. It's evident in the running, the laughing and shrieking, and the buoyant jubilation of a small boy who's ingested a large platter of energy – one that's begging to be spent quickly.

I pay the bill, and we all set off on foot back to the villa. It's 8.30 p.m. You should be dead to the world in bed or at least lagging, enduring the final embers of the day with dragging feet and fading enthusiasm.

Yet you march out of the restaurant as if you're on your way to collect the morning papers.

'Arlo, you must be knackered. Why don't you get in your buggy, baby?'

'No, Mummy, I'm not knackered – I'm not even a tiny bit tired. And I not sleep in my buggy – I just-tend for a little bit.' You then bound over to your buggy and lay your head on it for less than a second ('just-tend' is toddler speak for 'pretend') before returning to your energetic and purpose-fuelled striding.

I have so many questions. How do you understand what 'knackered' means? How have you constructed a sentence of that length and grammatical accuracy? And how were we ever in a place where we were worried about your speech development?

And now another question: where are you? You've vanished – into a shop.

Mummy calls after you, 'Arlo, don't go in there. We're going back to the holiday home.'

'I just checking it out, Mummy – for me and for Haylee and for my daddy and for youuuuuu!'

It's a twenty-minute walk back to the villa. Most of that journey is along the main road, which is lined on either side by restaurants, bars and still-open shops. And you insist on entering them all.

The bars are the best. You slide into each one we pass and announce: 'I just do a bit of dancing,' before adopting a feet-firmly-planted position and shaking your hips in time to no song that I can hear, that's for sure.

But you seem confident in expressing yourself, and I'm not about to shame you for how you 'should' be moving. After all, if you fall victim to the ruse that there's a right way to express yourself in any art form, you forfeit the right to call it art. Remember, art is the expression of truth.

Having long abandoned the idea that we can control your movements, we tell the others to press on ahead while we hang back with you to let you burn off the remaining excess glucose; this phase includes you singing 'Happy Birthday' on repeat for five straight minutes.

But then ... it happens: the crash. Your pace slows. Your enthusiasm wanes. One second, you're climbing the chairs in the café we've followed you into, and the next ...

'I just sit ... in my buggy now,' you say, with heavy legs and slumped shoulders.

'OK, baba, shall we get you home?' Mummy says.

'I watch a bit of *Peppa Pig* and have my bottle?'

'That's a good idea.'

With you immobilised in your buggy, we catch up to Nana See-See, who takes one look at you and starts laughing.

'Has the sugar crash hit you, Arlo?'

'I thought such things didn't exist,' I say.

'Oh, shush your nonsense.'

Holiday Reflection
Thursday, 12 May 2022

I'm at the airport. I'm flying home earlier than you and everyone else because I'm due to appear at The

Baby Show for the next three days (the same event we went along to when Mummy was pregnant with you. I covered this in *Dear Dory*). When I attended last time, it was as a clueless soon-to-be first-time dad. Now I'm attending as an exhibitor and public speaker – giving advice to other clueless soon-to-be mums and dads. Go figure.

Seeing as I've got some downtime, I figured I'd reflect on the holiday and write down what I've learnt.

First off, a relaxing holiday it was not. Despite the sun, the pool, the empty schedule and an adult-to-child ratio of 5:2, it's been exhausting (Uncle Matt, the fifth adult, joined us part way through the holiday). Granted, parenthood is almost always exhausting, but in my holiday excitement, I fooled myself into believing the tempo would drop. It didn't. The adults were getting up from their seats every few minutes to attend to your and Haylee's demands. This didn't mean we weren't having fun, but it was not a relaxing holiday.

A simple solution would have been to create a rota of sorts. Put Mummy and me on child-watch duty for an hour and then swap with Auntie Lisa and Nana See-See for the next hour. But the problem with that approach is that Mummy's family are not ones for sitting down and making plans – there's a lot of winging it. I find this challenging because where children are concerned, plans must be created to guide everyone through the day. A good plan reduces stress – if everyone signs up for the plan.

You and Haylee are close in age. Naturally, this means a lot of fighting and quasi-sibling bickering. That gets boring very quickly and adds to the exhaustion. You're cousins, not brother and sister, so Auntie Lisa has her way of parenting, and Mummy and I have ours. We didn't fall out over the treatment of each other's kids, but it was still a taxing scenario to police. One of your arguments occurred when Haylee was playing with the villa's decorative garden gravel. That pissed you off. Apparently, the gravel was 'Arwo's stones'. That said, that girl does know how to wind you up!

A phrase I quickly grew tired of saying was 'Arlo, don't do that' – to the point where I hated the sound of my voice. I usually encourage exploration and supervised risk-taking, but that wasn't in place on this holiday. Why? Because of this little red flag called a swimming pool. You can't swim yet, so I felt like I was permanently on self-appointed lifeguard duty.

Also, we were in someone else's home, an environment where – and I believe I speak for the majority of parents here – I feel less comfortable consenting to your demands to trash stuff.

The swimming pool, being in someone's home, the lack of a daily plan and you arguing with Haylee meant I was more uptight than usual. And the 'Arlo, don't do that' phrase spilt over into scenarios where it wasn't necessary. In the future, I'll have a quick word with myself about the dangers in any given environment and understand what boundaries I'm comfortable with.

Speaking of boundaries, Mummy taught me a crucial lesson this week. She said, 'We've not been setting expectations in new environments.' As soon as she said it, I mentally slapped my forehead in a moment of self-reproach. How did I miss that?

At home, we have our routines and our rules. You know where you fit in. But when we encounter new environments like aeroplanes, restaurants and swimming pools, we need to be clear about our expectations so that you can operate within those parameters. Sure – you'll stress-test them, but at least you'll know what they are. That's been my biggest takeaway from this holiday.

So with all that in mind, was it even worth going on holiday? Hell-fucking-yes! Playing in the pool was awesome. It didn't matter that you couldn't swim. I was happy to pull you through the water. And plenty of fun was to be had in the shallow end where you could just about stand. When you weren't fighting, watching you and Haylee play together was cripplingly charming. Finally, seeing your speech and confidence grow as you interacted with new environments was a huge proud-dad moment. And that's a good job, because as one holiday ends, another begins. Next stop – America!

Aeroplanes: Part Two
Tuesday, 17 May 2022

'Are we going on another aeroplane?' you say, through 3 a.m.-woken-up eyes.

'That's right, buddy. You, me and Mummy are going on another holiday. How lucky are we?' I say, shuddering at the thought of next month's credit card statement.

The car's already packed, so we get you dressed, leave the house and head to the airport.

'Digger! Look, Mummy, a red digger over there.'

'I can see it,' she says.

'And there's another digger, Daddy.'

'You are very good at spotting diggers, aren't you?' I say.

'Yes, I am, Daddy. Can I have my songs?'

'Can I have my songs ...'

'Please.'

'Of course you can.'

Side note: I hate that I've become that guy who condescendingly repeats sentences back to you until you add a 'please' or a 'thank you', but here we are; it comes with the whole dad thing.

'What song do you want?'

'I want "Alouette", please, Daddy.'

I press play. 'Search again – it's not the right version,' Mummy says.

'Does it matter?'

'Show me the pictures – I'll know when I see it.'

'No. This *is* the right version – we had it on for an hour on repeat yesterday, and he loved it. And one more thing.'

'Go on.'

'Maybe keep your eyes on the road instead of glaring at me?'

May

The rest of the journey proceeds without event, and before you know it, we're passing through the security scanners. We don't lose a single Fitbit device, and I remind Mummy that she's come a long way since our flight to Cyprus two weeks ago.

Next, we find somewhere to sit down and eat. We order food, but you're not in a waiting mood, so Mummy gives you a box of raisins, keeping you occupied for less than thirty seconds. Next, she unveils a *Peppa Pig* racetrack-puzzle game that we bought specifically for this journey. You love it so much that you refuse Daddy a turn.

It's 7.50 a.m. Remember that you've been awake since 3 a.m.

'Oh-my-God-we're-gonna-get-plane-food! Aren't we?' Mummy says, releasing four quarts of excitement over the airport-terminal floor space. 'We haven't had plane food since we went backpacking. I bet we get cheese and crackers. Eeek!'

8.20 a.m. We've eaten. We want to head to the gate, but the staff aren't in a hurry to take our money. You're bored and fidgety, so you pass the time by running off. I'm assigned the job of making eye contact with a waiter so that I can ask for the bill, while Mummy's job is to recapture you. She succeeds, but you run off again. This is now a game.

'Arlo, come here.'

'HAAAAAA!'

The restaurant's wood-cladded façade is a little over a metre high. From my vantage point, I lose sight of you each time you dash in front of it. But not of Mummy. She's taller, so I can see her from the waist up running towards you before bending down, momentarily vanishing from my line of sight.

When she reappears, it's with a beaming toddler in her arms. She brings you back and tells you to stay still and wait. You interpret her instruction as a signal that the game can begin again.

Every escape attempt yields a greater distance covered. I'm not the only spectator. You've amassed a fan base of weary passengers, silently rooting for you to beat your personal best a fourth time.

Finally, we pay and then wend our way to our gate. Your face is like a compass without a magnetic heading – rotating this way then that, absorbing the busy scenes and marvelling at the many points of interest; your wide, curious eyes are complemented by an open mouth pouring out a stream of wordless wonder.

The reason we're flying to America is to go and celebrate a very good friend's fortieth birthday. His name is Abdi, and I met him at university. After university, he reconnected with Steph, a woman he used to work with at a holiday camp, and they eventually moved to Pittsburgh and married. They have two children[7].

---

[7] We previously met Abdi and Steph in *Dear Arlo*, where I spoke of the effect on me of a social-media post that Steph wrote about a miscarriage she had. While no child can be replaced, I am pleased to say that Abdi and Steph went on to have a beautiful baby girl, one of the two children referenced above.

Pittsburgh is a somewhat inconvenient place to reach because the only direct flights available are extortionately priced, so we have no choice but to connect. First, we must fly to New York and then to Pittsburgh.

We board the New York flight and locate our seats in the central aisle, a four-seat-wide column. Our party takes three seats together, and a chap sits in the fourth. I look around the plane carrying out an inventory check of small humans. I spot one other toddler. *Great!*

'Looks like you've drawn the short straw. You're stuck next to one of only two families travelling with a toddler,' I say to my neighbour, making an effort to engineer some sort of social connection so that he'll hate us just that little bit less when you decide to move into full toddler-rampage mode.

'It's fine, honestly – I have to fly from London to Detroit in a couple of weeks with my three kids.'

'How old are they?'

'Twelve, seven and three.'

Strength be with you, brother.

'Hello, how can I help you?' says the flight attendant, who's just appeared by our side.

'Help?' Mummy says, confused.

'Yes, you pressed the button to call for assistance.'

Mummy and I look up to see that someone has indeed pressed the call-for-assistance button.

'I'm sorry, he must have done it.' Mummy turns to you and says, 'Arlo, we don't push those buttons, OK?'

'OK, Mummy.'

The flight takes off twenty minutes later.

9.45 a.m. As soon as the seat-belt signs vanish, we go about making preparations to ride the next seven(ish) hours out. Part of that strategy involves you sleeping. We've hired an inflatable footrest that we can stuff in front of the seat to create a makeshift mattress. You're too tall to spread out, but you can lie down OK, so long as you adopt the foetal position. You can even use it to sleep for … five hours if you want.

Another flight attendant arrives. 'Excuse me, before he gets too comfortable, I have to ask if that pillow complies with Virgin's policy because we don't accept all of them.'

'It's one hundred per cent compliant. I checked,' says Mummy, who didn't check.

'That's right. The website says it's compatible with Virgin. I also checked,' I say, having not checked.

'That's fine. I had to ask.'

'Of course,' Mummy and I say simultaneously.

Midday: the food makes dog shit seem palatable. I know aeroplane cuisine isn't known for three-star Michelin standards, but Mummy didn't even get her cheese and crackers.

Despite some understandable minor fidgeting, you are behaving beautifully.

12.47 p.m. We have a sleeping toddler.

2.35 p.m. We no longer have a sleeping toddler. He's woken and learnt the phrase 'Back off, Daddy' – a phrase he repeats regularly and at maximum volume.

May

And now the toddler wants to wander. And wander he does. Up and down the aisles, waving to passengers like a Z-list celebrity who's travelling to a shitty town to turn the Christmas lights on. It's a wave that says, 'Yes, hello, it's me. I'm here, the big celebrity, except I'm not that big, and deep down, I secretly know that. That's why the wave is half-arsed.'

But passengers are enjoying watching you in your unhurried, meandering state. They shower you with smiles, which you collect with swinging, side-to-side, grin-garbed glances.

2.50 p.m. You climb over your mother to return to your seat, but you kick *through* her headphone wires, the ones connected to the housing unit built into the armrest. You've ripped the whole thing out, and now Mummy is holding a headphone-jack housing and circuit board in her hand. Somehow, the wire connecting to the circuit board is still intact, so she quickly shoves the lot back in the armrest and discovers it still works.

3.30 p.m. You're watching your first-ever movie. It's basically a *Cars* rip-off, but with a tenth of the budget. I don't care; it's keeping you entertained and immobilised.

3.45 p.m. 'Let me check and see how long we've got,' Mummy says, pulling out her phone. 'Ninety minutes! YES! We have crushed this!'

4 p.m. 'Arlo, shall we change your nappy ... Wait, Arlo, come here!'

You've bolted, running the length of the fuselage and into the business-class section.

'Shit!' Mummy says as she hurtles after you.

A few seconds later, I hear you shout, 'Daddy, we're coming back!' as you return from business class and into my field of vision, wearing a pride-filled smile woven through every crease of your face.

With you escorted back onto our seats, Mummy and I work together to complete the nappy change.

Once again, there is a problem: you have an erection. And you keep hitting it.

'Arlo!' Mummy hisses. 'Deflate your willy right now.'

And now you're thrusting your hips up and down, making us laugh.

'I am funny, aren't I, Daddy?'

'Yes, you are. Now, are you going to listen to Mummy and make your willy go down?'

'I am not, Daddy.'

'In that case, would you like Mummy to take you to the toilet and change you?' she challenges.

You stop thrusting and tensing. Soon your willy transforms into that state that makes apparelling you with a fresh nappy easier.

'Thank you,' Mummy says.

Just then, the captain announces that the seat-belt signs have been turned on, and we are beginning our descent.

One flight down, one to go.

Life should be a cakewalk from here on out.

May

'Why is this taking so fucking long?' Mummy says.

We've been stuck in the queue for immigration for almost thirty minutes. When we got here, we explained to a staff member that we had to board our connecting flight in two hours. She said we would make it, no problem. But that was thirty minutes ago, and the queue has barely moved.

My phone goes off. 'Shit!' I say.

'What?'

'Just got a text. The departure gate for our flight has moved terminals.'

'Fuck!'

'Yes, fuck!'

'Mummy, I've done a poo.'

Mummy takes you out of the queue and finds me again ten minutes later in almost the same spot. Eventually, the staff make the inspired decision to put more people on the desks to process the newly arrived passengers quicker than the gestation period of an African elephant.

We get through and hurry around a corner and up an escalator. I watch a boy around your age step off the top of the ascending escalator and quickly run onto the one next to it, going back down. His mother isn't quick enough to stop him, so now she's also travelling back down the escalators so she can catch him. The toddler is laughing. His mother is not. I hope she doesn't have a connecting flight to catch. *Strength be with you, sister.*

Next, we collect our bags and check them back in. That's right, despite travelling on a connecting flight, we still have to collect our bags and check them back in. Never have I had to do this anywhere else in the world.

Welcome to JFK airport.

And if that wasn't bad enough, we also have to go through security again, which boasts a queue of similar length to the one we've come from.

We have thirty minutes left before our flight takes off. If this were easyJet, the gate would have closed.

But you're in good spirits. You set up several pop-up shops as we move around the snaking body of the queue, selling fruit and veg to other travel-stressed passengers and me. But then you tire of retail endeavours and go dead weight on the floor. I pick you up and drag you forward, but you're still limp. So I strap you in your buggy, kneel and explain the situation. 'Arlo, if we don't hurry up, we will miss our aeroplane. I really need you to help me. Can you do that?'

'OK, Daddy.'

The family in front overhears me and tells us to go ahead of them.

We get to the scanners, and my bag is picked up because it contains your filled-up water bottle.

'You know you shouldn't have any liquid, right?'

'Yeah, well, we're on a connecting flight, so anywhere else in the world, that wouldn't be a problem, would it?'

We have twenty minutes left.

'Mummy, I've done another poo-poo.'

Fuck me; we are not making this flight. 'Right, you change Arlo on the floor over there, and I'll deal with this,' I say to Mummy.

I tell the chap we're about to miss our flight. He looks at me, then you and then Mummy. He can tell we're genuine and not drug mules putting on a show to reduce the chances of anything getting picked up. He quickly empties the bottle and tells me I can go. I march over to you and Mummy.

'We've run out of nappies,' she announces.

'How? We had eight!'

'I know. He's gone through them all. What do we do?'

'We need to make that flight. Fuck it, let's go. This can be a problem for the staff at the gate.' *Assuming there is anyone still there.*

We leg it to a shuttle bus that takes us to the next terminal. We disembark and search for the trail again. But we can't see the sign we're looking for, so we ask a staff member. He happily points us to where we need to go. Still, he must be new here because we march fifty metres in the wrong direction before another passenger, one who overheard our exchange, is kind enough to chase after us and update our navigation database with the correct route.

You know that scene from *Home Alone* where the McCallisters (minus Kevin) are sprinting to the gate? That's us, except Mummy and I are snapping at each other.

We reach yet another set of escalators. You might recall from both *Dear Arlo* and *Toddler Inc.* that I have something of a love–hate relationship with escalators and buggies. Those books feature tales of triumphs and defeats.

But I give past events not a second's thought as I jog backwards onto the escalator with you in the buggy and with Mummy barely keeping up.

We have ten minutes before our plane is scheduled to take off.

Schtun!

And now the escalators have broken down.

Are you fucking kidding me? Luckily, the passengers below us have already started making their way to the bottom, which allows Mummy and me to carry you down in the buggy.

We make it to the bottom and once again sprint. We get to the gate and find a woman at the front desk. Through laboured breathing, I hastily explain we're on a connecting flight, and the queues have delayed us getting here.

'It's fine. You can still board. We've been delayed by a few minutes anyway.'

Thank God. 'That's great. Do you have any nappies?'

'Nappies?'

'I meant diapers. Do you have any diapers?'

'Erm, I'm not sure. Let me make a phone call.'

I leave Mummy at the desk. You and I search for a family so I can ask them for a nappy ... sorry, diaper.

How is there no one ... Gotcha! I march right up to an Asian mummy. 'Do you have a spare nap ... I mean, diaper?'

'Sorry?'

'Diaper, nappy, thing for a baby.' I enter charades mode, using my hands to point to my crotch area.

May

It looks as weird as it sounds, and the woman in front of me decodes it as such, shaking her head as she extracts herself from my company.

I look over to Mummy – she's about to burst into tears. But then I get a tap on the shoulder. I turn around to find Asian mummy smiling, holding out a Mickey Mouse-themed nappy.

'Thank you so, so, so bloody much,' I say, accepting her act of kindness. I then wave the nappy in the air like I'm the hero of the hour in a paintball round of capture the flag.

Mummy quickly changes you while I grab snacks from a stall opposite our gate. As we're boarding, I ask the woman at the front, 'How long until you'd have refused us entry?'

'Two minutes.'

I've lived in a car for a month, renovated a house without enough money while doing a full-time job, and I'm a parent to a toddler. And I write books as a hobby. And yet none of those stressful achievements rivals this connecting-flight experience. Seriously, to the JFK management team: fuck you all.

'Hey! You guys made it!' says a smiling Abdi, who's just arrived to collect us from Pittsburgh airport. Our connecting flight was incident-free.

'How was travelling on two flights with a toddler?' he asks.

'Arlo was a dream. The organisation at JFK airport, on the other hand – now that's fucking stressful!'

The time is 10.05 p.m. EST. Discounting your nap, we've been up for just over twenty-four hours. I need pizza, a beer and a pillow!

'It's not a long drive. We were thinking pizza and a couple of beers tonight, and then give you guys a chance to sleep in tomorrow. What do you think?' Abdi says.

'That I've bloody missed you,' I say.

May Monthly Review
Thursday, 19 May 2022

I don't have time to go through your monthly updates today, because I'm busy hanging out with my friends, whom I've not seen in forever, so it's a quick summary.

Your physicality and speech have continued to rocket.

Last year, you developed an adorable habit of exclaiming 'I did ittttt!' whenever you accomplished something, be it a small thing or a big thing. Now, you've replaced 'I did ittttt!' with 'Horayyyy', which is equally adorable.

And then there's … Nope, scrap that, sorry. We're done for today. You're still awesome. Keep it up!

Tarmac
Friday, 20 May 2022

Yesterday, we drove from Pittsburgh across the state border into West Virginia to one of America's famous holiday camps – the same camp where Abdi and Steph met. It's a stunning location with green foliage in every direction. And we've pretty much got the entire complex to ourselves, so it's a dream setting. Friends from the US and UK have travelled here to celebrate Abdi's fortieth. From the old university crowd, you've got Matty and me plus our families. Matty was at your birthday party with his eldest: three-year-old Oakley. You and Oakley are pals.

All we need is a nice big breakfast to tee us up for a day of adventuring ...

Breakfast

I'd love to get started on my pancakes, but I can't because—

'Daddy, I make you into tarmac,' you say before unleashing *whoosh* noises and some Dr Strange hand waving, signalling to me that you are performing a spell. I ignore the gurgling protest of my stomach and allow the spell to take effect, adopting a plank position – or that of a newly laid piece of tarmac. You and Oakley proceed to jump up and down on my back to test out the tarmac's durability. Spoiler: the tarmac is of the lowest fucking quality.

Lunchtime

We should be in the lunch hall, but watching workers laying tarmac on the tennis courts has naturally distracted us. The workman operating the roller is of particular interest to you.

'Arlo, shall we go and have l—'

'Look, Daddy, that workman on the roller, rolling the tarmac.'

'I can see.'

'Can we go in, Daddy?'

'We can't go in there, because they're working. But here's an off-the-chain crazy idea that might work – we could go and eat lunch.'

'And then, after lunch, can we come back here and watch the workman tarmac the road?'

'It's the tennis court, but yes, we can.'

'Thank you, Daddy.'

Dinner time

You've taken yourself off to sit at another table. It's the first time since we arrived at camp that you've sat still, so I'm taking this rare opportunity to eat in relative peace.

Abdi wanders over, laughing. 'Go and see what Arlo is up to, but don't be a killjoy and ruin his fun.'

So much for eating in relative peace. I do as Abdi suggests. You've all but emptied the salt and pepper shakers onto the table, and you are arranging the minute crystals and dust in a particular fashion; I can't tell what you're making, only that you seem to be driven by a specific purpose. 'What are you doing, Arlo?'

'Oh, hi, Daddy. I'm just tarmacking the road.'

'Of course you are.'

The Perfect Balance
Saturday, 21 May 2022

Self. Family. Fun. Friends. All critical pillars of our identity. Sometimes, when fate permits, you can pay tribute to them all in a single day.

It's the afternoon, and we're at the lake. The weather is warm, and the sights are worthy of a postcard. The camp's lake-based equipment is housed in a little inlet that opens up to a broad expanse of water, ready to welcome all manner of water sports.

Self

I take one of the kayaks out alone for twenty minutes while Mummy hangs back with you. Kayaking is my favourite water-based activity. I gain a different type of freedom from the one skiing affords, but it's just as nourishing for the soul. It's also nice to be by myself. I paddle out of the inlet and onto the lake. I may or may not have sneaked a beer on board with me. *And relax.*

Family

When I return, I invite you to join me. At first, you're not sure. You seem wary of the kayak and quickly request to get out. But when I paddle back to shore, you change your mind. So, I course correct, grateful that I get to take you out on your first-ever kayaking trip and that you're enjoying it.

Things get interesting when you spy a trampoline on the water. It's essentially a twenty-foot-wide rubber ring, with the net (the bouncy bit) cast over the top. To get there, I need to swim with you from the jetty to the far side of the trampoline using a set of steps to climb up. We're both in life jackets, and staff supervise the affair, ready to assist if things turn for the worse. But they don't. I swim while carefully dragging you through the water, before using one hand to hold on to the side of the steps and the other to launch you up. Then we bounce. We have a blast.

Fun

To cap off a wonderful afternoon on the lake, we make our way around the inlet to another jetty, and several of us take a trip on a speedboat. There's an option to partake in tubing. It works like this: you lie on a rubber disc attached by a rope to the boat, and you hold on tight while the skipper, Captain Morgan, manoeuvres the boat over the waves at such an angle that you capsize. I eagerly put my name forward to participate and have a thrilling three minutes getting the shit kicked out of me by nature and physics.

Mummy also takes a turn. She says it's important that you see her having fun as well as Daddy. I couldn't agree more.

Despite everyone's best efforts, Captain Morgan bests us all. I should also note that Captain Morgan is a stunning creature in her early twenties. The rest of the women present in our company are all mums, and they all suggest to Captain Morgan that she should make the most of her figure while she can.

Friends

It's now evening. We've all gathered in a communal lounge area. Steph has set up a surprise birthday video for Abdi, featuring birthday messages from those close to him who wanted to be here but couldn't. He's not heard from some of these people in years, though they hold special places in the different phases of his life. It means a lot to me that we've made an effort to be here in person and share this experience with such a close friend.

Today has been perfect ... OK, you did throw a tantrum halfway through the birthday video, and we had to leave before it finished, but before that moment – absolute star-studded perfection!

Cancelled Flight
Sunday, 22 May 2022

We've had an unforgettable time away at camp. But we've reached that point in our holiday where we're exhausted and ready to return to home comforts.

We arrive at the airport at 5 p.m., say an emotional goodbye to Abdi and head inside. Moving through security is surprisingly easy. As airports go, Pittsburgh International ranks higher than JFK. But then, so does being in the dentist's chair.

We find a restaurant and eat. Mummy triple-checks we have everything we need to ride out a short evening flight followed by a long-haul night flight, and I check the departures board to see what gate we need to head to.

FUCK!

Our flight is delayed by twelve hours – which means we won't make our connecting flight.

I return to you and Mummy. I tell her to sit down and remain calm. Then I break the news to you both.

Mummy's reaction is surprisingly supportive. 'OK, we just need to figure out a new plan then.' Five years ago, she would have lost her shit. Come to think of it, so would I.

'Why are we not going on the aeroplane, Daddy?'

'It's broken, buddy. We need the workmen to fix it.'

'Has it run out of batteries?'

'I think it has. It needs new batteries and a little rest before it can fly again.'

We locate a staff member at the airline help desk, a tense young woman. She stiffens up as we approach, preparing to field our complaints and weather the wrath of angry passengers who will surely arrive in our wake, demanding miracles and resolutions from the management team.

This is a test. As a family, we have every right to complain. How can such injustice strike a family like this? Doesn't the world know we have a two-year-old in our care?

Or, we could look to the stoics for guidance, leave our complaints on the floor, and figure out a solution.

First, I need to demonstrate that I'm not a threat. 'I know this isn't your fault, and I can only imagine what sort of shift you're in for,' I say, 'but I need you to help us figure out what we do now.'

She relaxes. She looks on her computer for alternative flight times. She also explains that bad weather is prohibiting us from landing in New York and that ours is not the only cancelled or delayed flight.

While she works, I turn around. The angry passenger queue has begun to form. I see not a single smile, only frowns and heads shaking. Actually, you and Mummy are smiling – you're playing a silly game.

'OK,' says the woman before presenting me with two options. Option one: fly out to New York tomorrow at 6 a.m. and board a connecting flight to the UK at 8 p.m.

'You want us to hang around in JFK for twelve hours with a toddler and then catch a night flight? No. I'm sorry, I need better.'

Option two: catch the same flight to New York tomorrow morning but somehow make a connecting flight forty-five minutes later. That's assuming we arrive on time and can get off the plane quickly.

'Again, I know this isn't your fault, and you're trying to help, but in what world do you expect us to make that connecting flight? If we're being honest, that's not an option, is it?'

In the end, she finds space on a flight to JFK tomorrow afternoon, followed by a night flight to Heathrow, but with enough time baked in to make the connection. I thank her for her help and leave, passing the newly gathered queue of angry passengers behind me. *Be kind; it's not her fault.*

Thirty minutes later and we're on our way back to Abdi and Steph's for an unexpected sleepover.

All things considered, I'd say we passed the test. To quote Seneca: 'Man is affected not by events but by the view he takes of them.' You can't control everything that happens to you; you can only control how you react.

The Weary Return
Tuesday, 24 May 2022

It's 8 a.m. We have just this second collected our luggage from baggage reclaim and stumbled outside, greeting the dawn light in the UK like a family of lost wraiths. Actually, not you – you're of a somewhat brighter disposition; that's the difference between someone who's slept through the entire plane ride and someone who hasn't slept at all.

While waiting to board our flight from New York to Heathrow, I marched up to the bar and said, and this sums up the entire experience, 'I need milk for my toddler's bottle, and I need a pint of cider for the toddler's mother.'

Still, we made it home and learnt that we could go anywhere in the world together. You have laughed in the face of my expectations about how difficult I thought flying with a toddler would be. You're still young, but there have been moments where you worked with Mummy and me to overcome hurdles rather than becoming a hurdle yourself. When it comes to parenthood, Mummy and I have always been an excellent team, but I can see how our work thus far has served to pave the way for another team member. You. We are a family unit: a supportive, loving network of three people. Connected. Relying on one another and becoming the best versions of ourselves in the process.

We couldn't be prouder of you.

Hogie: A Fallen Brother
Saturday, 28 May 2022

You won't believe this, but I've gone away again! I'm in Dubrovnik, Croatia, for a wedding that was postponed thanks to Covid-19. I went to university with the bride. I've left you and Mummy at home, but full disclaimer: Mummy isn't with me, because she's run out of annual leave. Had she not, she was more than prepared to offload you to the nanas, especially as the soon-to-be-married couple covered the guests' accommodation costs.

The big event isn't until tomorrow, but we've met up with the wedding party for welcome drinks at a gorgeous locale overlooking the Adriatic Sea, a body of water mirroring our actions and relaxing into the evening. The setting sun's beauty is unrivalled. Its vibrant glowing embers tell us that its work for the day is almost done and it will soon depart, making way for the night-shift team: the moon and the stars.

But there is a problem. The guy I've travelled out here with, Jamie, also an old uni mate, is a Liverpool fan, and Liverpool have made it through to the Champions League final. Not watching it isn't an option. Luckily, the groom is a football fan, and he and his bride-to-be have signed off on our side-excursion to leave early and watch the football without resentment.

We're not the only ones. In our group is another Liverpool fan, Jake, and another mate, James, who like me is a neutral but wants to come along regardless.

Enter Hogie.

Hogie's a close friend who married Lizzie, another of the girls from the uni crowd. I've known him almost as long as his wife and the rest of my university connections. He's a character whose drunken stories are the stuff of legend. Whenever a social event is organised, one of the first questions that invitees might ask is: 'Will Hogie be there?' Such is his value and his contribution to social dynamics. He's warm, friendly and funny – he ticks many boxes.

So naturally, I'm excited when he expresses an interest in joining us. He asks Lizzie if it's OK.

'Sure, you can go …' Lizzie says.

Yes, Hogie! Trumpets ring out across the Walls of Dubrovnik, announcing a hero's return as he's welcomed back into the arms of his friends after a long absence.

'... as long as you take the baby,' continues Lizzie.

The trumpet notes, once full of the promise of adventure, fall flat. The vibrancy of the setting sun is reclassified – the hues aren't vibrant; they never were. They're sombre. A reflection of the mood that now surrounds us, revealing the truth: five months ago, Hogie became a father. His once easily dispensed social endeavours have been restrained, rationed and all but withdrawn. He is now a man with responsibilities.

Despite Lizzie's on-paper approval for him to go, everyone knows it's a no – of course it's a no! He can't take a baby to a pub where they're showing the Champions League final.

And so, with a heavy heart and heavier footsteps, we depart, leaving Hogie and his longing to accompany us behind.

Jamie and James don't understand that Hogie is a fallen man – they don't have children. But Jake and I know. *Every dad knows.* As we leave, I say a silent prayer. *In nomine Patris et Filii et Spiritus Sancti.*

Goodbye, Hogie.

Hogie: A Mourned Man
Sunday, 29 May 2022

It's a wonderful day at the wedding. The venue looks like a wealthy Bond villain's lair. Impressive in scale and appearance, the sprawling mass of beauty is located on an island, meaning we had to travel by boat to get there. Many guests said it's like being in the film *Mamma Mia!* but I've not seen it. Besides, a wealthy Bond villain's lair evokes a cooler image.

We've eaten, the speeches have concluded, and we can now prioritise getting drunk and silly.

But not Hogie.

His wife is one of the bride's best friends, and it's only through their connection that he's here. Social law dictates that he must remain sober and look after the baby while Lizzie lets her hair down.

Jamie, who, I'll remind you, doesn't have kids, is slowly coming to understand what Jake and I already know. He sidles up to Lizzie and says, 'I miss Hogie.'

'What are you on about? Hogie is right there,' she says, pointing to her husband.

Jamie's face falls to the floor. 'That's not Hogie,' he says.

June

ignorance
noun

1. A lack of information on, or awareness of, a given topic.
2. Something that's overwhelmingly present when you have children because they ask incredibly complex questions such as, 'Daddy, why is that cat sitting on our wall?'

The Parenthood Dictionary
Adventures in Dadding Edition

Mine
Saturday, 4 June 2022

'Daddy, you're sitting on my purple travel pillow.'

'I've had that pillow since before you were born. It's actually *my* purple travel pillow.'

'No, Daddy, it's *my* purple travel pillow.'

'Fine.'

The pillow isn't the only possession that's had its ownership rights reassigned. My tape measure is no longer mine. Nor is my footstool in the basement. My work keyboard has been yours since you were a baby. When *Dear Dory* came out, Nana Hoover made me a book cushion with Dory on it, the same Dory from *Finding Nemo* that your pre-birth name was based on. Anyway, that's now your 'Dory cushion'.

You've even taken my Rubik's Cube. Admittedly, I have only ever spent five minutes playing with it, but that doesn't matter. You can't just point to shit, declare it your own and then take it. Although, if possible, perhaps you could start acquiring your possessions from other people outside of our family and friends – like bank managers, for example.

And when I decide enough is enough and say, 'No, Arlo, that's mine,' you lose all hostility, turn your head to the side and adopt that cute pose you do, the one you know I can't resist, and say, 'Daddy, can I please share that with you?' which beats me every time, especially with food.

Be warned, this ability to take what you want has an expiry label, though it seems you've got a while until you reach it.

'Daddy.'

'Yes?'

'Can I share some of your peanut butter on toast, please, Daddy? Can I, please?'

Sigh. 'Sure you can.'

'Thank you, Daddy.'

'You're welcome, buddy.' *You bastard arsehole.*

Bob The Builder
Sunday, 5 June 2022

I've endured the *Bob the Builder* theme tune on repeat for twenty straight minutes. 'Only twenty minutes?' you say. Try it, and then get back to me.

I Don't Know, Arlo
Monday, 6 June 2022

I don't know why the marketing team made the lid of the pot you're holding green. I don't know why blueberries are called blueberries when they turn purple when you squish them. I don't know why the manufacturers placed the on–off switch on our Shark vacuum cleaner where they did, but I imagine they had their reasons. I don't know why the bird outside is flying in the direction it's flying in, and I don't know why the binmen come to our house on a Monday but not a Tuesday. But thanks for asking me anyway.

I've always known that I don't know a lot, but being in your company forces the point home daily, making me feel very stupid. Being unable to answer the questions of a two-and-a-half-year-old does that to you.

But I do know some things.

I know that the yoghurt pot is empty because you ate the contents, and I know that you ate the contents because you were hungry, and I know you were hungry because you're always hungry. I know that my toe hurts because you stomped on it, and I know the reason you stomped on it was that you thought it would be funny, because you always find inflicting pain on a parent funny.

You only know what you know. Some stuff I know, and a lot of stuff I don't. That's just the way things are. What do you know? What do you really know?

The answer is almost always not as much as you think you do. Now get off my toe.

Pickups
Tuesday, 7 June 2022

Thanks to Covid-19 becoming less of a nuisance to humanity, as of today, parents are allowed into the nursery premises to collect their children. Luckily for me, I'm on pickup duty.

I arrive and walk through the entrance for the first time. One of the girls in the office nearby tells me you're in your favourite place, the garden. They give me directions, and I snake my way through to the back door and step outside to the top of a sloping garden. From my position, I'm afforded a view of the entire space. And what a space it is. The rear is populated with what Mummy tells me is her art barn on the left. To the right is a tree-house area where two wooden verandas surround two trees, joined together by a wooden sloped path. Welly boots cling to one of the fences like mountain climbers, with yellow plants sticking out of the tops. There's mud, tyres and wooden climbing obstacles. I understand why this is your favourite place to be.

I scan the area, searching. *Where are ...* There you are. You clock me a second later.

'Daddy! Come here, Daddy.' You trundle over, grab my hand and drag me back to the bottom of the garden, where Mummy is. 'Watch me, Daddy,

I'm going to destroy this,' you say, sprinting over to a green wheelie bin.

'Arlo, you will not be destroying anything!' Mummy says, who has to navigate her work responsibilities and her mumming ones simultaneously.

'I will, Mummy. I'm going to destroy that green bin. Daddy, watch me.'

Mummy halts your destructive intentions by blocking your path. I ask if you want to walk home. You say yes.

Every collection features a handover with a member of staff. 'He's had a really wonderful day. He's spent most of it in the garden playing with sand and water,' says Lucy, the colleague in charge of your handover today.

You lead us back through the building. We say thank you and goodbye to the staff at the front desk, and then we head home while allowing all manner of side adventures and distractions to accompany us.

'It's six forty, and Arlo isn't dressed for bed,' Mummy says.

'You said you wanted me to bath him,' I respond.

'Yes, but surely it doesn't take that long. You picked him up just after five.'

'It took us ages to walk home.'

'Why's that?'

'I'm thrilled you asked. It's a fascinating tale. First, we had to discuss which way up the road we would walk.

In the end, I managed to convince Arlo to go in the direction of our house, but then we got held up again because we both got into a dirt-throwing contest, which we took very seriously. Then we had to splash in a few small puddles – notice I said "small" and not "big". That's because he only had his trainers on, and I knew that to permit big-puddle splashing in trainers was irresponsible, and I am anything but an irresponsible father.'

'Uh-huh. Anything else?'

'Yes. Then we had to cross the road and look at a digger, and then we had to collect stones – not a job that can be rushed, I'm afraid. Finally, we played hide-and-seek. Actually, that's not quite right. We then had to inspect some bird poo, followed by a Q & A session about said bird-poo inspection.'

'But then you were done, yes?'

'Correct. Then we made ingress and moved immediately to bath time. All in all, a bloody enjoyable walk home. Wouldn't you agree, Arlo?'

'Yes, I would, Daddy.'

A Classic
Wednesday, 8 June 2022

Mummy has arrived home with a story from nursery that made me chuckle. Apparently, you didn't have your listening ears on, and Mummy full-named you in front of several parents who had arrived to collect their children. 'Arlo Kreffer, take those stones out of your mouth right now!'

She then had to explain to the parents that that's not how she usually speaks to the children, but the one she was shouting at was her own.

While initially concerned, every parent dropped their judgemental frowns, transitioning to looks of understanding and solidarity – all of them knowing what immoral behaviours their children exhibit to warrant full-naming.

For your part, you just laughed and ran off – probably with a mouthful of stones.

'Can I Watch Peppa, Nana?'
Monday, 13 June 2022

'Can I watch *Peppa* on your phone, Nana Ooofer?'

'No, Arlo, I only let you watch it earlier because I was changing your nappy.'

'OK,' you say, as your face contorts in a way that suggests you're wrestling in a psychic battle of the mind, fighting to repel whatever evil is trying to take control. There's grunting and some red blotchiness while a single tear forms and falls.

And then ...

'Nana.'

'Yes, Arlo?

'I've done a poo. Can you change me? And can I have your phone now?'

Well played, son. Well played.

Todd

Tuesday, 14 June 2022

Todd is the name of the groundskeeper at the camp we stayed at when we went to America to see Abdi. One of Todd's many responsibilities is to ensure the grass is kept to a respectable length, and he has an array of machinery to assist him. You even witnessed him in action using a strimmer and his John Deere lawnmower.

But what you and I can't agree on is Todd's jurisdiction. I'm certain his remit only extends as far as the camp borders. You disagree. You believe he's responsible for all of the grass in Northampton. Why do I say this? Because we're walking back from nursery when …

'Daddy, Todd needs to cut that grass. What you playing at, Todd? Daddy, what's Todd playing at?'

'I think Todd only cuts the grass at camp.'

'No. Todd needs to get on an 'elicopter, fly over here and CUT THAT GRASS!'

'Oh, I see.'

'What you playing at, Todd?'

'Yeah, Todd, what are you playing at?' I say.

I'm sorry, Todd, but I like an easy life where possible. Today, life's easier when I side with a toddler and blame you for your subpar work ethic.

Gulliver's World
Saturday, 18 June 2022

To the managerial team at Gulliver's World.

Today, I attended Gulliver's Land Theme Park Resort in Milton Keynes with my partner and our son (two and a half years old). I wanted to share some feedback with you and begin what I'm sure will be a productive conversation on aesthetics.

Look, I'm the first to agree that all art is subjective, including theme-park design, but I implore you to rethink your commitment to drenching your soft-play sections in six different whiffs of piss. I know everyone's a critic these days, but one of the flavours was so intense that my nostrils now resemble the aftermath of a bonfire: a scorched, crispy, blackened wasteland – you know what I mean? It's a bit like when Gary from next door has a few too many beers, takes his eye off the BBQ and grade-one fucks it on steak-sizzling duties.

Try as I might, tears and prayers could not dilute the pain.

Where do we go from here? The oldest vintage I could detect was at least six months old, so what say you to a compromise, where you meet me in the middle and clean up the place every three months or so? You still get to boast that no odour of piss can rival Gulliver's Land, but your visitors don't gag their way to an early grave.

Failing that, Febreze?

The ball's in your court. You have an opportunity to learn. So why not do something with the ball? Just don't urinate on it.

Kind regards

A father with an eroded nasal septum

Father's Day
Sunday, 19 June 2022

Yo, yo, yo – what up? Where all my dads at? You know who you are: warriors, ronins – silent wanderers. You who stagger through life alone. You who raise no complaint or objection. You who bury your emotions because contemporary social norms and 200,000 years of evolution dictate that you do so. You who are stoic, emotionless, ready to shoulder it all – ready to comply with the demands of the day. Ready to suck it up and be a man.

You perform your duty admirably. No one knows the truth. You are your wife's rock, your son's cape-wearing action hero and your daughter's smiling white knight. At work, your boss views you as a dependable employee because you always volunteer to take on more responsibility.

But I know the truth.

I know that the hard-man exterior is a mask – a stage show. Should the audience look closer, they'd see the cracks and cement-filled fractures.

The clues are everywhere.

Be it one more reminder of your credit-card debt, one more notch on the scales, one more directionless day in the office peppered with meaningless small talk while you're battling pressures to deliver that project on time and on budget, one more day spinning too many plates and juggling too many balls, one more instance of your children rejecting you in favour of their mother.

It is a cruel fate dished out by the gods: you work to support your family by sacrificing time with them. And when you do spend time with your family, you worry you're not doing enough to provide for them. Either way, you're chained to guilt.

Money. Health. Relationships. Meaning. Emotional well-being. You worry about them all, but you can't possibly attend to everything. Something's got to give.

So you give yourself.

You forgo so much: time in the kitchen preparing healthy meals; going to bed early; going to the gym; taking time out for yourself, like beginning that side project you've always dreamt of doing.

You stare in the mirror and lie. You tell it that you're OK, that you can handle the self-neglect in favour of the greater good, that your shoulders are strong enough to carry the burdens that surround you.

But therein lies a path to your destruction. This way of life is not sustainable. The foundations will snap, and your shoulders will give way. The bill always comes due, and you cannot avoid paying. And if you don't select a way to pay, life will do it for you. Often, the cost is paid by the people you love most, the ones you work so hard to protect and provide for.

Everyone needs help.

Life can be really fucking tough. It is the ultimate adversary, the matchless opponent. Failure to concede that means you've already lost the battle. And I fear for you. And I fear for those that love you for who you are and appreciate everything you do for them.

There's no shame in admitting you need help – there is only strength.

Everyone needs help.

Let your children see your flaws, your struggles and your burdens. Let them know you're not invincible. Inspire them to do the same. Encourage them to talk. Teach them to reach out and say, 'I am not OK.'

Where is the scripture that tells a man how to navigate modern life anyway? Where is the blueprint? Where is the operating guide? Nowhere. It doesn't exist.

Remember that.

And remember that the biggest priority in your life right now is you. Accept that, and those around you

June

will benefit. The ones you care so deeply about will thrive by your example. Your kids will learn how to navigate modern life because the blueprint now exists. You have created it, and you have shared it with the world. You have become the best version of yourself, and that's what those around you get, the best of you.

Everyone needs help.

For those that have cracked it, my heart commends you. Bravo. Now go and help the person next to you.

And to those of you struggling out there, falling further each day, not knowing if you will make it to the next sunset, do me the biggest favour on this Father's Day, and ask for help. If you can't do it for me, then do it for yourself, and if you can't do it for yourself, then do it for your children. Do it for those you love and for those who love you back.

I stake all my worldly possessions on one undeniable truth – that you are more than you realise and that you have the strength to crawl out of the hole, climb up that mountain and free yourself from your inner turmoil. I believe in every one of you. You just need a helping hand. That's all. Because we all do.

Everyone needs help.

Happy Father's Day to all you dads out there in the world doing a badass job at dadding. Now, go to your children, hug them, play with them, give them your undivided attention for an hour, and tell guilt and shame to fuck off for the day.

Maybe – just maybe – if you can do it today, you might be able to do it again tomorrow.

June Monthly Review
Monday, 20 June 2022

With the majority of May spent travelling, I was hoping to return to a slower pace of life this month, but it sure hasn't felt that way. We've all experienced illness. I've just enjoyed a bout of shingles. Fingers crossed you contract chicken pox. Why? Because the younger you are when you get chicken pox, the easier it is to endure.

With all the holidaying, you've found returning to the regular routines of our lives difficult. You're less enthusiastic about starting nursery, often welcoming the news with a few silent tears, though they never last long. And your mood soon brightens when you lay eyes on Abi and she asks you if you want breakfast.

Speaking of Abi, Mummy and I went to see her last week for parents' evening. She tells us what we want to hear and what we already know: you are doing brilliantly. You're confident, intelligent and quick to grasp new concepts. She says you favour the comfort of your own company, but that's through choice rather than social wariness. Mummy and I have noticed this as well, mainly when we go to children's parties.

Since the start of the year, I don't think a monthly update has gone by where I've not spoken about your imaginative play increasing. This month is no different, and I'm glad I'm not the only one who's noticed. Abi commented on your love for 'small-world' play. You play out scenes from your favourite cartoons. *Peppa Pig* has been your go-to for months, but she's about to make way for *Bob the Builder*. Fortunately, you favour the newer CGI version (you call it 'new Bob') over the old stop-animation version featuring Spud, a character who sounds like his throat was ravaged by a flamethrower and repaired with gravel.

I was an only child without a dad, so I often had to keep myself amused. My playmate was my imagination. I once spent hours one afternoon recreating the great city of Agrabah, from *Aladdin*. I stacked books in varying-sized towers, nestled closely together to replicate the proportions of the narrow elevated alleyways through which the guards chased Aladdin. I'd play out the chase scene from the start of the animated Disney movie.

I think you get the depth and breadth of your imagination from me. This will be something I will pay close attention to and foster if necessary. I always wanted to tell stories, but it wasn't until you came along that my dream became a reality. If you show the same desire, I will help you find a path towards your goal.

One thing Abi did say was that we need to get a move on with potty-training. 'He's been ready for a while,' she said. As you know, we purposely held off because of our holidays. But now they're done, we need to progress through this famous milestone. We've earmarked a weekend in July. We plan to follow a programme that promises to help crack it in three days, though we've budgeted for a fourth.

You've been sleeping well, rarely waking at all in the night. But you've forgotten that you can get out of bed by yourself in the morning, and it's something you've stopped doing, which is a shame. You walking into our bedroom is much more pleasant than you screeching 'MUMMY, DADDY' and expecting us to retrieve you.

That's about us done for June. As usual, thanks for another fun month on the wonderfully fulfilling gig that is dadding.

I Am Ready!
Friday, 24 June 2022

It's 7.30 a.m., and I have this second announced I've woken up enough to parent, for which I'm rewarded with a 'Yay, Daddy' comment from Mummy, a piece of praise that I bloody well deserve. Why? Because you were up seven times last night. It's not your fault; you've been ill.

That said, six of those seven times were to request a drink from your bottle of water next to your bed, a location that you can, as we've previously indicated in revolutionary fashion, reach yourself with an outstretched arm.

I forget what other reason you shouted us for, but that's probably because I was so fucking tired.

We need to have a serious chat. Unless you're about to die or you have a request that's more complex than picking up a bottle that's right next to you, can you please fend for yourself and stop screaming for assistance between the hours of 9 p.m. and 6.30 a.m.?

You might be thinking that if you were up seven times, then surely Mummy is feeling the same way and also deserves praise. Almost, but not quite. I got up four of the seven times, which means I got up more, which means I'm the better and more exhausted parent.

And before you ask, the answer is yes, we are going to forget every single previous night where Mummy got up more times than me, because if we don't do that, then I won't have a reason to moan, and I really need a reason to moan today.

Glasses
Thursday, 30 June 2022

'I'm leaving with Arlo to go to the optician's and choose his new glasses.'

'OK, but can I count on you not to let your selfishness get in the way of this mighty but simple task?'

Mummy sighs. 'I will ask to see their *Star Wars* selection, but be warned they might not have—'

'They *will* have, and I'll be forced to call bullshit if you come at me with your excuses.'

'Oh-kaaay.'

'There aren't any *Star Wars* glasses here,' Mummy says via her phone on a video call.

'That's just not true. Why are you lying? They had loads last time!'

'Yes, but I'm in Boots in the hospital, not Specsavers.'

'What about Marvel?'

'Nope.'

'Why do you hate me and Arlo? We've given you everything you've ever wanted.'

She turns her attention away from me to speak with someone nearby whom I can't see. A second later, an older woman comes into the frame. She has a name tag that identifies her as Jean.

'She's not lying. We don't have any of those here,' she says.

'Oh, really, Jean? How much cash has made its way into your back pocket for you to say that?'

'None,' she says, laughing. Apparently, she assumes I'm messing about.

'So, if I check our joint account right now, I won't see a cash withdrawal for thirty quid.'

'What are you like?' Jean says, shaking her head and disappearing.

Mummy returns on-screen. 'See, I told you, didn't I?'

I can see another mum and her son over Mummy's shoulder. The mum is also looking at me, shaking her head in agreement with Jean and Mummy, telling me that the words Jean and Mummy speak are true, adding even more lies and deceit to this whole piece of subterfuge that your mother has roped everyone into.

'Oh dear,' I say, 'she's paid you off too. That's a shame. You look like a nice person, but you're just like Jean and Arlo's mother, a liar!'

I end the call. Mummy returns home with you fifteen minutes later.

'I've got him a gorgeous pair of red glasses that really suit him.'

'But are they *Star Wars* or Marvel?'

'You know they're not.'

'Yeah, just like I know you were lying the whole time because of your prejudice against *Star Wars*.'

'Shut up, and go and make me a cup of tea.'

'Fine!'

July

milestone
noun

1. A significant stage in the development of a skill or capability, such as a child's learning to walk.
2. A bittersweet moment for parents, who feel pride in the achievements of their children but are saddened they have grown and left a stage behind forever.

The Parenthood Dictionary
Adventures in Dadding Edition

The Dummy Fairy
Friday, 1 July 2022

Start the camera – and we're off.

'Hello, Dummy Fairy,' I say to the camera.

'Hello, Dummy Fairy,' you say.

'If Arlo gives you all of his dummies tonight, will you leave him a present? And if you will …' I turn to you and say, 'Tell her what you would like.'

'Chocolate.'

'And what else?' Mummy says.

'A hard hat.'

'Pleeee …' parents Mummy.

'PLEEEEASE, Dummy Fairy.'

'And also,' Mummy says to you, not to the camera, 'ask the Dummy Fairy if she's going to give your dummies to the—'

'Babies.'

Wrapping up, I summarise: 'OK, Dummy Fairy, we're going to leave Arlo's dummies out tonight, and if you get time to stop by, you can have them and give them to any babies that need them. And if you do bring him a gift, then he would like a hard hat and some chocolate. Thank you very much.'

'Bye, Dummy Fairy,' we all say together before I end the video.

Like potty-training, saying goodbye to dummies is something we should have done a while ago. But you've never been totally reliant on them. You use them at night and sometimes when you get upset. And because we've never foreseen this particular milestone as something that you'll find difficult, we've sort of let it carry on. Also, the dentist commented that you had 'perfect teeth' during your last appointment, another reason why we chose not to prioritise it (some believe long-term dummy use can lead to incorrect positioning of teeth).

So why now?

For one, it's not something we can put off forever. Two, we've earmarked next week for potty-training, so we figured we'd get this one out of the way quickly before we take on that more daunting milestone.

I remember the very first time we gave you a dummy. It was the middle of the night, and you wouldn't settle. You were less than a week old. So we tried it, and it worked, and we've never looked back. I know the use of them can be quite a divisive topic among parents, but I'm not really for or against.

Come bedtime, we again set the camera up to record the moment. It's a beautiful scene. Mummy has given you a bag to take around your bedroom while you find all of your dummies and deposit them in there. Mummy is fighting back tears.

You playfully insist that in addition to your dummies, the Dummy Fairy would like to take the empty glass candleholder that we use to store them.

'Arlo, the Dummy Fairy does not want that.'

'Ha ha! Yes, she does want that,' you say, dropping the candleholder into the bag for a third time.

'Is that all of your dummies?' Mummy asks.

'Yes.'

'What about the last one? The one in your mouth.'

You pull it out from your mouth and stare at it. You're about to throw it in the bag when you change your mind and stick it back in your mouth to get a few final sucks in.

'That's right, get the last few in,' Mummy says, losing her battle to keep tears at bay – not that I'm all that far behind her.

You extract the dummy from your mouth and drop it in the bag, saying goodbye to yet another phase of your life.

Next, you need to decide where you want to leave the bag for the Dummy Fairy. You're concerned as to how she'll gain access to our house, especially when your bedroom window is shut.

'She'll probably come in through the spare room window,' Mummy says.

'Hmm … Leave it open when you go to bed,' you say.

'We will,' she promises.

In the end, you opt to leave the bag in our bedroom, which was bloody mighty of you because it makes the Dummy Fairy's job a lot easier.

Sleep well, son. I'm proud of you.

Has She Been?
Saturday, 2 July 2022

It's morning, and it's taken you all of two seconds to discover that the Dummy Fairy has been to see you. She left you this note:

Hi Arlo,

I received your video message. Thank you very much for leaving out your old dummies for me to collect. I know a few tiny babies who will love them.

As a thank you for being so kind and thoughtful, I have left you a gift.

Have a great day.

Love,
The Dummy Fairy
xxx

She wasn't lying. In addition to fulfilling your request for a hard hat and some chocolate, she also brought you a *Peppa Pig* Grandad Dog soft toy. I know you didn't ask for this, but the Dummy Fairy may have found it at the back of the wardrobe in the spare room, and meant to give it to you months ago.

A Day In The Life Of Arlo: Television
Monday, 4 July 2022

Hmmm, I think I want *Bob the Builder*.

'Daddy, *Bob the Builder*, please.'

'Sure. Which episode?'

'The spinny one.'

'UFO restaurant, gotcha.'

I believe I said the spinny one, but as long as you understand me, then we shouldn't fall out.

'Here you go, Arlo.'

'Actually, I want *Cocomelon*.'

'OK–'

'I want *Bing*.'

'OK, *Bing* it i–'

'Actually *Bluey* … please, Daddy. No, I want *Peppa Pig*.'

Why is Daddy sighing? What's up with him, Louie? He looks exhausted. All we're doing is sitting on the sofa watching a little bit of television before bed, having some quiet father-and-son time. He looks like he needs to go and have a lie-down.

'What *Peppa Pig* episode do you want?'

'I want the one with the baby.'

'"Babysitting". OK, I know where that one is. One sec.'

'Thank you, Daddy.'

'You're welcome, Arlo.'

'Daddy?'

'Yes, Arlo?'

'I don't want that one.'

'For f– Arlo, can you please make up your mind?'

'I want *Bob*.'

'*Bob the Builder?* The spinny episode?'

'Yeah.'

'Right, that's what we're having. No more faffing about.'

'OK, Daddy.'

Louie, I love the new *Bob the Builder* because it has an awesome theme tune. It's catchy, and I already know all the words. Can you hear it, Louie?

'Right, *Bob*'s on. Shall I go and get you some milk?'

'Yes please, Daddy. Daddy?'

'Yes, Arlo?'

'I don't want *Bob*. Can I watch diggers on YouTube?'

Louie, why has he turned into a grumpy statue?

'Daddy? Daddy? Daddy? Daddy?'

'Yes, Arlo, my darling little boy?'

'I said I wanted diggers on YouTube.' You deaf twat!

Full Circle
Wednesday, 6 July 2022

It's bedtime. Mummy has just dressed you in a pull-up nappy. It's a big moment because, if all goes to plan, this is the last nappy you will ever wear. It's fitting that Mummy has the honour of dressing you in your last one because it was me that had the first.

I remember that moment like yesterday. You were minutes old. The midwife asked if I wanted to change you. I couldn't believe my daddy-tenure began so soon after your birth. Mummy had gone to hell and back to bring you into the world, but I too had my own mountain to climb in those initial moments after your birth – though, out of the two, childbirth probably takes the podium position in terms of difficulty.

That feels like a lifetime ago. Tomorrow we officially begin potty-training. I'm not sure what we're in for, but if I know you, you'll likely smash through our expectations.

Sleep well, buddy. We have a big few days ahead of us.

Potty-Training: Day One
Thursday, 7 July 2022

It's morning. 'Can you build me a track with my Toot-Toot cars, Daddy?' you say.

'Sure. But shall we do something first?'

July

'What?'

'Shall we take that nappy off and throw it in the bin? And then shall we get all of your other nappies and put them in a bag to give to another little boy? Because you don't need them any more, do you?'

'No, I don't!' you say, jumping up and down.

'And why is that?'

'Because I do my wee-wees and poo-poos on the potty.'

'That's right. Come on then, let's go and find a bag.'

While I don't envision any of us being in for an easy few days, our potty-training adventure starts out well enough. It's a big moment, working our way around the house searching for all your nappies. We find some in your changing bag, some in your bedroom and a pack in the spare room. They're being donated to one of Mummy's friends' little boys. Next, we present you with a pair of boxer shorts.

'What are these, Arlo?' I say.

'These are my big-boy boxers.'

'That right.'

Mummy helps you into them. You've worn boxer shorts a few times before, but this feels like 'the moment', the one where we officially say goodbye to one stage of your life and welcome in another.

Once we're done with that, you and I build a Toot-Toot racetrack and generally mess around a bit before breakfast.

7.30 a.m. 'Arlo, tell Mummy or Daddy when you need to do a wee or a poo, OK?'

'OK, Daddy.'

7.32 a.m. 'Do you need to sit on the potty?'

'I don't, Daddy.'

7.34 a.m. 'Arlo, baby, do you need to sit on the toilet?'

'I don't, Mummy.'

The constant asking might seem excessive, but we're following a programme that promises to help us crack it in three days. The programme, *3 Day Potty Training*, by Lora Jensen, requires us to spend as much of the next three days as possible at home. It says to continually ask you if you want to sit on the toilet, but only to ask. We shouldn't be forcing anything, as that won't help you to understand body control. And the way we ask is equally important. Notice we haven't said, 'Do you need to pee?' Instead, we're asking you to tell us if you need the potty, or to sit on the toilet. The subtle difference in positioning will apparently help you learn your own body signals.

We're counting on a few accidents. This is so you can feel what it's like when you have wet boxer shorts and trousers. We should also be keeping your fluid intake high during the day to give you more opportunities to use the toilet or have accidents and start to learn how your body works.

9 a.m. 'Arlo, are you sure you don't need the toilet?'

'I don't, Mummy.'

I shrug in response, and we get on with our day. I'm working, but I've brought my laptop upstairs from my office so that I can support Project Potty-

Training. It also means I can get away with extra playtime between meetings.

10.20 a.m. 'Daddy, you must eat all of your pretend pizza if you want some pudding, OK?'

'OK, Arlo. Look, do you need a wee-wee or a poo-poo?'

'I don't.'

Christ, even I've been for a few wee-wees since I got up.

10.50 a.m. 'Arlo, do you need the toilet?'

'Yes, I do, Mummy.'

'OK, quick, quick, let's get you to the toilet. Has it started coming out yet?'

'Just a tiny bit.'

We get you to the toilet and sit you on the potty, and you release a huge stream of amber liquid. I'm not surprised – this is the first time you've been all morning.

Mummy inspects the damage to your boxer shorts. There is literally the smallest dribble, which means you've already demonstrated excellent control. Top job. It's so small that we only need a fresh pair of boxers. You can keep your pyjama shorts on.

Midday. Mummy has taken the car for an MOT, so it's just you and me. Because you're about to go down for your nap, the programme allows me to break protocol and insist you try and have a wee on the potty before you go to bed.

You don't resist. Once again, you release a healthy volume of urine.

'Oh my God, what is that?'

'That's my wee-wee on the potty, Daddy.'

'Have you done another wee-wee on the potty?'

'Yes, I have.'

'That is so good! I think that deserves a double high five.'

We go a few rounds of double high-fives before washing our hands and heading into your bedroom for story time.

By the way, I'm usually conscious of how much I praise you because, as a family, we're guilty of overdoing it at times. We can't help it; you make all of us incredibly proud each day. But sometimes, the praise embarrasses you, so I make a conscious effort to be mindful of that. Mummy, by the way, does not, and she will 100 per cent be the more embarrassing parent out of the two of us, though I'm sure I'll have my moments.

Story time aptly consists of a *Hey Duggee* book about potty-training. I love *Hey Duggee*, but this book is complete and utter dog shit of the highest degree. There's no rhythm in the prose, and the speaker attributions are clunky. But I should probably stop right there before I get readers writing in and saying 'pot, kettle'.

As I'm about to lay you down for your nap, it strikes me as a good idea to sit you on the potty once more. 'Arlo, can you just try and go on the potty for me one last time? We don't want you to have an accident while you're asleep.'

'OK, Daddy.'

A few seconds later ...

'Daddy, I'm doing a poo.'

Yes, yes, YES! 'OK, buddy, take your time,' I say calmly, but I'm anything but calm. On the inside I'm dancing on the bar, letting off streamers and party poppers, blaring out celebratory notes of triumph on a trumpet, writing poems about your awesomeness and eyeing up a big piece of rock from which to carve a sculpture – a tribute to you becoming a 'big boy' and moving through the transition so smoothly.

You complete your business, which includes another wee-wee, and then you assume a position with hands on the floor and bottom up so I can clean you up. Then it's off to bed while I skip my way out of your room.

2 p.m. 'MUMMY!' you shout from your bedroom.

Mummy is back home, and we both leap our way upstairs to inspect your bed for signs of any accidents.

Nothing! Not a single fucking drop!

4 p.m. Another wee on the potty. Admittedly, we encouraged you to try more than we should, but you and Mummy were about to go knee-deep in a serious vacuuming session, and she knew you would be distracted. For my part, I was downstairs working.

6 p.m. Another wee on the potty.

6.30 p.m. We go up to bed. You try and go again, but nothing comes out. We have stories, brush teeth and crack on with a bit of silliness.

7.20 p.m. Last chance to use the potty before we say goodnight. You do one tiny wee and one tiny poo.

Sleepy time.

You have fucking crushed it today. What's more, you personally know you crushed it, so you've been able to enjoy the achievement almost as much as Mummy and I have.

Full disclaimer: I'm anxious about you staying dry at night. I had a bed-wetting problem as a kid, and I don't want you to have it. It's certainly nothing to be embarrassed about, but as a child, I found it embarrassing, and I'd love for you to be spared that. It can impact on your social life, your sleep and your mental health. I still have memories of waking up in wet sheets. It wasn't pleasant.

Is there any reason to think you've inherited this from me? Well, yes. The programme says that if a child wakes up and their nappy is full, that suggests they haven't yet learnt bladder control. This could be the result of you treating your nappy as a 'safety blanket' of sorts. Or it might not. All I know is that your nappies are *really* full, and my childhood experience of the subject, coupled with what I've read in the programme, is responsible for my anxiety. That said, I'm almost forty now; the research into bed-wetting has surely come a long way. Still, the scars of childhood aren't easily forgotten, no matter how many layers of clothing you cover them up with.

I'm also worried about sleep. It looks like we're in for a few nights of broken sleep, which is the lowest-ranked of all my concerns, but it's still a concern.

July

We are well prepared, though. We've got spare bedding ready to go should we need to change your sheets, and we've added an extra waterproof sheet on top of your already waterproof mattress protector. Also, following the programme, we will get you out of bed and sit you on the potty after you've slept for an hour. Mummy says these are called dream wees. It's 7.30 p.m. now, and you're still tossing around, but you should be asleep any minute. We will also get you out of bed at 5.30 a.m., about an hour before you wake up, for another dream wee.

Now then, let's see what the night brings ...

8.30 p.m. 'Arlo, darling, let's sit you on the potty,' Mummy says quietly, gently lifting you out of bed and carrying you over to the potty. You're naturally groggy.

'I can't do it, Mummy. There's nothing coming out.'

'OK, baby boy, well done for trying. Let's get you back to bed.'

Keep going son, you're doing great!

End-of-day report – Day 1:

- Number of accidents: 0
- Number of wees: 6
- Number of poos: 2

Potty-Training: Day Two
Friday, 8 July 2022

1 a.m. Another dream wee. Nothing. But you're dry, so we let you get back to bed.

4.45 a.m. 'MUM-mee,' you shout–slur.

Both Mummy and I roll out of bed and tiptoe-sprint to your bedroom. My first move is to put a hand under your cover and inspect for dampness. Nothing! You're dry. 'He's dry,' I say to Mummy, both astounded and impressed.

'Quick, let's get him up. Arlo, darling, come and sit on the potty.'

'No, Mummy.'

We feel awful for doing this, but you surely have a full bladder. Mummy helps you out of bed with that gentle maternal touch that she's so famous for. Once again, we go through what is already becoming a familiar sequence of events. Mummy sits you on the potty, and you try and go. But …

'It's too hard, Mummy. Nothing is coming out.'

'OK, baby. Well done for trying. Daddy will lift you back into bed,' she whispers.

I do, and you roll over and go back to sleep. Mummy and I leave the room and look at each other in shocked delight. *Dry!*

5.30 a.m. I can't sleep. I know it's way too early to start a victory lap, but given what I confessed to you last night, you have to understand why I'm elated for you. And sure, we might still have a way to go, but I no longer feel any pressure. I mean, you did it,

July

didn't you? You demonstrated day-and-night bladder control. You haven't had a single accident. Of course, there will be accidents, but I was never worried about that. I only wanted reassurance that you *could* do it. Reassurance that I now possess. I cannot envision a scenario where this becomes a battle. I know I keep telling you how proud of you I am, but I'm going to say it again: I'm proud of you, son.

6.30 a.m. You wake as normal and shout for us to come and get you. Once again, both Mummy and I quick-march into your bedroom to carry out an on-site inspection. Dry.

Mummy sits you on the potty. You release a big fuck-off wee-wee and ask to go downstairs and watch TV like it's a normal day.

8.30 a.m. 'Mummy, I need the potty.'

She quickly gets you seated for you to do your stuff. Similar to yesterday morning, there is a tiny dribble in your boxer shorts. Again, this shows excellent bladder control because you had the awareness to clench up and tell us you needed to go.

8.45 a.m. I can hear banging and crashing and laughter. It's you and Mummy. You're upstairs dancing, and it's lovely to hear. One of the complaints Mummy has about motherhood, and I know this is widespread, is that when she's at home with you, she's often preoccupied with managing the house. But for now, she's dedicated her time to you for potty-training, which means she's able to forget the domestic chores and indulge in some silliness.

Soon after, Mummy and I discuss your progress. We conclude that, owing to you smashing the fuck out of life, we can accelerate our schedule and bring the time frame forward. This means you're going out!

This isn't overconfidence on our part, but it's fair to say you've got the hang of the potty while you're in an environment you feel comfortable with. So why not proceed to the next level? Mummy will ensure she's well prepared, but remember we *want* accidents, preferably out-in-public ones, so you know what the experience is like.

Mummy is taking you first to collect your new non-*Star-Wars*-or-Marvel glasses and then over to Nana See-See's, while I stay home and work. But first, she needs to repack your ... er, your going-out bag? What are we calling it now? I always referred to it as your changing bag, but that now feels wrong. Let's call it a going-out bag. That feels like an appropriate name to etch into the stonework of this coming-of-age marker.

'Three changes of clothes, three pairs of socks and three pairs of shoes. Why do we need socks and shoes?' Mummy says, testing me.

'Oh, I know. Is it because everyone forgets that accidents drip down legs and dampen socks and shoes?'

'Correct!'

'Yes!' *I was listening.*

'We also need a fold-up toilet chair. Which we have because Taci gave us one.'

You crank out another piss before you leave.

11.12 a.m. Another wee on the potty. This one is at Nana See-See's.

2.30 p.m. 'Right, so we've had our first accident,' says Mummy, who has called from Nana See-See's.

'Right.'

'But it wasn't his fault. He was out in the garden with Haylee, and he shouted that he needed a poo, but I didn't hear. By the time I got to him, he'd already made a start, but he finished on the toilet.'

'Is that an official accident?'

'I don't think it is.'

'Me neither, so stop wasting my time and trying to sabotage my perfect son.'

'OK, bye.'

The afternoon proceeds without event. You continue to request the potty whenever you need to use it.

End-of-day report – Day 2:

- Number of accidents: 0 (I'm not counting the poo; that's Mummy's fault for being an absent parent.)
- Number of wees: 5
- Number of poos: 2

Potty-Training Day Three
Saturday, 9 July 2022

5.17 a.m. First official accident. I woke up to go to the toilet, checked on you and noticed your wet sheets. In one way, this was a good thing as it meant we got to go through changing your bed sheets while in sleep-deprived states. Mummy sat you on the potty, and I sorted the bed. I don't know how I would have approached it had I been on my own, but the trial run meant we could reflect and devise a plan. Which we've done. From now on, if one parent gets up and you've had an accident, they'll use a flannel to clean you and then put you in our bed before changing your bed covers. And even that is something we've systemised. We've layered the mattress like this:

- Waterproof sheet (bottom layer);
- Normal sheet;
- Puppy pad;
- Normal sheet (top layer).

This means we have only to whip the top sheet and pad off, and we're good to go. We have another duvet made up that we keep in the spare room, so I can probably put up a decent performance to rival any F1 pit-stop crew should the need arise.

I don't see this as a setback. But I'm annoyed that I can't figure out why or when you went. I got you up for a dream wee about 10 p.m. Fine. But when I touched the wet sheets this morning, they felt cold, telling me it wasn't a recent accident. Were you in a deep sleep and unable to wake yourself? Or perhaps you did wake, but you couldn't be bothered to shout for us. Who knows?

July

I have two pieces of good news. First, I've stopped tallying how often you go on the potty because there's no point – you've mastered it during the day. There hasn't been a single dribble in your boxer shorts, and that's despite you spending much of the day being distracted and playing.

Second, I have a working theory on last night's accident. I think the temperature was too high. There's not a lot we can do about it, as that's down to the weather, but you were a very sweaty toddler, and I believe that could have interfered with things. As I said, it's a working theory, and it's not something I've been able to back up online, but hey, I'm a parent; it's my right to make up diagnoses on a whim!

And now, some not-so-good news. Nana Hoover has ordered you a toy, which she claims is 'just a bit of harmless fun'. It's a purple turtle. It has a list of features that add up to it achieving the status of being a 'proper wanky toy'.

I'll walk you through it. First, it repeats what you say in a gimmicky voice. Toys that copy you are fun for sixty seconds. Never any longer. Next, it uses sand. You spoon-feed it the sand, and then the turtle digests it and 'poos' it out into a toilet accessory that comes in the box. Of course, you first have to fill the toilet with water.

So, to recap, we've got sand and water as the main components necessary to access the full range of the toy's capabilities, with sand and water being well known as stupid choices for indoor use with toddlers. Finally, it's battery-operated. I still don't understand why toys aren't like smartphones. Why can't we charge them and reduce the risk of leaky batteries?

Think I'm exaggerating? I have this app on my phone where you enter the toy's name, and it returns the results of how good it is. Here, take a look:

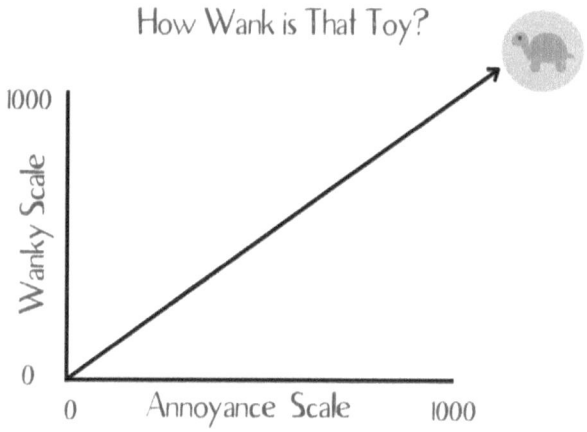

It's now evening, and Mummy and I have agreed that we'll set our alarm for 4 a.m. for one of us to check on you. I wish you the best of luck for your third night, son. And remember not to worry if you have an accident. Accidents are a natural part of life as you learn new skills and embed new routines.

Sleep well.

Potty-Training: Reflection
Sunday, 10 July 2022

3.10 a.m. I've woken up, and I need to use the bathroom. Given the time, it makes sense to check in on you and only wake Mummy if she's needed. But she's not. Once again, you're dry. *YES! YES! Yes, yes, yes, yes, yes, yes.*

I get you up and sit you on the potty, but you're having none of it, so it's back to bed we both go. *Do I set the alarm again for 5 a.m.?* No. No point.

7.05 a.m. I'm awake. You and Mummy are still sleeping, so I sneak into your room for another inspection. Again, dry. Again, I'm transported to the moon – carried there by my pride and elation for you. Well done, son. Well bloody done. As far as I'm concerned, that's potty-training complete!

Sure, there might be setbacks, but could the last three days have gone any better? Remember, we went straight in and tackled day *and* night, so your achievements cannot be understated, though I accept I'm one biased parent right now.

I attribute your success to many factors. First, you have been ready for a while, and you've had plenty of practice using the potty. You have always guided us on that front.

Also, we were well prepared. I read the guide twice. I highlighted important sections and referred to them constantly. And we were consistent. We brought the programme forward and left the house, yes, but your progress informed that decision. We were on it at all times. Apart from when Mummy abandoned you in the garden.

I also believe we nurtured you the right way, praising you and continually reminding you that it didn't matter if you had accidents and that we could always try again. I've said it before: I would love to know what the nature–nurture split is in your character. I suspect that, on this occasion, nurturing has had a significant impact. Imagine if we told you off every time you had an accident. That wouldn't do your confidence any good, would it?

Finally, we can credit you for being you, someone who is remarkably pliable and accepting of change. I've seen it time and time again.

It's clear my theory that you had a potential bed-wetting problem was incorrect. Mummy and I have re-examined the theory, and we think we know where we took the wrong path. Historically, you'd always asked if you could have your morning bottle before we changed your nappy. We never said no to that request. This meant you probably got shot of a couple of morning wees *after* you'd woken.

Another factor is the clock in your room. It's blue at night but turns yellow at 6.30 a.m., signalling that it's morning and it's time to get up. Sometimes, you wake when the clock is blue, so you chill out while waiting for it to change. If you had needed a wee then, of course, you'd go in your nappy. Never have I been so happy to readjust my position on something.

And now I end on a sad note. Potty-training was the penultimate major milestone that I had marked out for early childhood. The final one will be when you start school.

Congratulations on your achievements this weekend. You are now a young man who does his wee-wees and poo-poos on the potty and the toilet.

I couldn't be prouder.

Mixed Messages
Monday, 11 July 2022

It's evening, and you and I have been playing. We got a bit carried away, and you stuck your tongue out and started spitting. 'We don't spit, Arlo. That's not very nice,' I say.

You respond to my words with a look of confusion. 'But Mummy says yes, and Daddy says no,' you say, slumping your shoulders in the posture of someone on the receiving end of mixed messages.

First, I'm amazed at how you've been able to articulate that we've given you mixed messages at such a young age and that you find it confusing. This means I'm awarding you a ton more proud-parent points to add to the pile you've accumulated from your potty-training success.

Next, we need to find out why and how we've given you a mixed message.

It doesn't take long.

It transpires that Mummy was blowing raspberries at you the other day, with her tongue out. You guys had fun, so you've sought to replicate the experience with me. Instead, you landed yourself in trouble. No wonder you're confused.

This is why parents must ensure they align with one another in every decision they make, at least in their children's eyes. Mummy and I know this, and we strive for it all the time, but tonight's episode demonstrates how easy it is to get it wrong.

But it's also been simple to correct. I explained to you the difference between blowing a raspberry and spitting. You accepted the explanation and tried again. Admittedly, more saliva landed on my face from you trying *not* to spit, but that's irrelevant.

In future, you are entitled – and encouraged – to call Mummy and me out for mixed messages whenever they occur. We'll sit down together as a family and discuss it. Thank you for speaking up.

To The Person In Charge Of Warehouse Visits
Tuesday, 12 July 2022

Good afternoon

I hope my email finds a patient and understanding ear – or even better, two ears.

My name is Tom. I'm an author from Northampton. I'm also the father of a two-and-a-half-year-old boy named Arlo, who absolutely adores your NRV240 Henry vacuum cleaner. I believe he is Henry's number-one fan.

July

Let me share my reasons for that belief:

- If you ask Arlo who his best friend is, he will tell you it's Henry. His second-best friend is Hetty.

- At night he personally oversees his toy Henry vacuum cleaner's bedtime routine, often settling Henry into our bed while issuing stern commands not to touch 'my Henry'.

- He once body-slammed his mother because she told him that she would eat Henry. I've never seen a more protective primate in all my years of watching David Attenborough documentaries.

- When he's not playing with his toy Henry, he's begging me to let him watch the abhorrence that is *Henry Hoover TV* on YouTube. Are you aware such evil exists in the world?

Arlo's second birthday was Henry-themed, and it featured a rather splendid Henry cake. In the months since then, he has amassed an impressive collection of Henry paraphernalia. This includes (as well as his toy Henry) a Paladone Henry Vacuum-Novelty Desktop Cleaner, a Henry T-shirt, a Henry jigsaw puzzle (and a Hetty one), a Henry mug and, finally, several upcycled Henry and Hetty bases that have had their innards removed to make way for soil and seeds. Two of the bases grow spinach. Two more grow courgettes. I'm not making this up; I have photos to prove it.

I told you he was your biggest fan, didn't I?

But why am I telling you all this? Well, I was wondering if your facility in Somerset offers factory tours to Numatic enthusiasts, especially lovers of your NRV240 model. If so, do you allow under-threes?

You may recall that, way back when I began this communication, I told you I was an author. I write non-fiction parenting memoirs about fatherhood that have been warmly received by readers, especially my mum, who has bought two copies of each of my books and tells me she is very proud.

I'm writing my latest book about raising toddlers, and, were you to graciously extend an offer for us to come and visit, I would guarantee you some excellent PR. I'll even dedicate a whole chapter to you. It's no big deal; I'll just remove one of the others, like the one where Arlo told me he loved me for the first time. Here's a sample from the chapter that I will write (I welcome your feedback):

Numatic is the best company in the world – full stop. For me, the experience of using an NRV240 is better than playing Goldeneye on the Nintendo 64 with my mates (Multiplayer – Facility: Licence to Kill with pistols. #IfYouKnowYouKnow). It's better than your mum cooking you a full English breakfast when you have a hangover, and it's better than getting a rare first-edition holographic Charizard in a pack of Pokémon cards. It's even better than a provocative and highly sexualised poster of Jessica Rabbit.

What do you say? And remember that I'm asking on behalf of Arlo, a hopelessly adorable two-and-a-half-year-old boy who would be really upset if you said no. Please don't disappoint.

Sincerely yours
Tom (an optimist)

My Least Favourite Type of Parenting
Wednesday, 13 July 2022

There are many forms of parenting. There's the fun stuff, like chasing-a-naked-Arlo-around-the-house parenting or assault-course-construction parenting. One of my favourites is trash-the-shit-out-of-Mummy's-cushions parenting.

Others aren't as much fun. Like Arlo-would-you-keep-your-fucking-head-still-while-I-clean-your-teeth parenting, or the please-don't-scratch-Daddy's-face kind of parenting. Those aren't as pleasant.

But there is one I detest more than the rest. And that is parenting in the car.

Where do I begin?

Let's start with getting you into the thing – a coin toss on whether or not I whack your head on entry as I bend my spine in the shape of a theme park ride. I'm not kidding; I have to loop under the door frame and then back up again to slide you into your seat. That's assuming you permit me to lift you in the first place. Often, you deign to be the one to climb in, a course of action that takes longer to complete than a full rotation of the planet.

We can divide the next section into passenger-seat parenting and driver-seat parenting. Let's start with passenger-seat parenting.

Within sixty seconds of any journey commencing, you can bet you'll drop the thing I gave you to keep you occupied. I then have to rotate my body like I'm auditioning for the part of a screw at the local theatre. The part requires the screw to curl its already twisted torso around the back of my seat and then go on a fishing expedition to find the thing you've dropped in the footwell.

As soon as I complete my mission, I enjoy a relaxation period of eight seconds before the inevitable *thud* happens, followed by a 'Daddyyyyy, help'.

I do help. Many times. Until you assume this has become a game, even though I use my serious voice when telling you not to drop your toys in the footwell.

Thud.

I keep still, refusing to go out on another toy-rescue mission.

'DADDY! Arwo's?'

'I told you not to throw it on the floor. I can't keep twisting around like that.'

'AHHHH,' you say, kicking the back of my seat.

And now you've stopped kicking and screaming because the door handle has drawn your attention. These days, child locks are a given, but that doesn't help me sleep soundly at night, because things break, and watching your brutal attempts to wrench the handle free from the car door does nothing to settle my nerves.

'Arlo, we don't pull the handle.'

'This, Dadda?' you say, punching the buttons that operate the window, which is also child-locked.

'Those you can touch.'

'But not this, Dadda,' you say, simultaneously shaking your head and trying to open the door again.

'That's right. We don't touch the handle.'

'OK, Dadda.'

The next item on the agenda is for you to request a snack, usually an orange. But an orange requires me to peel it and inspect each segment individually for pips. Naturally, I don't do it as quickly as you would like me to.

Then there's music. It's bad enough that your music tastes hijack our car journeys, but it's not like we can just pick a playlist and move on. No. You want to listen to ten seconds of one song before demanding another, but before we've loaded up 'another', you want to return to the one we started with.

What about driver's-seat parenting? It's very similar to passenger-seat parenting, except I also have to drive the car. Of course, I can't feed you orange segments, reclaim lost toys and drive the car safely at the same time. I have to prioritise. Selfish of me, I know, but I typically prioritise road safety, which can be challenging when you're screaming at me for not fulfilling your every whim and desire at the drop of a hat.

And just when you thought it couldn't get any worse ... 'Dadda, Arwo done poo-poo.'

This is parenting in the car, and it's my least favourite kind.

Ring, ring.

It's Mummy. 'All right, how we doing?' I ask.

'I got distracted by Arlo asking me a question, and I hit the car in front of me.'

'Oh ... you guys OK?'

'We're fine. It was only a tiny bump. It was my fault.'

Do you see, Arlo? Do you see why you should learn to be a decent back-seat passenger? This is what happens. I'd love to know the stats for road collisions that are exclusively down to children distracting their parents. I bet they're high!

Cold Fire
Thursday, 14 July 2022

'What's that you've made there with the watering can? Is it a puddle?'

'No, Daddy, it's a fire.'

'A fire made out of water?'

'It's a cold fire. You can put your hand in it. It's not a hot fire.'

'Oh, I see.'

'Put your hand in it, Daddy, it's just a cold fire.'

I do as instructed. 'You're not wrong, Arlo. It doesn't burn at all.'

'No, because it's a cold fire, Daddy. I made it on the paving slabs.'

'I love it.'

Mummy Deserves A Holiday
Sunday, 17 July 2022

'Did you have a chance to look at those dates?' says Auntie Lisa to Mummy. We're all over at Nana and Grandad See-See's house.

'No, not yet,' Mummy responds.

'What dates?' I ask.

'Lisa's booked a caravan down at Camber Sands, and she wondered if Arlo and I wanted to come. I assumed you couldn't because you don't have enough holiday allowance.'

Interesting.

I momentarily exit the conversation along with my physical plane of reality and head to the situation room in my mind for a meeting with Other Me.

OK, first, just calm down, and don't give off any information through body language. We do not want to self-sabotage this wonderful opportunity, says Other Me. *Find out more information first, then report back.*

'How long would you be going for?' I ask.

'If I managed to get Wednesday off, we would drive down Tuesday night and come back Friday afternoon,' Mummy says.

I relay this information back to Other Me.

Fuck, that's three nights and three days to yourself. You could watch whatever you wanted on the television. You could enjoy a few lie-ins, maybe even listen to some music. The possibilities are endless.

I'll admit that some time alone does sound appealing to me, Arlo, and by appealing, I mean it would feel like our local council rang me and said I never have to pay council tax again.

It's settled then. Play it cool, but encourage her to go.

'I think you should go,' I say.

'Really? You sure?'

'Of course. Look, you deserve a break. You'll enjoy having the time away from me, and your mum will be there to help out with the kids, so it shouldn't be too stressful, right?'

'I don't think it will be stressful at all. They've been playing nicely together.'

'Exactly. You'd be silly not to go. You need this.'

'OK, I think I will. Lisa, Arlo and I are coming.'

YES! FUCKING YES! Lie-ins, movies that you want to watch and not one single cunting children's television programme! Hoist the bunting, pop the champagne corks, and give a toast to a few days of glorious peace.

'I mean, there's nothing to stop you coming—'

'NO! I mean, no, it's OK. You guys go and have fun. I'll crack on with some distraction-free work or something. No biggie.'

'Only if you're sure.'

'So sure.'

We couldn't be surer.

July Monthly Review
Tuesday, 19 July 2022

The no-dummy-at-night regime has produced a surprisingly charming benefit, and that's listening to you chatting with your soft-toy companions. You've done this before, but without a dummy inhibiting your vocals, this is now happening more and more. For over a year, I've questioned, through scowls and tuts, why we still have a baby monitor. I never use it. If you're awake, you shout. A camera serves no purpose any more.

Until now.

You parade around your bed, rounding up your pals for a chat, and it's delightful to watch. The other night, Mr Moo Chow Cow didn't have his listening ears on, so you told him off. Another night, you lined everyone up and sang the *Bob the Builder* theme song to them. Your isolation at night coaxes out the full force of your imagination because there's no social anxiety. Like I said, delightful.

I'm still reeling from pride and shock at how quickly you got the hang of potty-training. You've had the odd accident since then, but any accidents usually occur within the first two hours of you going to bed. It's now on Mummy and me to figure out the best time to get you up for a dream wee. It's a structure we're still experimenting with. The heat doesn't help. It was 38 degrees yesterday.

You like to have company in the bathroom. You'll position the potty to face the toilet and demand I sit with you while we both enjoy a sit-down wee. It's one of those bonding experiences we'll only have for a short time, so I treasure it all the more – a father and son having a sit-down wee together. Sit-down wees are the best.

Recently, you've begun announcing that you need to get your jumps out and then proceeded to find a good jumping spot. This is especially prevalent at bedtime when Mummy and I are trying to get you to pay attention to the story we're reading.

Your favourite book at the moment is *Monkey Puzzle* by Julia Donaldson. You like it because when I get to the end, I pretend to keep dropping the book before I can reveal the final page, which sends you keeling over with laughter. I'm surprised it's not run its course yet, but you still find it funny. Admittedly, I lean into the theatrics and give my bestest performance each night.

Your taste in television has developed. *Shaun the Sheep* has wandered into our lives, and I'm thankful for that. Because it's pretty good. You also enjoy *Peppa Pig*, *Bob the Builder* and *Tractor Ted*. Your favourite activity is watching diggers on YouTube. I don't mind this, as anything is better than watching *Henry Hoover TV*.

We've noticed another leap in your intelligence. I mentioned the other day about you being able to articulate your confusion from receiving mixed messages. But there's more. Just yesterday, I was trying to answer you, but Mummy kept blurting out distracting, pointless interruptions that were not serving any purpose aside from pissing me off. You noticed, so you gently took my hand and said, 'Daddy, talk to me.' You said it so calmly that I realised you were reacting to in-the-room feedback. Incredible!

And you ask intelligent questions. I forget the exact phrasing, but while on the train with Nana Hoover, you asked why no one person owns a train like they do a car. We all agreed that was incredibly insightful for a boy of your age.

You smile, you play, and you explore. You test boundaries, but you respect the rules and routines that we've built. You are a joy. Thanks for another happy month.

Ref, Time Out!
Sunday, 24 July 2022

I've taken you to the trampoline park to allow Mummy some downtime to battle a hangover. Usually, when we go, it's to a parent-and-toddler session, costing me £6. Those sessions don't run on weekends, so we've had to book a regular session with a delightful price tag of £25 – yes, that's despite you officially being a toddler for a few more months. *Yay!*

It's been a while since you were last here, so it will be interesting to see how you take to the environment with your increased physicality and confidence. You get involved in the warm-up video that the park's policy insists we follow. This is new; usually, you just stand there staring at me as if I'm a moron while I wave my arms.

Once in the park, you test out your abilities. You're miles more confident on the trampolines, bouncing higher and remaining on them longer. Then there's the ball pit. You waste no time launching yourself off the side and into the pit before scrambling to get out. When you do, you announce: 'Daddy, I saved myself,' rather than requesting crane support from me to rescue you.

We're having a phenomenal time of life right now.

Just then, two bigger boys (about seven or eight) approach and ask if we'd like to play football. It's not an odd request given where we are. The trampoline park has a section decked out for the sport. I'm torn. I want to say yes, but you're too young, and I'm worried you'd get hurt. But then I look at your face. You're looking at the bigger boys with an expression of reverence.

'Arlo, do you want to play football?'

'YES!'

'OK,' I say, before turning to the boys: 'We're in.'

The pitch is small – about 30 metres in length. But it's caged in by nets, so there's no danger of kicking the ball into next door's garden and having to play rock paper scissors with your mates to determine who has to climb over the fence and retrieve it. It's us versus the boys, Alby and Cillian. I explain that they need to go easy on you and that we'll have to stop the game immediately if you get hurt. They agree. I take you to the side and do my best to explain the rules.

'Right, you see all those circle lights at the end?'

'Yeah.'

'That's called the goal. We need to kick the ball into the goal. Do you understand?'

'Yeah.'

'And another thing, we only use our legs in football. We don't use our hands to pick the ball up, OK?'

'We only use our legs,' you say, picking up the ball and presenting it to me.

'That's right, so put the ball on the floor, and only kick it.'

I need to be on high alert for red flags and threats in an area where I've volunteered for a game full of red flags and threats. I'm sure there's a lesson in that, but there's no time to dwell on it, as the match has started.

I go easy at first, but as soon as I see the opposition means business, I turn it up a notch. I'm famously hopeless at football, but the fact we're playing a gimmicky version of the sport and not real football is to my advantage, as is being fully grown.

I pass the ball to you, causing you to jump up and down in excitement. You eventually calm down and think about kicking it, but the ball left the space you're standing in hours ago, something you find utterly hilarious.

Your excitement levels are maxed out. You're laughing, shrieking and jumping, and now you're running alongside me as I reclaim possession and go on the offensive. You have no desire to kick the ball yourself, because you don't know what's going on. You don't care. Neither do I. I divide my time watching you enjoy the moment while trying to put up a half-decent performance.

I score two.

But then we concede three.

Being in goal is challenging. You're right by my side, continuing to exhibit all the behaviours that tell me you're still in that good place. My job is to prevent the ball from crossing the goal line and hitting you in the face. Cillian exploits the weakness and scores again.

To their credit, the boys are careful to avoid getting too close to you. As payment for their respect, I try and give them as good a game as I can, but within five minutes, my lungs march out onto the picket line and begin protesting, complaining that they cannot compete with the vitality of youth. Eventually, reinforcements arrive – two similar-aged boys. We tag them in and leave the pitch. The smile on your face is as wide as it is telling.

'Was that fun?' I ask.

'It was so much fun.'

'Wasn't it?'

'Daddy, can we play in the ball pit now?'

'We can, but Daddy just needs a break for a minute.'

'Why, Daddy?'

Because I'm a tired old man. 'I've lost all my energy playing football.'

'But will you get more energy?'

'Absolutely, buddy. I'll get lots more energy.'

Sneaking
Thursday, 28 July 2022

'Sneak – sneak – sneak – sneak – sneak,' you whisper.

You're creeping up on me while I sit quietly on the sofa minding my own business, supposedly having no idea of the terrible fright that's about to assail me. For your part, you believe you're invisible; you're moving slowly and only whispering as opposed to shouting or talking at a normal volume. But I'm afraid no fright will assail me. Instead, I'll have to put on one helluva performance to avoid disappointment and a possible tantrum. In addition to your auditory warnings, I can also see you in my peripheral vision. Again, you're not really making the stealthiest of approaches.

'RAAAAA!'

'AHHHH! Oh my God, you sneaky little monster, you scared me.'

'Daddy, I was sneaking.'

'Hmmm ... Yeah, OK then, I'll give you that one. You got me good.'

August

listening ears
noun

Organs of hearing that are similar to regular ears but detachable; they can be hidden at will, especially when a parent asks their child to do something for the hundredth time.

The Parenthood Dictionary
Adventures in Dadding Edition

Listening Ears
Monday, 1 August 2022

No one wins when your listening ears go on sabbatical. Usually, we can convince them to return through some sort of distraction. But sometimes, you're in the mood for a battle, and we're the only opponents around.

You pair up not listening to us with repeatedly asking the same questions, such as why you can't have another lolly. Those two strategies, while effective on their own, are lethal when combined. Life becomes exhausting, and, like money left in the bank, the exhaustion compounds itself.

But there's a third variable, and that's when a parent's 'not feeling it' either.

Those three variables are mixed up in a bowl and served as a dish of heightened emotions and flaring tempers. Last week, Mummy was on the receiving end of this. Today it's me.

I've got this hereditary genetic marker – you might also have it. I discovered it *after* you were born. Doctors can't tell me much, but it's led to an autoimmune condition. One of the side effects is anterior uveitis, where my immune system picks an eyeball and attacks it for bantz. I'm midway through a flare-up right now. My right eye is red, sore and sensitive to light. The only way to combat it is to throw a fuck-ton of steroids at it until it calms down.

No one from the eye department can tell me what triggers it, but they have said that long-term use of steroid eye drops isn't the best thing in the world. *No shit!*

The lack of answers means these flare-ups stress me out, and my attempts to practise stoic philosophy have a higher-than-normal failure rate. Add to that you being in a non-listening mood, and you have a situation where I'm not enjoying my dadding job, which is a shame because I've engineered a scenario that has all the ingredients for an epic dadding memory.

I've taken us to the park with our scooters and Nana Hoover. While going to the park isn't a new experience, going there with our scooters is, as this is the first time I've taken mine out as well. Mummy got it for me for my birthday last year. She said, 'When Arlo's big enough, you can both take them out together.' I've been looking forward to that day ever since. And now it's here. But unfortunately, I'm not – well, physically I am, but emotionally, I'm somewhere else.

'Daddy, why don't you need a helmet?'

'Erm, because I'm a grown-up.'

That right there is the first sign of me being on the back foot. Rarely do I default to such an unhelpful explanation. But I'm tired, in pain and not in the best of moods. And then I remember that this isn't your fault, and I try again. 'Arlo, I have a licence because I passed a test, and so I don't have to wear one.'

'When I pass my test – when I'm bigger – I won't need to wear a helmet as well?'

'Yep.'

'I don't want to ride my scooter.'

Fuck's sake. This happens every time we take your scooter out. We say you must wear your helmet, so you say you don't want to ride your scooter, and I end up carrying it the entire time.

'Here, give me your helmet,' I say, making an executive parental decision to rewrite the scooter section in our *How To Parent Arlo* manual.

'Don't I have to wear it?'

'Not this time.'

'But why don't I have to wear it, Daddy?'

'I'm honestly not sure what answer I can give you other than to tell you it's OK because we're in the park.'

Believe it or not, this isn't me giving in; it's a calculated risk. And if it means you actually ride the damn thing, then I'm happy to shoulder the blame if any mishaps occur.

But they don't. It was the right call. You go up and down the path demanding we watch you. You're in your element.

Until it's time to go home.

We came to the park on foot, but now I wish I had remembered to bring the buggy. I need more eye drops, and I need to start dinner.

'Come on, Arlo. Please hurry up,' I implore.

You don't.

Nana Hoover plays the part of the calm intermediary, suggesting we play hide-and-seek and encouraging the person doing the hiding to run up the road in the direction of home.

It works.

But then it doesn't. You keep running into shops.

'Arlo, if you don't stop running into shops, then you'll have to hold Daddy's hand, OK?'

In through one ear ...

... and out the other.

ENOUGH ALREADY! 'Right, Arlo, you're holding Daddy's hand.'

'NOOOO! Daddy, I don't want to.'

'Have you been using your listening ears?'

'No, I have not.'

'Then you have to hold on to my hand.'

You wriggle and convulse your arm to jerk it free, but your pissed-off, evil daddy's grip is too firm.

This is the first time I've intervened using physicality outside of picking you up from a precarious position, like on the stairs. Walking down the street playing tug of war does not qualify as me feeling great about myself.

We get around the next corner and I drop down to your level. 'Are you going to switch your listening ears on now?'

You don't say anything, you just give me a rebellious toddler glare, but you lift both hands to your ears simultaneously and 'switch them on'.

'Excellent. Now, let's try again.'

We spend the rest of the journey not talking to each other.

It's evening. You're asleep, and I'm mulling over the events from today. I'm sorry things didn't go the way either of us wanted.

Often, I'll find online articles about parenthood that point out that saying no to your kids is hard, but you do it because you love them. I understand that – saying no is hard sometimes, like when I've got family members asking if they can give you ice cream or when you ask for one more story or cartoon before bed. I say no because I want you to eat well and rest so that you wake up the next day a happier version of yourself. If Mummy and I start flipping a coin about whether we're enforcing the rules, then they're not rules.

The hardest part is when we give you a warning. Because if you ignore the warning, we are obliged to follow through with whatever threat we issued as a deterrent. Today, it was holding my hand. You hated that, and I hated enforcing it. But you know what? I'd do it again in a heartbeat rather than contribute to a world view where warnings are empty, where the more you scream and shout, the more likely we are to buckle. Not a chance.

And no, the helmet doesn't count. I made a conscious decision. Yes, I was pissed off, and my explanation for the rule change was awful. But as I sit here now, calmer than I was a few hours ago, I'm at peace with my decision. That wouldn't have been the case if I hadn't enforced the hand-holding.

Despite writing books on the subject of parenting, I've not once publicly or privately pretended to be anything I'm not. What I am is an average guy doing an average job of something that arrived with no preparation or training, and there's no continued supervision or appraisals. I do my best with what I've got, accepting that limitations and failures are two immutable clauses in my parenthood contract.

But here's something I do stand by: if, as a parent, you say you're going to do something, you must follow through with it! If not, you'd better have a good reason because your children will hold you accountable.

Once again, I'm sorry about today, and I'm sorry I lost my temper with you. Sleep well. I love you.

Bad Idea
Tuesday, 2 August 2022

I put you in the bath and attempt to remove the sand stuck to your skin after a day at nursery.

'Daddy, I need a wee-wee.'

Ah, man. 'Couldn't you have told me that before you got in?'

'I need a wee-wee, Daddy.'

'OK, I'll tell you what, you can just go in the bath.'

'OK.'

Ten seconds later ...

'Arlo.'

'Yes, Daddy?'

'Please stop drinking the bathwater.'

A Medical Emergency
Wednesday, 3 August 2022

'I think Arlo has broken a rib,' says Mummy gravely.

'Really? Why do you think that?' I ask.

'Have you not seen that bruise on his ribs? It's awful.'

'Sure, I can see a bruise ... [Insert awkward silence, and maybe some tumbleweed.] It doesn't mean he's broken his ribs, though, does it? It could just be a bruise.'

'But if you put your finger on it, it feels lumpy, like one of his ribs is broken.'

'Oh, so you think it's a complete fracture?'

'Maybe. I'm gonna call one-one-one.'

'Please don't do that.'
'Why?'
'Because I promise you, he hasn't broken his rib.'
'How would you know? You're not a doctor.'
'Nevertheless, I'm pretty confident.'
'How?'
'Because he's currently doing handstands on the sofa next to you. That's in between bouts of jumping up and down and climbing all over us. Do you not think that screams "guys, I haven't broken any of my ribs"?'

'Well, I'm gonna keep an eye on it just in case you're wrong!'

'You do what you think best.'
'Oh, I will. Don't you worry about that.'
'I'm not worried.'
'Good!'

The Consequences Of A Toddler Licking The Carpet
Thursday, 4 August 2022

'Daddy, I've got hair in my mouth.'

'Do you think that might be because you keep licking the carpet?'

'Yeah. Can you get it out?'

'Let's give it a go.'

It takes me a few attempts, but eventually, I extract the hair from your mouth. 'Have you learnt your lesson about licking the carpet?'

'Yes. I shouldn't do it.'

'That's right, and— Arlo, what are you doing?'

Coming up for air and grinning, you say, 'I'm licking the carpet, Daddy.'

'Of course you are.'

'Daddy.'

Sighing. 'Yes, Arlo?'

'I've got hair in my mouth. Can you get it out?'

One Rule To Rule Them All
Sunday, 7 August 2022

'God, it wasn't that long ago when shops were closed on a Sunday. Now everywhere is open,' Mummy says as we make our way to our favourite restaurant in town for breakfast.

'Not long ago? You know shops started opening on a Sunday when we were kids, right? Like, thirty years ago.'

'No!' exclaims Mummy, refusing to come to terms with how much time we've spent on the planet.[8]

We arrive at the restaurant and get settled. We like it here because it's easy to get a healthy meal and the environment is relaxed. We've managed to secure one of the sofa-by-the-window spots, which are great for families because they can spread out the eight bags of toys and tricks that wise parents bring with them to keep bored toddlers amused and entertained long enough for the food to arrive.

---

[8] Right, folks, who's ready to feel super old? The Sunday Trading Act 1994 came into effect on 26 August of that year.

Your first order of business is a spot of trampolining. 'Arlo,' I say, 'can you take your shoes off if you're going to jump up on the sofa?'

'Oh, it's fine. Let him crack on,' Mummy says.

'OK, Mummy,' you say, before unloading a few more jumps.

'Hang on one minute,' I say to Mummy.

'What?'

'You batter him if he jumps on the furniture at home. You've always said it sends him the wrong message and will encourage him to mistreat other people's furniture the same way he mistreats yours.'

'That's right,' Mummy says, getting annoyed that I haven't made my point yet, even though I've just made my point.

'Well, you're full of s-h-i-t. You don't care about furniture etiquette. You only care about *your* furniture.'

'Oh, have you only just worked that out?'

'So it would seem.'

'Daddy, look at me. I'm getting all my jumps out.'

Unbelievable.

The Shoe On The Other Foot
Monday, 8 August 2022

Remember the planned trip to Camber Sands? The situation has developed. First, Mummy couldn't get the extra day off she needed, but she still planned to drive down with you on Wednesday evening after work and stay away for two nights, meaning

August

I would still get two evenings and two lie-ins. Not bad!

But then ... Nana See-See asked if she could take you with her today so you could hang out with her, Haylee and Auntie Lisa before Mummy arrives on Wednesday.

We've agreed, but it's been a difficult decision. We've had instances where we've left you behind so that Mummy and I can go away and have fun, but never the other way round. It's not that we mind you going. But we're worried you'll get overexcited from being outside the comfort of your routine and need a Mummy- or Daddy-cuddle. Then there's Haylee. You love to wind each other up, and such endeavours can often lead to tears. Again, you won't have a parent there should you need one.

On the flip side, when we explained that you would go on your own for a couple of days and then Mummy would join you, your little body began vibrating with excitement. You were incredibly vocal and animated, and so the decision was made for us.

But do you know what the hardest thing was? Today is Mummy's birthday. She only got to see you for ten minutes in the morning before she had to get ready and leave for work. Hats off to her for letting you go.

I've often spoken about the need for parents to take breaks and time for themselves. Not once have I thought about how children might need a break from their parents.

Have the best time, son. I'll see you on Friday.

PS: tell Nana to lay off the fucking ice cream!

Time Away Versus Time Together
Tuesday, 9 August 2022

Mummy and I video-called you to see how you were enjoying your holiday. *And if you were coping.* You managed a 'hello' before running off to do laps of the campsite with Haylee. It's safe to say you're doing OK.

And that's reassuring because homesickness is horrible. A few days away can feel like a lifetime at your age if you're not enjoying yourself.

Your going away is a good test for Mummy and me because it will happen more often. In *Dear Dory*, I spoke about an article called 'The Tail End', by Tim Urban. Tim uses illustrations and basic modelling to calculate how many more books he'll read or how many more winters he's got left before he dies, assuming he lives to the age of ninety. He then uses the same modelling techniques to determine how much more in-person contact he'll be likely to have with his parents. He calculated that he had already used up 93 per cent of his in-person parent time when he graduated from high school.

The article had, and continues to have, a profound impact on me and how I spend my time with others. It's one of the reasons why I wanted Nana Hoover to come to Northampton. It's also why I say yes to any social invitation from my closest friends.

Generally speaking, children spend much of their time with their parents. But as they grow, they begin to draw away. First, they go to nursery and then school. Then it's after-school activities and play dates, then sleepovers. Before you know it, they're spending all their free time hanging out with their mates, partying, and going on trips away before heading off to see the world or settling down in another city to work and maybe start a family of their own.

Your going away is the start of that process, the start of the tail end. Sure, we have plenty of time together, but we never have as much as we think, and we must never take the time we have for granted. For the most part, I don't, though I'm not perfect. Your absence reminds me how precious our time together is. Though, conversely, I stand by what I said: time away from us is also important, despite the stress it places on my heartstrings. If that sounds paradoxical, then that's because it is. It's another parenting paradox.

One day, you'll understand this yourself. You might be in my position, sitting in a quieter-than-usual house, wondering how your children are getting on. Maybe Mummy and I have taken them away. Perhaps you'll be grateful for that time alone. But if you are, I'd wager your thoughts will nonetheless drift to your children: how they're doing, what they're doing, how much sugar they've had and if their emotional needs are being met.

I'm glad you're having fun.

Silence
Wednesday, 10 August 2022

Mummy drove straight from work to join you on your mini holiday. Nana is working nights which means I'm by myself.

Everything has slowed. There's no rushing through routines; no clanking sounds piercing the air as teacups are thrown into the dishwasher; no television background noise; no pitter-patter of Arlo feet running away from bedtime. Everything is ... silent.

And the silence is surreal. Like when you see an old friend you've not seen in such a long time. The last time you saw each other you were different people with different priorities and world views. Life has changed you both.

But it's not unwelcome. It may be a while since I've socialised with silence, but I remember why I was drawn to it in the first place. Silence is an ally, a chance to reflect on what matters and be still.

I journal.

I take a bath.

I meditate.

I slow down.

But then my thoughts return to you. And they're hard to shake.

It's been great reacquainting with an old friend, but now it's time for us to say goodbye and for silence to go home. We vow not to leave it as long until we next meet, though neither of us has a proven track record of honouring that promise.

I sit on the sofa, switch the television on and begin a six-part documentary on ILM (Industrial Light & Magic), which is fascinating and distracts me from you.

After a while, my eyelids tire of being open. So, I take myself upstairs and position myself in the middle of the bed. Then I ... *ZZZZzzzzzzz*.

FFS
Thursday, 11 August 2022

'Hi, Arlo, are you having a good time?'

'Yes, I am, Daddy. Can I see Hetty?'

Sigh. 'Yep, I'll bring you down to her now,' I say, flipping the camera around and getting ready to stand off to the side like a spare part.

This happened before when you went away to Ireland last year. *And it will happen again.*

Despite missing you, I don't mind being shunted aside in favour of a pink vacuum cleaner, because there is still plenty of value for me to distil from this experience as you have your chat with Hetty. You're excited, and your excitement emanates something that I can soak up and absorb, something energising, something that's enough to keep me going until you return home tomorrow.

Enjoy the last day of your holiday. Safe journey home.

Back Home
Friday, 12 August 2022

Mummy said it was one of the worst drives she's ever had to do, but you guys are home now and safe.

Do you agree with my philosophy? Everyone needs time away from loved ones, don't they? Because it makes you realise why they're your loved ones. It's good to have you back.

Another Party
Sunday, 14 August 2022

We're at a birthday party at Taci's house for her two girls. Haylee is with us. I get ten seconds of Taci's time before she dashes off to oversee another task. During those ten seconds, she tells me how stressed she is, how nothing has gone according to plan and that the place looks awful.

Taci is the most creative person I know. Her version of 'this looks shit' is my version of Disneyland – she's incredible. When I used to work with her, she once transformed our entire bank of desks in the office into Australia's famous Bondi Beach, in celebration of the Olympic Games. Today, she's not enjoying the moment, because of her responsibilities and, in part, because she's unable to comprehend the height of her creative talents.

'I think we should host a party for Arlo this year,' Mummy says.

'That is still a terrible idea,' I say.

'Why is it?'

'Why is it? Why are you asking for my opinion when I've given it multiple times? We have this conversation every month – have you seen how stressed Taci is?'

'But if we pay to have it at soft play or something like that, then it will cost us loads, and they won't be able to have a digger theme.'

'From the top: it might cost us, but it's worth every penny because hosting a party is a form of self-harm, and we can dress it up in whatever theme we want. All we need is a digger cake and a few digger banners. He'll fucking love it.'

'Well, I think we should host.'

To be continued ... next month, I guess.

The theme today is a splash-and-play fairy party. At one end of the enormous garden is a shed – sorry, a 'fairy shed' – for dressing up.

'Look, Mum, I'm a fairy!' screams one young boy of about six as he runs towards his mother, proudly showing off his new threads.

The fairy shed is not the main attraction. The main attraction rests in the middle of the garden: a plunge pool covered with a tarpaulin.

Party invitations instructed all children to bring swimwear. And they listened. And now they keep asking when they can go in.

'It's up to Taci,' parents say.

'Not until after food,' declares Taci.

Lunch is served inside a sweatbox of a marquee. I try to get in to help, but it's crowded ... which I take as a message from God to vacate, find a quiet spot and relax. I do. I find a rocking chair and catch up with a couple of girls I used to work with and whom I've not seen in some time.

After food, the children, including you and Haylee, get changed into swimming gear and loiter near parents, patiently waiting for the flagship attraction to open. I conduct some basic maths. The pool measures about 3 metres by 1.5 metres, and roughly thirty children are here. If even a third of the attendees get in it at any one time, then it will be over the maximum occupancy by some margin.

This should be interesting ...

Everyone is getting fidgety; lunch included several E-number-laden delicacies, and the sugar highs have arrived, sending the kids buzzing into unstable states. They need to begin burning it off quickly, but Taci, the big meanie, is taking her sweet time over conducting the pool's opening ceremony.

But then ... the tarpaulin is lifted, revealing that, in addition to water, the pool also contains a swollen layer of balls – basically, a ball pit on top of a paddling pool. The scene is dazzling.

'Right, kids, the pool is open for business,' declares Taci.

And just like that, thirty overdosed-on-sugar children, including you and Haylee, charge forward in unison towards the ball pit–splash pool, screaming battle cries.

Carnage.

Chaos.

Destruction.

And noise – such ear-piercing noise. Getting stranded on Isla Nublar is less lethal than this cocktail of swinging limbs. The balls explode out of the pool – it's like the whole thing is one giant multicoloured popcorn machine.

Did I mention that you're the youngest one here?

Duty soon calls. I've lost sight of you, so I'm no longer sitting in the rocking chair. But you're hard to locate. Imagine playing *Where's Wally?* But you're standing next to a festival speaker listening to a band that can't harmonise, looking for a toddler and a preschooler in a picture that's full of moving colour and other children who closely resemble the toddler and the preschooler that you're looking for.

There they are! You and Haylee are having fun and are, for now, uninjured. But you're wary of your surroundings, and the noise is too much. You linger at one end of the pool, practising getting in and out.

And then Taci makes another announcement. 'OK, kids, come and get your water bombs!'

A rare moment of silence as thirty meerkats freeze in the middle of the mayhem and look towards the sound of Taci's voice. They find it right next to her husband, Adam, who places a large black bucket on the ground, one filled with water bombs.

I don't know who's the first to respond, but when one does, they all do. They come crashing out of their environment like escaping convicts, scrambling over one another to reach the bucket and load up on ammunition.

You don't know what the fuss is about as you've yet to acquaint yourself with this vital component of summer fun. And even if you did, you don't boast the build to wade through the curtain of bigger kids.

But you know who does? Me.

I force my way to the bucket, load up on bombs and distribute them between you and Haylee. Watching the other kids is all the education you need. You squeeze one bomb, exposing a tiny hole and creating a mini-hosepipe effect. Grasping the game's concept, you aim it at me, and I play the part of beaten victim, though I'm already very wet from having to threat-watch by the pool a few moments ago. Everyone is enjoying the outdoor hydro-skirmish.

Enter Dolly.

Dolly is the youngest of five. Her four older siblings are boys, so she's had to learn to survive in a male-dominated environment. And she has indeed learnt. Because Dolly is a fucking monster.

She tears through anyone who gets in her way as she pursues her targets like a broke bounty hunter, delivering wrath and devastation. No one can best her. She is ruin personified, automatically choosing the biggest boys she can find. I watch her make one lad cry on three separate occasions in three minutes.

Dolly's mother, Christine, takes Dolly to one side. She chastises her daughter for being too rough, telling her to lay off the kid she keeps destroying. Dolly nods in understanding before bolting off and grabbing a water-balloon slingshot. She loads it, aims it at the same poor teary-eyed lad and fires.

The watery missile misses, but it doesn't matter. Dolly was so close to her quarry when launching her attack that the rubber from the slingshot struck him in the face. He's crying again.

'Dolly, that's enough,' shouts Christine.

'OK, Mum,' Dolly says, releasing another missile. *Splat.*

Another kill. Dolly has now amassed more scalps than anyone else here.

Mummy sidles up to me. 'Well, this is—'

'Barbaric. Still want to host?' I say.

'Erm, well, let's talk about it later.'

'Sure.'

'Dolly! I mean it this time. You must *not* punch him.'

'Sorry, Mum.'

And there you have it, son – another children's birthday-party memory to add to the pile stored in the trauma section of my long-term memory.

I Don't Want Daddy!
Wednesday, 17 August 2022

You're unwell. Mummy has taken the day off to look after you. It's been a rough morning spent on the sofa watching cartoons, threaded through with tears and bouts of frustration.

But now you're napping, and, hopefully, a rest will perk you up. Failing that, it's not long until your next dose of Calpol is due.

'Mummy,' you shout.

I'm anxious to see how you're doing, so I follow. You're sprawled out on your bed. I can tell immediately from your angry, pissed-off toddler eyes that you're not happy.

'Do you want to come downstairs?' Mummy says.

'No!' you say, wriggling like someone who's had a bag of ants tipped over them.

When you're ill, our sympathy levels are automatically overstocked, so we can handle whatever you throw our way. Mummy sits next to you and begins calmly stroking your face.

After a couple of minutes, you decide you don't like Mummy rubbing you.

And that's when it happens.

A transformation in you that I've never witnessed before.

You roll onto all fours and start wailing, 'No, Mummy.'

The sound you utter is scary and off-putting, like a distressed cat you sometimes hear in the middle of the night when everyone is in bed and a feline scuffle breaks out. The sounds from such an encounter are always memorable, but not in a good way – an out-of-tune violin handled by someone who's never played before.

Mummy pulls you into a warm, loving embrace.

'NO, MUMMY!'

'It's OK. Mummy's got you. We don't—'

'I! Don't! Want! You!'

'OK, that's fine. Do you want us to leave?'

'YES!'

Mummy puts you back in bed, and you revert to sounding like a talking gargoyle that's had its throat slashed. As we're leaving, you roar, 'NO!'

'Do you want one of us to stay?' Mummy says.

'Yes.'

'Who do you want?'

'Not Mummy.'

Mummy leaves, and I tag in. I do what I can to comfort you, but when you're in this state, you want Mummy (despite her banishment). So Mummy returns and sends me out of the room. Eventually, you calm enough for her to bring you downstairs to the sofa. I'm in the kitchen.

'Go downstairs to the basement, Daddy. I don't want you here.'

Ouch! 'I'm just making my lunch, and then I will,' I say.

'Nooooo. I don't want Daddy here. Go away, Daddy. Go downstairs.'

OK, now that stings. And I'm in a tricky position. Had you said something like that when you weren't ill, we would have discussed your choice of words and how you used them. But seeing as you are sick, you get a hall pass. But I'm also hungry and not about to leave my lunch, only to come up in five minutes and have you revert to this state again and undo Mummy's hard work.

'Arlo, I will go downstairs once I finish making my lunch.'

'No, Mummy. I don't want Daddy to be here.'

You're really going for it now – lots of tears and anger.

'He does love you. He's just very upset,' Mummy says, reading my body language.

She's never had to support me in that manner before. You've gone through stages of favouring one parent over the other, but it's never come close to what's on display now. Usually, you have a storyteller preference, or you prefer one of us to play a particular game. But my occupancy of the room is causing you great distress, as if my presence is an airborne acid that will only go away when I do.

After an excruciating few minutes, I take my lunch downstairs to the basement and leave you to calm down. The experience has left me shaken. Maybe I assumed the bond we share had inoculated me against such treatment.

Am I angry? No. I'm not. You have nothing to be sorry for, and I have nothing to forgive. But it's next to impossible not to take the rejection personally. I can't get over the wailing-cat sound, coupled with the anger and distress you felt while I was in the same room as you. Is this a sign of things to come in the future? Probably.

It's evening. You're calmer and receptive to my company. We're having a cuddle on the sofa, and you're stroking my face because you like the feel of my stubble.

If this afternoon was hell, then this is heaven. I hope you feel better soon, son.

August Monthly Review
Friday, 19 August 2022

You love building dens. And you like it when we watch you do stuff. You'll say to me, 'Watch the whole thing, Daddy,' before doing the whole thing. Another phrase you say regularly is, 'I've got a good idea.' You said it to Haylee the other day. She rolled her eyes before replying, 'Arlo, you've always got a good idea.' She will be four in December.

If I ask who made all the mess, you point to yourself and say, 'This guy right here.'

Whenever we part company, you ask for a hug and a kiss. And when we reunite, you charge into me, giving me 'a big, maviss hug'. It's spirit-nourishing stuff. 'Maviss', by the way, is how you mispronounce 'massive'.

What's less nourishing for the spirit is you ignoring us when we talk to you. That, my boy, pushes buttons. At least acknowledge our presence!

And when you do acknowledge us, it's often to present a counterargument as to why you don't need to do what we've asked you to do. Now, the arguments I can handle. You ignoring me, I can't.

The worst bit is how in command of your timings you are. You'll push me right to the brink, and then, as I'm about to march to war and take a toy, your listening ears turn back on – prohibiting me from carrying out the punishment, even though you've stressed me out enough to warrant it.

Nana Hoover doesn't help. She uninvitedly inserts herself into the dynamic with a grin that says, 'You were just like that as a toddler.'

FUCK OFF, MUM! You're not helping!

Your confidence continues to increase, and you are becoming comfortable in your skin. This tells Mummy and me that we're doing something right. But then you'll go and destroy the game Haylee's playing quietly in the corner, for no reason and with no regard to consequences. *Maybe we don't deserve that pat on the back.*

Another thing you love is being naked. After using the potty, you ask if you can leave your trousers and boxer shorts on the floor. I'm fine with that. You were in nappies for over two and a half years; you're entitled to naked time, especially as you'll soon become self-conscious of such appearances.

Your excellent use of the toilet or the potty continues. We still get the occasional accident at night when the weather is hot, but that's rare. I'm still shocked at how easy potty-training was for us, but I'm no less grateful.

And the language around pottying is also very special, something I take full credit for. You'll excuse yourself for a code brown, and then you'll shout from the toilet, 'Daddy, I'm just curling out a big, maviss log, OK?' – a sentence that beckons a warm smile and a large dose of pride.

Keep doing everything you're doing except for switching those listening ears off. Don't do that! Because it's annoying as shit!

I love you.

Some Damn Fine Helper Action
Saturday, 20 August 2022

'Mummy,' I say, 'Arlo and I are coming upstairs and reporting for duty.'

'We're coming upstairs, Mummy!' you scream.

'Oh, no, I don't think that's—'

'We're here! What can we do? We've come equipped with some damn fine helper action,' I declare.

'Some damn fine helper action is what we've got Mummy.'

Mummy has bought new baskets for the bathroom, a purchase which I decreed unnecessary, but I was ignored. But now I'm happy I was ignored because there are a bunch of rolled-up towels that need to be unravelled, placed in a pile and then jumped on. From there, we'll recycle the pile of unfolded, trampled-on towels to make a den, one that will house a couple of lads, whence they will offer words of encouragement to Mummy while she scowls at us.

If that doesn't sound like the perfect Saturday morning, then I don't know what does. Wouldn't you agree?

'Oh, Arlo, why have you tipped everything out?'

'Because I needed to, Mummy. You see?'

'Yes, I can see ...'

'Isn't life so much easier when you have a couple of damn fine helpers?' I offer.

'Is life easier, Mummy?'

Stair Gate
Monday, 22 August 2022

You and Nana Hoover are pissing about by the top of the stairs. Your antics have led to you demonstrating your ability to shut the stair gate.

'Oh wow, that's very impressive. Can you open it—'

'NO!' I say, arriving on the scene instantly, before adopting the persona I use when I have to explain to you about sharp objects. 'Arlo, Nana didn't realise that what she suggested was a VERY silly thing to ask, wasn't it, Nana?' I say, turning my attention to her and adopting an are-you-fucking-mental expression. 'We don't want a toddler opening the gate once it's locked. Otherwise, it negates the purpose of its existence, doesn't it? Silly Nana.'

'Silly Nana,' you say.

'I just thought—'

'What a terrible idea? Good, we had the same thought.'

Seriously, I love and rely upon grandmothers. But both of yours could do with an electrician coming in and rewiring the part of their brain that decides what is and isn't a good idea as far as their grandchildren are concerned. Because teaching them to open a stair gate isn't.

Don't Tell Mummy
Friday, 26 August 2022

Arlo, can you keep a secret? OK, here goes – and don't you dare tell Mummy this – but Daddy went upstairs with his shoes on. There, I said it. I confessed. Let's keep that between you and me. Otherwise, Mummy will visit upon me a fury of untold devastation.

There'll be some shouting and some flapping and some frowning and some tutting and some sighing. Then snarling. Her entire body will vibrate with rage and wrath – a biological nuclear bomb that cannot be tamed or disarmed.

So best to keep quiet, OK? The fallout isn't worth it.

Do You Like Yourself?
Tuesday, 30 August 2022

'Daddy, do you like yourself?'

What the— 'Where did that come from? You know it's only 7 a.m. Are we really going there this early in the day?'

'Do you?'

I guess we are. 'I suppose I do, yes. Not always, but a lot more than I used to. And it's easier than it used to be.'

'OK.'

The answer seems to satisfy you because you've returned to the television, but my God, what a question to spring on me.

Let's unpack it a bit more.

First, a definition of what self-love is not. Liking and loving yourself is not about longingly staring into the mirror, captivated by your own good looks. Vanity is not self-love, though, conversely, being comfortable with your reflection is absolutely a form of self-love because it means you are accepting of yourself – something that's not easy.

Self-love is about being kind to yourself.

Be kind to your body. Feed it with healthy food and exercise it often. Your body loves it when you stretch and go for walks in nature, and when you splash out on a sports massage.

Be kind to your mind – your spiritual self. Take time to notice your surroundings. Meditate. Slow down. Accept your limitations and welcome failure. Surround yourself with people with whom you can be open. Remove people who draw out the worst in you.

If you can learn to listen to your voice, you will understand your basic needs. And if you can learn to respect yourself and be kind to yourself, you will work to ensure those needs are met.

Berating yourself for what you haven't done or can't do, or for what you don't have, is not being kind to yourself.

Is this easy? No. It's hard. It takes daily practice. Often, towards the end of the day when I'm tired, I find my self-kindness slipping. When that happens, I know it's my body telling me I need to stop what I'm doing and go and relax. Feedback is important. But it's often ignored.

So, to answer your question, yes, I do like myself. Not always, but I do. And I will help you learn to do the same. Acceptance of *what is* facilitates an easier life. Rejection of *what is* invites misery.

Toddler Inc.: Panic Stations

tipping point
noun

An improbability so improbable that it's not worth going into any more details, because the chances of it occurring are staggeringly and inconceivably remote.

Toddler Inc. Employee Handbook
Third Edition

Klaxons blared through the corridors of Toddler Inc. Employees panicked, fearing the worst. Some cancelled their meetings for the day so they could update their CVs. Others ran up and down the corridors waving their arms in terror. The savvier employees began quietly relieving the company of as many possessions as they could hide in their jackets. Within ten minutes, the pencils had gone. The rubbers went next. Then the staple guns.

Even Mr Jacobs was rattled, though he knew better than to advertise the matter.

I need to calm the situation, and quickly, he thought, as he passed a wall where someone had graffitied the words *WE'RE DOOMED*. He turned a corridor and met his assistant, Karen, who stepped into line with him.

'Talk to me.'

'They're calling it a tipping point, sir.'

'A tipping point? Nonsense. Are you sure?'

'I'm afraid so, sir.'

'I thought the perils of modern life prevented that from happening.'

Karen shrugged, unable to respond. Like her boss, she didn't have any answers. Only questions. 'Perhaps the other department heads will have more information.'

'They've arrived?'

Karen nodded.

They came to a large, intimidating steel door. Access required three-factor biometric authentication. Mr Jacobs pressed his thumb on the fingerprint-capture pad, glared into the retinal scanner, and then, into a microphone, said, 'A toddler's charge in life is to stand tall because a toddler's fate in life is to rule over all.'

The door's locking mechanisms relaxed, allowing Mr Jacobs and Karen to enter the Situation Room.

A twenty-foot-long oak table stood in the centre of the rectangular room. On its far side was a large display monitor. The heads of department were waiting, standing by the table next to their chairs. No one would sit until Mr Jacobs gave the word.

'Please, everyone, sit,' Mr Jacobs said.

They did.

'Let's get down to business. Mr Keithy, as head of Damage Control, what can you tell me?'

Mr Keithy, a small, wiry, bespectacled man dressed in a walrus-patterned Hawaiian jumper, cleared his gravelly throat. 'Tipping point, I'm afraid.'

'How?'

'There are ... rare moments when a parent feels in control. Like they know what they're doing. Usually, those moments depart as quickly as they arrive. We call them "moments of sublime ignorance".'

'I know this.'

'Right, and we also know if two parents in a given support network experience a moment of sublime ignorance together, it creates a bond of sorts. The parents' shared feeling of empowerment generates enough energy for the moments of sublime ignorance to linger on together.'

'Yes, but they still only last a few seconds at most, right?' said Mr Jacobs, who then turned to face another woman in the room. 'Sheila?'

Six feet tall, Shelia McNamara, the head of analytics, was a goddess of a woman with perfect features and natural blonde hair. She wore an Easter Bunny onesie. 'Two moments of sublime ignorance, birthed at the same time and connected in some way, can last up to five seconds, though there have been rare occasions where we've monitored moments lasting for six. The record is seven.'

'Right, so what's the problem? Are you telling me it's possible three parents in a room shared a moment of sublime ignorance? Not a chance.'

The room turned to Mr Keithy to hear him deliver what Mr Jacobs quickly realised would be a devastating statement.

'Sir, at seven p.m. GMT, a UK influencer went live with a tutorial teaching parents how to practise calm parenting techniques and self-forgiveness.'

Silence.

No one knew what to say. Karen started crying.

'We've got a clip,' continued Mr Keithy, holding up a remote and pointing it towards the large display monitor that blinked to life.

On it was a video with a young father in his thirties talking directly to the camera. 'And remember, every day is a new day – a new opportunity to parent our children.'

Mr Jacobs noticed the streaming participants. 'Seventy thousand people watched this?' he exclaimed.

'I'm afraid so, sir. Since then, things have got worse.'

Mr Keithy clicked the remote again, and the video footage dissolved into a grid-like pattern, showcasing on-the-ground reporters from around the world. Each took their turn to deliver blows to the company:

'One mum has started free online breathing-technique classes.'

'We've got dads organising Sunday walks in the park with their kids and practising what they call "talking about one's feelings".'

'There's a TikyTokko—'

'You mean a TikToker?' corrected Mr Jacobs.

'Yes, one of them, a TikyTokko, who's teaching parents how to deal with tantrums and explaining what they are and why they happen.'

Mr Keithy pressed a button, and the screen went blank.

'For the love of God,' Mr Jacobs said, 'we cannot allow parents to know the truth, that tantrums are nothing more than verbal frustration. They need to believe these are cruel, malicious acts, calculated attempts by their children to shear through their mental health.'

'It's too late for that, sir.'

'So it is a tipping point,' Mr Jacobs said, more to himself than anyone else. 'Sheila, is there any hope?'

'We've never seen momentum like this before, sir. It's everywhere. The word is out that burnout awaits anyone who tries to take on too much and doesn't ask for help.'

'But silent sufferers equate to almost sixty per cent of our annual turnover. It pays employee bonuses.'

'I know. I was planning to buy my husband a jet ski for his birthday.'

'Well, we're not dead in the water yet. We still have one ace up our sleeve, and I say it's high time we play it.' Mr Jacobs turned to a short dark woman with no hair. She was covered in the most exquisite tattoos, all pop culture references from her favourite television shows as a child in full-colour vibrancy. 'Zainab, I hope you've got some good news for me. Has your team completed the latest psychological evaluation on Arlo's parents?'

'They have,' Zainab said nervously.

'And?'

'I'm afraid that, despite the quick succession of parenthood challenges, including multiple flights and holidays, potty-training and repeat episodes of absent listening ears, Arlo's mummy and daddy are not just sound of mind but still infatuated with Arlo. They have zero regrets about becoming parents.'

'Well, we're fucked. We're all fucked. Everyone in the room is fucked. Michelle, I can see you're crying. I'm so sorry, but you are also fucked. Everyone in the fucking building is more fucked than when the dinosaurs played softball with an asteroid.'

Ring, ring.

The noise came from a phone console in the middle of the table. Mr Keithy pressed a button and put the call on loudspeaker.

A crackly, panicked male voice broke through. 'I'm here with the shareholders. Disturbing reports are flying in from all over the planet. We're looking for some reassurance.'

The heads of department looked to Mr Jacobs.

'Oh, haven't you heard? There's a lot of complexity and finer details, but in short, we're all fucked,' Mr Jacobs said, before standing up.

'Sir, where are you going?' Mr Keithy said.

'To defenestrate myself!' Mr Jacobs said, before marching out of the Situation Room.

From outside, everyone heard their boss's final thoughts on the matter.

'FUCK, FUCKETY, FUCK, FUCK!' he said.

September

Santa-isn't-real moment
noun

A point in time when one learns a disappointing truth about life – such as the fact that it isn't always fair.

The Parenthood Dictionary
Adventures in Dadding Edition

A Day In The Life Of Arlo: Evil Mummy
Thursday, 1 September 2022

'BUT I WANT IT!'

'Arlo, this is Mummy's toast. And I've already given you some.'

'But Mummy, you said I could have the middle bit.'

'I didn't, darling. I said you could have this bit here, which I'm holding out for you. Mummy has just eaten the middle bit.'

'Where is it?'

'It's in my tummy.'

'Get it out. I want it.'

'I can't.'

For fuck's sake, Louie! Mummy never listens. I was very clear. I told her I wanted the middle bit. She usually gives it to me, so why the one-eighty? And how dare she eat it herself? Selfish Mummy!

I'm afraid I can no longer remain in her presence. I'm off to lay some grass and then cut it.

'Arlo, where are you going?'

Oh, do piss off, toast stealer. Ah, here we are, Louie: one roll of turf ready for me to lay down and sculpt. I will do a magnificent job. You know how skilled I am at cutting the grass, Louie, especially inside grass.

'Arlo, can you please put the toilet roll back where you found it?'

I don't believe this, Louie. That monster is at it again! 'I'm just laying some grass, Mummy. I need to cut it.'

'That's fine, but can you please not use the toilet roll, as it's a waste of paper.'

September

Lord, I beseech thee. Rid me of this happiness mauler, this destroyer of joy, this fun-killing dictator whose foul actions know no bounds.

'Why, Mummy?'

'Because I've explained that it's a waste of paper. Can you use something else?'

'NO! I need to use the toilet roll.'

'Arlo, have you got your listening ears on?'

Err, more like, have you got *yours* on, because I've already told you no.

'Arlo?'

'But Mummy, Mummy. I need to cut the grass.' Can I not have this one simple pleasure in life? Can't you at least give me that, woman? Or are you to take everything away from me ... Shit, Louie, she's coming over here. Oh no. I think she's ...

'I'll take that, thank you.'

'NO! MUMMY! GIVE IT BACK! Whhhhaaaaaa!'

'I know, it's very sad. Would you like a cuddle?'

'Yeah.'

'Come here then. Let's have a cuddle.'

'OK.'

No middle bit of the toast and now no indoor grass. Louie, today is a shit day.

Daddy-And-Arlo Day
Saturday, 3 September 2022

Mummy's gone to Brighton for the weekend with Auntie Lisa. So, it's just you and me, buddy, and I need it. I've been working too much lately; I haven't given you enough quality time. But I plan to make it up to you. No laptops. No emails. Nothing. Just a Daddy-and-Arlo day. And it starts with soft play!

The Kitchen

'OUCH!' That's me twatting my head on the door frame in the kitchen's play area.

'Would you like a coffee, Daddy?'

'I'd love one.' *And some painkillers if you've got any.*

'I'm gonna do some cooking as well.'

'Coffee and dinner? You're spoiling me today.'

Next to the kitchen is a shop. You dash in, clear its shelves of ingredients and return. You divide your haul, placing half in the kitchen sink and half in the microwave.

A young lady approaches. She comes to inspect the percentage of play food that's in your possession. The look she gives you suggests you need to share.

I stay silent. This is for you guys to figure out.

After a few moments, she sheepishly selects some items and retreats. You debate kicking off, but you don't. Instead, you say, 'Daddy, I want to go somewhere else.'

Beautician's Parlour

'Daddy, shall I brush your hair?'

'Yes, please.'

You do a fantastic job. You're gentle and calm in your movements. And I feel very relaxed ... 'Hey, where are you going?'

'Come on, Daddy, let's climb the big mountain.'

'But I was enjoying that.'

'Come on, Daddy.'

The Big Mountain

It's the star of the show, the flagship feature, the crowd-puller: four storeys of colourful obstacles daring any would-be adventurer who wants to test their physical limits. But you've conquered the mountain many times since you turned one. Now, it's as easy as climbing the stairs.

In fact, it's too easy! I can't keep up.

There's a mini maze. Some of the pathways are blocked by hidden-passage-type doorways that swing on a central axis, so unless I'm directly behind you, which I'm not, I get smashed in the face by the opposite side of each door you pass through – something that's happened four times in as many seconds.

I bet chiropractors have a lot of dads in their care who think they can act the same age as their kids.

'Arlo, wait for Daddy.'

'I can't, Daddy. I'm going.'

A poignant response if ever there was one.

'Let's go down the slide,' you say.

We do. Then we climb the mountain again. Then we go down the slide again. I'm feeling battered and bruised, but the look on your face as we slide down each time is worth it.

After thirty minutes, I announce that it's time to think about leaving.

'But, Daddy, we didn't have a go on the cars.'

The Great Race Track

The vehicles are supposed to be motorbikes rather than cars, but their protective bumpers give them a bulky appearance that makes them seem more car-like, although the handlebars give the game away. The last time we were here, you weren't tall enough to reach the pedals or strong enough to steer the handlebars.

Today, you're both tall enough and strong enough; you require little help from me. *My second poignant moment of the day.* With parenthood, you rarely know when you will do something for the last time. I don't know when the last time was that you wanted to sit on my lap and go down the big slide (these days, you always ride solo) – it's another reminder for me to cherish each moment we share.

Once the ride is over, I shower you with praise, recognising how you drove the bike all by yourself. You are a beaming block of self-esteem.

'Daddy, can we come here again one day?'

'Of course we can.'

'Oh, thank you, Daddy.'

On the way out, we pass the lockers. When you were a baby, you would spend most of your time bashing them, swinging the doors open and shut. Today, you don't even notice them.

Another Daddy-And-Arlo Day
Sunday, 4 September 2022

We're at the fair. 'What do you want to go on first?' I ask.

'Can I go in here?' you say, pointing to a mini two-storey soft-play cage with trampolines, a ball pit and a slide.

'Sure.'

The cost is £1.50 for five minutes. When your five minutes are up, you show no desire to leave, so I pay for another five minutes.

I'm distracted by a dad next to me who's losing his marbles at his daughter because she won't stop jumping on a trampoline so he can take a photo: 'For God's sake, stop moving so I can get a photo of you having fun.' Sadly, the irony of that remark is lost on him.

Once your time is up, we head off, searching for the next thing. The next thing is a visit to the House of Fun. And it's fun we have. We laugh. We play.

Next, you go on two merry-go-round rides. Then you go on these water-based rubber-ring bumper cars – sorry, dodgems; you're not supposed to bump, are you? Even though society universally accepts that's a rule we should ignore. You spend most of your time going backwards (admittedly, the controls aren't easy), but your desire to tackle such a challenge by yourself reminds me again of how much you've grown.

'Arlo, it's almost time to go home, but you can pick one more ride to go on, OK?'

'OK, Daddy.'

And that's when you see it – my arch-nemesis. A knot forms in my stomach and drags it to the ground as I read your face before the words spill out.

'Daddy, can we go on those?'

Enter teacups.

I hate them. I've always hated them. I hate anything that spins. My body does *not* respond to the sensation in a thrilled way. Give me roller coasters. Give me the fastest, most terrifying roller coasters in the world. Or give me bungee jumps or skydives. But please, for the love of God, don't stick me in a teacup.

'Daddy, come on with me.'

'Err ... OK, sure ... Can't wait.' I begrudgingly pay the fee to the young lady who looks bored as fuck. I hoist you in, clamber in after you and allow bored-at-work lady to drape a thin sliver of rope across us. A fat lot of good that will do. Nothing can save us now.

I need you to understand that I'm not exaggerating when I say I hate teacups. I need you to know this so you can recognise how much of an amazing dad I am. Because I do not want to be here. OK? I feel I've made that clear, right? I FUCKING HATE TEACUPS!

The ride begins. I feel sick after one rotation. 'I do not like this at all, Arlo.'

'Why, Daddy?'

'Because it's spinny, and it's evil.'

'I love it.'

'No, we do not love the spinning.'

'I do, though.'

'No one loves spinning in the teacups. Why is there so much spinning? I don't like this.'

You laugh.

There's a central pole in the middle of each cup, one that the rider – if they so wish – can use as leverage to spin the cup around even faster.

'Wait, why are you spinning us even faster?'

'Because I love it.'

'No! Arlo, that's a terrible idea.'

'It's a very good idea.'

I'm gonna vom.

Eventually, the cups slow until they're stationary. I undo the safety bar, and, stumbling, I get us out.

'Daddy, do you not like the spinning?'

'Nope.'

You jump up and down laughing while I wait for the world to resume a non-spinny state.

'Have you had the best time?' I ask.

'Yeah! I love the fair.'

'Me too. Except for the teacups. But listen, we need to say goodbye to the fair now.'

You don't make any fuss. You simply turn around and wave. 'Bye, funfair. See you another time.'

You have been a delight this weekend. You've behaved beautifully, and you've been tons of fun and a pleasure to hang out with. As we're leaving, I can see you eyeing up the soft-play cage you went on at the start. But you don't say anything.

I stop you in your tracks and bring myself down to your level. 'Arlo, because you've had your listening ears on all day, would you like another turn in soft play?'

'YEAH!'

'Come on then.'

'Oh, thank you, Daddy.'

'You're welcome.'

No Expense Spared
Monday, 5 September 2022

It needs to be at least seven storeys high, made of gold and silver and diamond-encrusted to accentuate its magnificence. And it will require a grand unveiling. Maybe Oprah or Sir David Attenborough for ribbon-cutting duties. After all, I deserve nothing less for my achievements. I am—

'What are you doing? You look like you've zoned out or something,' Mummy says, having not long returned home from her weekend away.

'I was just working out what it would look like.'

'What do you mean?'

'The statue in my honour for me babysitting Arlo for an entire weekend – *by myself* – while you went off and got pissed with your mates.'

The response from Mummy is a silent, furious stare, one that advises me to stop talking immediately. But it's difficult. I have more information to share with Mummy. I need to tell her that I was planning to build Cyril 2.0 this weekend, but I didn't, because she begged me to keep the house tidy. And I listened. I actually listened and respected her wishes, even though yesterday, someone in the street had thrown out the cardboard box for a fridge – a fridge! It was fucking huge. And unspoilt. Perfect for Cyril 2.0.

And the other thing I wanted to tell her is that I didn't realise you could suffer from such bad jet lag after a two-and-a-half-hour drive from Brighton. But you obviously can. That's why she's in such a foul mood, I guess.

Set The Timer
Tuesday, 6 September 2022

'Arlo, it's time to get out of the bath now.'

'Just two more minutes, Daddy – set the timer.'

'You got it.'

Setting the timer became a thing we did before bed when we had the television on. We used it as a tool to help you emotionally prepare for saying goodbye to *Bob the Builder*, going upstairs and cleaning your teeth. But you – genius that you are – have made it a device we use for everything, including bath time.

Now, I don't have to think about when to get you out, because I've outsourced the decision, allowing me to commit to the next two minutes fully. I don't have to half play or humour you or keep one eye on the clock approaching bedtime. My focus is on you and in the moment.

And it's bliss.

Time to leave the park? Set the timer.

Time to stop playing and leave the house? Set the timer.

Time to get dressed? Set the timer.

I love it! I've started using it myself for personal tasks, and the results have been surprisingly productive.

Bored with working on that important project? Set the timer and give it everything for another ten minutes.

Athletes take creatine as a supplement. It gives them what they need to lift one more rep, but it's often the most critical rep of the set, the one that adds the most value to the muscles they're working on.

So, I say to parents everywhere around the world: set the timer. Outsource guilt, waning concentration, decision-making worries and flickering presence of mind. And then get on with the thing you're doing, especially if that thing is spending quality undistracted time with your kids.

Set the timer. You taught me that. Thank you.

Staying In Bed
Friday, 9 September 2022

Beeb, beeb, beeb.

My alarm clock. I usually get up at 5.30 a.m. to write. If I don't, I forgo my only distraction-free period of the day. But in doing so, I miss out on you walking into our bedroom and climbing into bed for snuggles before issuing commands to 'get my vitamins and milk, please'.

I miss out on that. Though I accept it's my choice to write at that time.

I don't want to get up.

When something becomes a habit, you free yourself from the reliance on willpower and discipline. You no longer need them because your actions are automatic. That's why building good habits is critical. That's what I've done with writing.

But sometimes, for whatever reason, there's a glitch. That's what's happening now. Something is overwriting my habit protocols, telling them to behave in direct opposition to their programming. In the past, I would berate myself for displaying such 'weakness'. But I have since learnt how unhelpful, not to mention unkind, a reaction that is. You remember our 'Do you like yourself?' chat, right?

I no longer see it as weakness but as cause and effect, though I'm struggling to join the dots up this morning. Our minds and bodies are a series of complex interconnected systems that coexist in ways we don't always fully understand. Today something is happening inside mine.

Fuck it. I don't have to understand. I'm not getting up! I remain where I am and enjoy being awake and warm in my bed.

I stretch out.

I think of nothing.

After a while, I hear the sound of small feet padding on the hallway carpet and then a small exclamation of effort as the small feet climb the step into the next section of the hallway. Our bedroom door opens quietly. You make a beeline for Mummy, who's closest, but then you see me.

'Oh, hello, Daddy.' You walk around to my side of the bed. I lift the covers, and without saying a word, you get in and we snuggle. It's bliss.

'Daddy.'

'Yes, Arlo.'

'Can you go and get my vitamins and my milk, please?'

'Sure thing. After I have one more little cuddle.'

'OK.'

Hello, Old Friend
Saturday, 17 September 2022

'What's this, Arlo?

'That's a clock.'

'Good boy. And now this?'

'An apple.'

'Excellent. And now what can you see?'

'A cup.'

'Brilliant.'

The ophthalmologist is happy with the sight in your right eye. Now to see about the left eye. Remember, in March we were told we could do away with the eyepatch altogether, and you've not worn one since.

'OK, Arlo, look this way and tell me what you can see.'

I can tell something's off immediately. So can Mummy. We say as much to each other through a glance. For your part, you're leaning forward in the chair as much as you can and squinting.

'A clock?' you say, guessing because you can't see the object clearly.

'Almost. Let's try another one. What can you see now?'

'A house?'

'Not quite. Let me make the pictures a little bigger for you.' She adjusts the size.

'An apple.'

'Good boy. Now what?'

'A boot.'

'Excellent.'

With your confidence back on the up, she presses a button; the pictures flicker back to the smaller size. But it's no use; your vision in that eye is compromised.

The ophthalmologist turns to her computer and reviews your notes. I don't carry cash, but if I did, I'd bet it all on what she's about to say.

'Right, so obviously there has been some degradation in the left eye again, which we need to correct. You're going to have to start patching him again.'

Fuck! You won't like this. Not at the age you are now. When we initially began the patching treatment, you were a baby. And you coped brilliantly. But I don't see it being as easy this time. You've physically and emotionally matured a lot since then.

'How long?' Mummy asks.

'At least two hours a day, but more if he can tolerate it.'

'How much more?' I ask.

'As much as you can.'

'What would give him the best and quickest route to improvement?'

'Between four and six hours.'

No one says anything for a few long, drawn-out seconds while Mummy and I absorb and accept the news. Part of me is angry. If you were at risk of setbacks, why weren't your appointments scheduled more regularly so we could identify this sooner and fix it?

Due to some recent health issues concerning *my* eyes, I have first-hand experience understanding how the brain can shift allegiance to a stronger-performing eye, essentially abandoning the weaker one. Clearly, this has happened to you. You've got used to relying on one eye and probably haven't noticed the declining strength in the other.

Until now.

That must be terrifying. And to top it off, you're expected to adjust to wearing an eyepatch again for up to six hours a day.

We thank the ophthalmologist, leave with a fresh box of child-friendly eyepatches, and drive home.

'This is going to be horrendous,' Mummy says.

'It might not be that bad,' I say, which I admit is a sentence devoid of any backing or belief because I agree with Mummy. This will not be pleasant. For anyone. You will be frustrated and scared. All of us are about to have our hearts torn to shreds.

We park up, and while we're still in the car, we do our best to explain things to you.

'Arlo, so you know how you found it a little bit difficult to see some of the objects on the screen?' I say.

'Yeah.'

'Well, that nice lady we were with has given you some really cool eyepatches that will help make your eye see better.'

'Really?'

'Yeah. So tomorrow, we'll put one on you in the morning, OK?'

'Can I have one now?'

'Erm, I guess so,' I say, turning to Mummy to see if she agrees; she nods.

I select an eyepatch from the box. *OK, here we go. Hands nice and steady,* I say to myself as I perform the task I didn't think I'd ever have to perform again.

Within seconds, you're hit by the full realisation of what wearing an eyepatch means for your vision. At least for the time being.

'Mummy, take it off. I don't want it on. I can't see.'

'I know, darling, but it's going to help make your eye stronger.'

'But I DON'T WANT IT!' you say, thrashing.

We explain that this isn't forever and that it will help. You're still not happy, but you listen.

'So when I wake up tomorrow, I'll be able to see again, will I?'

That's the most gut-wrenching, emotionally piercing thing you've ever said. Like physical pain, emotional pain has different strains. Your last sentence was uttered from a place built on hope. We now have to respond and shunt that hope aside as delicately as we can – an unenviable position for any parent.

'Maybe not tomorrow, but if you keep wearing your eyepatch every morning, your eye will get stronger and you'll see better,' Mummy says.

You nod, not with the enthusiasm or the hope you held only moments ago, but with a calm, saddened acceptance.

I'm so sorry this is happening – I would do anything to trade places with you. I believed we'd left all of this behind, but we haven't. Not yet.

You have a doll. His name is Bobby. Mummy promised you we could go to the charity shop and look for baby clothes for him. So we do. I get you out of the car and put you down. You stagger as soon as you start moving, but you don't go to ground.

You perk up when we reach the shop. You hide in the clothes rails and look at the toys. There's a thing – I have no idea what it is exactly – that looks like a model swimming pool that you could use with your toy figures.

'Daddy, I think Bobby would like that very much.'

'Do you?'

'I do, yes. Shall we get it for Bobby?'

'I'll tell you what. If you do a good job with your eyepatch this week, Daddy will get it for you and Bobby. What do you think?'

'OK.'

It's a cheap trick, I know. But for now, while you're adjusting, I'll happily do whatever it takes. Have I made the right decision? No idea. I don't have a blueprint to work from. Previous experience counts for nothing, as you were a baby then. Now, you're about to turn three. The two stages are entirely different.

Mummy and I agree that you'll wear your eyepatch for at least two hours a day over the next few days while you acclimatise. Next week, we'll up it to a longer period. We are committed to doing everything we can.

After two hours, we take the eyepatch off.

Well done.

Once again, Mummy and Daddy are super fucking proud of you. And remember, doctors initially said that the condition of your eye was much worse than the revised diagnosis. We took that as a win. And it's still a win. This is a setback, that's all. Life is full of them. Setbacks are part of what makes us who we are. We can't control what happens to us, but we can, with time and practice, control how we react. You go into this challenge with my faith in your ability to respond accordingly. It's not blind faith. It's based on data. Because you always overcome the odds. I love you, buddy.

Santa Isn't Real
Sunday, 18 September 2022

It's morning, and Mummy and I have forgotten about your eyepatch. So have you. But then I remember. I grab the box that houses them and invite you to choose the one you want. You select the digger pattern. As soon as I apply it, you crumble in distress.

'But I can't see the television, Mummy.'

'Here, put your glasses on, baby boy.'

She helps put them on, but you're still very upset. 'I still can't see, Mummy,' you say while crying. 'I want Daddy to leave.'

'OK, I'm going. No worries.'

As it turns out, I'd arranged to go on a bike ride. I assumed I'd have to drop out to help support you and Mummy, but it seems I'd only make things worse. So I get on my bike and pedal away a few calories, trying to distract my mind from the scenes playing on repeat in my head, scenes of you crying and telling us you can't see, scenes that constrict the soul as it chokes out a wordless apology.

After a couple of hours, I stop for a break and check my phone. I have three messages.

> **8.19 a.m.:** He's crying uncontrollably. He dropped the Sellotape dispenser on his foot as well! He won't let me go to the loo. He's screaming at me from the living room.

> **8.23 a.m.:** He's OK now

September

8.47 a.m.: We are doing OK, Daddy xxxx

The final one includes a picture of you and Mummy having a cuddle.

I return home at 11 a.m. to find you asleep on the sofa, still wearing your eyepatch.

'He just got himself so worked up and knackered himself out. He's been asleep for over an hour. The worst thing was him saying, "Mummy, I can't see my Henry Ooofer" when it was only three metres away,' she says, tears falling from her eyes.

This sucks, doesn't it, bud?

Welcome To My Shop
Monday, 19 September 2022

'Hello, sir, welcome to my shop. I have some lovely colourful eyepatches in stock and some yummy vitamins. Would you like to take a look?' I say, pretending to be a shopkeeper at the side of our bed.

'Yes, please,' you say.

Like a magician fanning a deck of cards and asking an audience member to pick one, I display the eyepatches. 'We've got rocket ships, robots, dinosaurs, diggers and a blue camouflage option.'

'Diggers, please.'

'Certainly, sir. That will be two pounds.'

'Here you go,' you say, handing me some imaginary money.

'Excellent. Thank you very much, and here is your change,' I say, handing you back some imaginary money of my own.

'Can I help put it on, Daddy?'

'Sure.'

You peel open the pack and also the flaps. Then together, we apply the patch. You utter not one syllable of protest. Even your body language is positive.

'Would sir now like to see the vitamins I have in store?' I say, chancing a *Can you fucking believe it?* glance at Mummy.

'Yes, please. Put them out in your hand.'

'Absolutely.' I tip a selection of yellow and orange bear-shaped gummies into my hand and allow you to peruse the sample.

'Ermmm ... I think I'll have this one ... No, this yellow one.'

'A fine choice.'

You eat your vitamin, and then you get comfy in our bed and begin a round of cartoons. I go downstairs and make drinks for us all.

I don't know if you've noticed a slight improvement in the eye or if you're already coming to terms with the new routine. Either way, you'll believe me when I tell you how relieved Mummy and I are.

You have the best day today.

It's evening. Today has been a much better day for us all. Your personality and disposition are worlds apart from the weekend. You wore your eyepatch for four hours today and you didn't complain once! Nor did you ask us to remove it. I'm speechless! And now you're wiping your bum with a yellow crepe-paper streamer and presenting it to your mother as a mighty tribute. You do this while laughing.

Some days, you swim against the tide. Others, you swim with it.

September Monthly Review
Tuesday, 20 September 2022

Tough month – for all of us. Toughest in as long as I can remember. However, I'm happy to report another incident-free morning regarding eyepatches. You've adapted to the new routine already, as I suspected you would. I've underestimated you before, and it looks like I've done it again. Well done. I've swung by the charity shop to pick up the toy you wanted. It's a Playmobil swimming pool. A staff member was able to help me put it together because her granddaughter has one.

Even if we discounted the eyepatch saga, I'd still be reporting that you've become more emotional. You're quick to anger. You become inconsolable at times for seemingly the smallest thing. Of course, in your world, there's nothing small about it. You make a lot of huffing and harrumphing sounds, accompanied by appropriate body language, illustrating to those in your company that you're pissed off.

Mummy has found working at nursery challenging because you've decided not to share her. You're jealous when she's with other children, and you behave accordingly. You've also been a bit of a bugger towards Haylee. You won't let her play with anything when she comes over. The other day, you screamed at her for touching the sofa.

We're not worried. Haylee went through a similar thing at your age, so we know this is a toddler-transitioning-into-preschooler thing and not an Arlo thing. Mummy says this is what parents refer to as the terrible twos. I'll confess I thought it was all a myth. It didn't take long for us to figure out our response to tantrums, and we've had an impressive success rate in resolving them all year. But this month, the intensity has ramped up, particularly around other children.

When you're alone, though, you're *mostly* your chirpy, happy self.

If explaining why you need to wear eyepatches again ranks as the hardest thing about dadding this year, a close second is dealing with rejection. It's horrible. It will never not be horrible, though I'm slowly getting used to it. Ironically, it's a good sign, as it shows you have strong, trusting relationships with those closest to you. This is healthy behaviour. But, oh boy, does it suck to be on the receiving end. The phrase 'I don't want Daddy' is a serrated dagger to the heart.

On a brighter note, we've started cooking together

a lot more. We make banana pancakes and homemade granola. You get involved with every step. Yesterday, you cracked three eggs in the bowl by yourself, and we didn't have to fish out any shell fragments.

I still cherish our walks home from nursery. We stop and explore things on the side of the road, and we put the world to rights, vocalising our outrage at the litter on the street. You say, 'Come on, guys, it's not that difficult. Just put your rubbish in the bin.'

Sometimes, you sing 'Twinkle, Twinkle, Little Star' before bed. You've never been one for singing before; now, though, you put your little lungs and big heart into the performance – it's beautiful.

You still ask me for a kiss and a hug in the morning when leaving for nursery.

Nana Hoover has been back with us for almost six months now. I was apprehensive about how she would settle in, but I'm pleased to report that, so far, it's working out brilliantly.

This is encouraging, especially when you consider the cost-of-living crisis that's struck the UK due to the ongoing fallout from Russia's invasion of Ukraine. The price of energy has already shot up, and it may very well do so again in the future. I take comfort that we'll all be under the same roof for the winter while we ride out yet another piece of history.

Not long until you turn three.

The Bath Is Not A Toilet!
Sunday, 25 September 2022

'Mummy, Daddy did a wee-wee in the bath.'

'Did he now?' she says, turning to face me.

'Oi! Arlo, you grass! At least give the full context.'

'And what would the full context be?' Mummy says.

'I'm gonna tell you. What happened was Arlo and Daddy badly needed a wee-wee at the same time, but Arlo selfishly commandeered the toilet. I can't fit on his potty, so it was either the bath or the sink. Would you have preferred the sink?'

She says nothing.

'Exactly. I made the right choice, and I'm ready for you to apologise and say well done.'

'Hmmm.'

'And as for you,' I say.

'Yes, Daddy?'

'What happened to the whole "Don't tell Mummy that I'm weeing in the bath" thing?'

'Mummy?'

'Yes, Arlo?'

'Daddy weed in the bath the other day as well.'

Human Rights
Monday, 26 September 2022

It's bedtime, and you are not using your listening ears.

September

'Arlo, do you want Daddy to stop reading the story?'

'No, I've got my listening ears on,' you say, continuing to play with your toy tractor.

'But you're playing with your tractor. Can you put it down, please?'

Silence.

'OK, that's it then. Story time is over,' I say, fuming that you've forced a battle right before bed.

'No, Daddy, I want a story. I've got my listening ears on.'

'Mate, I gave you lots of chances, and you didn't listen. That's enough stories for tonight.'

You go to ground. Mummy comforts you but backs me up. 'I know it's sad. Maybe tomorrow you can have some more stories,' she says.

'Noooo! I want a story now.'

'But story time is over. It's bedtime now.'

It takes us a while to get you into bed. You're not happy. You're staring at me like I left Louie in the oven overnight. The effect is almost palpable. Saying no to you is hard, but I'm not going back. I'll weather the travails of sticking to my guns any day. But my God, it stings!

I lean in to give you a cuddle, and you recoil as if pushed back by magnetic repulsion. 'I don't want a kiss and a cuddle from you.'

The pain passes through me like a freight train crashing into a hay bale. I am reduced to nothing – utterly destroyed.

You cannot do that to me! I need a kiss and a cuddle from you. It's how we end the day – full of love. Not like this. You realise that's my evening gone, right? I'm not recovering from this one in a while. *Fuck you!*

The Human Rights Act 1998 sets out the fundamental rights and freedoms that everyone in the UK is entitled to:

> *Article 3: Freedom from torture and inhuman or degrading treatment.*

A child rejecting their parent breaches Article 3. It's torture. Your well-being is my air. The happier you are, the better the quality of the air I breathe. Any sadness you display chokes me, cutting off my oxygen supply. But withholding love and affection is something else entirely. When you shut me out, you are cleaving my identity into pieces.

Can you do me a favour? Get a good night's sleep, and make restoring your daddy your top priority.

Good night, buddy. I love you, even if you don't like me very much at the moment.

Let's Make Up
Tuesday, 27 September 2022

It's morning. I'm standing at my desk working in the spare room with my noise-cancelling headphones on. Out of nowhere, I feel a little pair of arms wrap themselves around my leg. I turn to see you standing there with a big grin on your face. I take my headphones off.

'Good morning, Daddy.'

'Morning, buddy. Did you sleep well?'

'Yes, I did.'

'Can I have a big cuddle?'

You reciprocate, repairing the damage from last night's heartache.

'Daddy, can you open up the eyepatch shop downstairs?'

'You betcha.'

'And can you carry me downstairs?'

'I sure can.'

Guess Where We're Going?
Wednesday, 28 September 2022

Remember that email I sent in July to Numatic International? Guess what? They only went and bloody responded!

'Arlo, can Daddy tell you something?'

'Yeah.'

'You know how I told you that you, me and Mummy are going on a little holiday tomorrow?'

'Yeah.'

'Shall I tell you where we're going?'

'OK.'

'You know how we've been watching that YouTube video where all the Henrys and Hettys are made?'

'In the factory?'

'That's right. Would you like to go and visit the factory?'

'In our car?'

'Yes.'

It takes a moment to sink in. But when it does …

'They-might-have-loads-of-Henrys-and-Hettys-and-forklifts. And will we see trucks? And is Arlo going and Daddy going and Mummy going?'

'Absolutely.'

'Whoaa.'

Whoaa, indeed.

'When you wake up in the morning, we'll get straight into the car and drive down to the factory. It will be a long drive, but it will be totally worth it. What do you reckon?'

'I think that's the plan, Daddy.'

'I think you're right, son.'

Now then, Numatic International, let's hope you don't disappoint!

The Home Of Henry
Thursday, 29 September 2022

We're up, packed and on the road by 6.45 a.m. The Numatic headquarters are based in Chard, Somerset. Our satnav reports a journey time of three hours and thirty-two minutes.

An iPad and downloaded episodes of *Peppa Pig* ensure a stress-free journey. The sixty-minute nap you take also helps.

We make it to Chard with enough time to stop at Greggs for a sausage roll and a pumpkin spice latte before heading in search of the labour ward for Planet Earth's most famous vacuum cleaners.

The arrival

'Is this where they make all the Henrys and all the Hettys, Daddy?'

'That's right.'

It's a sprawling complex of buildings. Some look like small aeroplane hangars, while others are standard brick-built structures. The roofs are of industrial-strength corrugated steel. Some of their edges are laced with the same red as you-know-who's skin colour.

Mummy drives at a crawl, pulling up next to the gatehouse. A security chap sticks his head out of the window and says, 'Are you here with Arlo for a tour?'

'We are.'

'OK, great. I'll let you through. If you can get parked up and then come inside so I can sign you all in.'

You're wearing your Henry T-shirt. And you insist on bringing your toy Henry with you on the tour as well. Your expression is neutral, but I can tell that you're excited. Your actions are a touch more animated, even if your face is playing it cool.

We make it back to the gatehouse on foot as it begins to rain.

'That's right, get yourselves in here and keep warm,' says the chap who let us in. He introduces himself as Eric. Eric's colleague is also present, sitting at a control console overseeing control-console stuff.

'You've really lucked out today. Paul will be showing you around, and he's amazing with children. He'll be along shortly,' Eric says.

The dazzling array of security monitors on one side of the gatehouse draws your attention.

'Look, Daddy, forklift loaders!' you say, pointing to a screen linked to one of the many outdoor cameras.

There are indeed forklift loaders, lifting pallets of Henrys and Hettys onto lorries, ready to be shipped off to retailers. Eric presses a few buttons, and the display monitors blink. Now we can see what the indoor cameras see.

'Is that the inside of the factory?' you say.

'That's right,' confirms Eric.

We stand around, waiting for Paul. You continue to ask questions and point out forklift loaders. Eric gives Mummy and me visitor passes and hi-vis jackets.

Enter Paul.

Paul is instantly likeable. I'd say he's in his mid-fifties and is of slim build. He keeps what's left of his grey hair cut short and boasts a warm, kind smile that I'd wager he uses often.

'Now, we can't start the tour without one of these, can we?' he says, handing you a Numatic badge holder to keep. 'That's better. Right. Ready, Arlo?'

'Yeah.'

'Come on then, let's go and see if we can find a few Henrys.'

The showroom

Paul leads us to what was once the showroom. 'We're still getting it back in shape, as this was the main Covid-19 testing site in Chard.'

You don't care. Your face is alive with delight as we arrive at the room's main attraction, a large white A-frame assembly with a few Henrys and Hettys sitting on it, like youths hanging out on a climbing frame in the park. Surrounding the structure are more smiling Henrys and Hettys and even a few green Georges. There's also Henry's liquid-sucking cousin, Charles, who's blue, and a bunch of charcoal-grey ride-on floor cleaners.

'If you stay here for a few minutes, I just need to go and get Arlo something,' Paul says.

You continue exploring, dashing from one smiling unit to the next, punctuating your manic zigzagging with some excitable jumps, vocal outbursts of glee and utterances of 'LOOK, ANOTHER HENRY RIGHT THERE!'

This is fucking brilliant!

Paul returns with another hi-vis jacket. 'Here you go, Arlo. You need one of these for a factory tour, don't you?'

You smile, beaming at Paul, warming to him more and more. You allow him to apparel you in your new oversized bright-orange jacket that hangs below your knees. 'And when you're done here, you can take that home with you.'

'Thank you,' you say.

'You are most welcome. Would you like to have a go on one of these?' Paul says, pointing to the nearest ride-on floor cleaner.

You can't accept the offer quick enough. I help you up, and, encouraged by Paul, you start pressing buttons and tweaking dials like you're a DJ.

The museum

From the showroom, our route takes us through a side door to a corridor housing more vacuum units. However, these are extra special.

'This is our museum collection that will eventually go back into the showroom,' Paul says, directing our attention to some of the original Numatic vacuum cleaners. 'The bloke who founded Numatic is a man named Chris Duncan. He's still the sole owner of the company. When he started, he used everyday components to put the units together. Here,' Paul says, pointing to various old models, 'these are made from oil drums and washing-up bowls. And these handles are from suitcases. Chris would use anything he could get his hands on. He once tried to buy four hundred washing-up bowls, but the supplier only had them in white. Chris said, "Well, they won't stay white for very long."'

Arlo, I level with you, I wasn't expecting to find the tour fascinating. This was all for you. But I'm fully engaged, and so is Mummy. All of us are having a blast.

'Now, here's something very special,' Paul says, holding up what is clearly a very old Henry prototype. It's the same shape as the Henrys you see today, but the drum and motor – or hat – are made from metal and painted in a faded, washed-out blue, and they have various rusty lesions and more than a few bumps and bruises. But the Henry has two eyes and that smile that all Numatic enthusiasts are familiar with. That said, the face looks ... drawn-on? With permanent marker, maybe?

'This here is the original Henry,' Paul says.

NO FUCKING WAY! The original Henry! Arlo, we are in the presence of royalty right now.

'WOW!' I say.

'Yup. It's the first unit that had the face. Do you know the story?'

'Weren't the faces added to cheer cleaners up?' Mummy says.

'Nope. What happened was a member of staff was at a trade show, and he was bored. So he drew the face on for a laugh. And then Chris, the owner, caught him. The staff member thought he was going to get the sack. But instead, Chris had the idea to incorporate the design for all the vacuum cleaners in the product line.'

'So, a global phenomenon that children around the world, to this day, still gravitate towards all started from one bored employee at a trade show?'

'That's right.'

Mind blown. That's incredible.

'I think it's time to look inside the factory now, Arlo. What do you think?'

'Yeah!'

We head back outside and make our way to the factory floor. We pass a car with the number plate F5NRY. 'That's the owner's,' Paul says.

'He still comes in to work?' I ask.

'Oh yeah. Almost every day. Even though he's in his eighties.'

What an inspiring work ethic.

We enter one of the large shed-like hangars.

'Welcome,' says Paul, 'to the factory floor.'

The factory

I've never been inside a working factory before. The first thing that hits me is the noise and the smell of machinery – it's loud but not uncomfortable. Rows of assembly lines, machines, and shelves full of parts populate the room in a grid-like format.

The floor is made of concrete, with red-painted walkways. We follow Paul.

'This is where we assemble the ride-on cleaners you saw at the start of the tour. We build seven a day from scratch.'

You're a little overwhelmed, but you're taking things as they come, listening to Paul and allowing him to guide you forward. At one point, he takes hold of your hand, and you don't shrug away.

'Right, Arlo, I think it's time to go and see where we make all the Henrys. What do you think?'

Your eyes widen, and your pace quickens. We follow Paul through yet another side door … and into another vast expanse of floor space.

The labour ward

More machines.

More noise.

September

More activity.

And also ... more colour!

'This is where we make all the Henrys and Hettys. Let's go and meet one of them.'

We arrive at a complex arrangement of machines and assembly lines, where automation works harmoniously with manual labour. A forklift-like instrument carries familiar red Henry bases from the plastic injection-moulding unit to a conveyer belt.

'The drums cool quickly, enabling us to manually assemble the rest of the components, which we also manufacture here,' Paul says.

Sure enough, a young lad is standing at one end of the conveyor belt, adding the wheels, the vacuum bag and other vital organs to the newly birthed Henry drum. He also adds the face, a separate piece that slots over the nose.

'Would you like to have a go at putting one together, Arlo?'

You enthusiastically nod your head. Paul, who is clearly high up on the employee food chain and can pretty much do whatever the fuck he wants, wanders over to the assembly line and pulls off the next Henry to arrive on the belt.

Together, you, me, Paul and the assembly-line worker fit the wheels and other pieces.

I cannot overstate how much fun this all is.

We finish our team-effort assembly and then place the Henry drum back on the conveyor belt, leaving the young worker to continue his daily quota. But it seems he'll have to work harder because Paul yanks the Henry back off the line and gives it to you. 'You best take this home with you, Arlo, seeing as you were the one who built it.'

You are speechless.

So is Mummy.

I turn to you and say, 'That's very kind of Paul. What do we say?'

'Thank you.'

'You're very welcome.'

But Paul's budget for giving stuff away isn't spent. Next, he takes us to a section where they store the different Numatic face-pieces. He grabs one of every colour and gives them to you. We have a pink Hetty, a blue Charles, a green George and several others.

'Now you can swap the faces around at home,' Paul says.

But he's still not done.

He dips his hand in a small bucket bolted to the side of one of the cage posts, extracting a handful of what looks like silver coins. 'Here, take these,' he says to me, giving me a fistful of treasure: Henry key rings.

Next, we wander over to an area where employees are responsible for inserting into the headpieces the motors and the other electrical components that enable Henry and Co. to do their thing. A young lady holding a soldering iron turns and does a double take when she sees you, mouthing the words 'How adorable' to herself.

'Once the hats are ready, they're attached to the bases, and then we slide the units to the end of the production line, where they're boxed up and ready … for … shipping.'

Paul has become distracted, though I've no idea why. He's lost in thought.

'Here, can I have Arlo's red Henry base? I'll show him how we put the hats on.' We double back a few metres and eagerly await the demonstration. 'On second thoughts, take this back,' he says, handing the red base back to Mummy. 'Let me put the head on one of our blue Henrys instead. That way, Arlo can swap them over at home.'

He dashes off before we can respond. Mummy and I look at each other confused. *Swap them at home?*

When you wish upon a star

Paul returns with the following items: a brand-new blue Henry base, a large box and another colleague carrying a clear plastic bag containing the usual accessory pieces. Paul attaches the black hat to the blue body and slides the fully assembled unit across to the new colleague, who starts boxing everything up.

Surely, he can't ...

'Here you go, Arlo,' says Paul, 'Your very own complete Henry Hoover.'

Jaw. Shattered.

Mummy is crying.

And I'm now the one who's speechless.

Eventually, I manage to stammer out a response. 'Er, are ... are you sure? That's very kind of you. Arlo, what do you say to Paul?'

'Thank you very much.'

'You are very welcome, Arlo.'

Mummy turns to me. 'As if he's just given him a Henry Hoover! Where are we going to put it?' she says, before smiling.

From there, we begin to wrap things up. Paul leads us all outside the factory and into another room with an adjoining office. I'm carrying your brand-new Numatic vacuum cleaner while Mummy carries your other red Henry base and the ten different-coloured plastic faces.

Paul's penultimate act of generosity is to hand you a small white duffel bag that's waiting in the office adjoining the room. The bag is branded with Henry's eyes and smile. Inside are a hat, a jigsaw puzzle, some Henry and Hetty socks, a sticker and some books.

'Wait here a sec. I need to nip upstairs and grab a few more books for Arlo.'

I cannot take much more of this. I'm genuinely stunned. Talk about exceeding expectations. Paul returns moments later with several more official (and beautifully illustrated) Henry children's books, his final act of generosity. Then he escorts us back to the gatehouse.

Mummy starts packing up the car while I drag you to the side. 'Here, Arlo, quick – sign this for Paul,' I say, shoving a copy of *Toddler Inc.* under your nose, which I brought from home, thinking it might come in handy. *Thank God I did.* You sign it with your trademark squiggle, one that's different every time you sign one of our books, and then I add my untidy inscription, along with the message *Thank you for making a small boy's dreams come true.* We then present our tiny token of gratitude to Paul. 'I have no idea if you read, but if you want to see how Arlo's fascination with vacuum cleaners began – it's all here.'

'I do read. I look forward to checking it out. Thank you. And thank you, Arlo. It's been a real pleasure meeting you all.'

And with that, we say our goodbyes and leave Paul to get on with his day. We then hand back our visitor passes and hi-vis jackets to Eric (you keep yours), sign out and exit the compound.

'Mummy, Paul gave me my own Henry Ooofer.'

'I know he did. You're very lucky, aren't you?'

You start inspecting the long list of Henry swag you've amassed while Mummy and I sit in silence.

What's amazed me about today is how a small bit of kindness has created a wonderful lifelong memory, certainly for Mummy and me at least. Yes, Paul has been beyond generous, and yet it's not only about the value of his gifts. He knew you were a big fan, so he made every effort to ensure you had the best possible experience. And that is something you cannot put a price on. This might have been easy for him to arrange, and you can tell he had fun doing so, but the point is that you valued this experience more I thought possible. And for that, Paul and Numatic International will always have my gratitude.

But Mummy is right – we need to find somewhere to put all this stuff!

October

nap dropper
noun

A person who does a really shitty thing to a parent. This is the lowest of the low and is worse than a sucker punch.

The Parenthood Dictionary
Adventures in Dadding Edition

Symptoms To Terrify
Saturday, 1 October 2022

There have been changes. Symptoms, if you will. Ones that are, quite frankly, shit-your-pants terrifying. At first, they were barely visible, like when the temperature goes up or down by half a degree. I wasn't worried until Mummy noticed as well. She was the one who first suggested what this might mean for our family.

She said, 'This should have happened months ago. Most kids—'

'Shut up, God damn it! It's not true! It can't be true.' *It can't be.*

But the symptoms are now more prevalent, harder to ignore. And I have no choice but to confront the reality of what's in front of me.

Are you ready, son?

Mummy ... and I ... believe you are coming down with a condition called *toddlerus non napperus*.

Now do you understand? A toddler that doesn't nap!

'Like I said, most kids his age have dropped their nap already. We've been very lucky,' Mummy says.

'But how are we supposed to get through the day without a break?'

'What, did you think he would nap until he started school?'

'I did, actually.'

'Why did you think that?'

'"Oh, I don't know," he said sarcastically, scratching his head, "maybe BECAUSE THAT'S WHAT YOU TOLD ME!"'

'I didn't say that.'

She did, Arlo. Check the first journal entry of this book if you think I'm lying.

'You did. I asked you at the start of the year if he would drop his naps, and you said, and I quote, "No, don't worry. He should nap now until he starts school."'

'I don't understand why you're so scared. It only affects you on weekends.'

'Err, and bank holidays and family holidays and when you're home and I fancy watching television on my lunch break in peace. Oh, and Mondays when my mum has him and they stay in the house. And what about when he's ill?'

'Welcome to my world.'

'That's what I'm saying. I have no intention of visiting your world. You choose to work in childcare and be around the small satanic things all day. I choose to work at a desk in order to sit in silence and look out of the window. I don't know if I have the strength to fight such odds. He will tear me down quicker than a tsunami going to war with a model village made of sticks and twine.'

'Well, it's looking like he'll drop his nap before he turns three. You watch.'

'I DON'T WANT TO WATCH. I WANT TO LOOK OUT OF THE WINDOW!'

Selling Books
Sunday, 2 October 2022

We've driven down to Cheltenham to The Baby Fayre, where I've got a bookstand. I've started doing more of these events. I enjoy them because I meet couples about to begin their parenthood journey. I'm usually the only exhibitor with a message aimed at dads.

You've been a great salesman. You tell people the books are about you, and you 'sign' them with me. Readers love it. It's a fitting practice when you consider how all of this started.

You're also great at distributing my business cards. You've yet to realise the card content is identical from one to the next; you handed five of them to one young lady and another five to the same young lady's friend, but hey, no such thing as too much publicity, right?

I meet another couple and I give them the pitch. I start with the *Dear Dory* origin story and then talk about the rest of the series. You and Mummy are lying on the floor behind me, colouring in.

I finish, and then I stop talking to allow for any questions.

'So, in this one, *Toddler Inc.*, can we expect a few stories on tantru—'

'NO, MUMMY, THAT WAS MY RAISIN, AND I DIDN'T SAY YOU COULD HAVE IT!'

'That's right,' I say, 'as is being demonstrated by the star of these books right now.'

'Oh, I see. Err ... how much?'

The Next Thirty Minutes
Monday, 3 October 2022

What to do, what to do.

I'm downstairs working. You're upstairs with Nana Hoover. You've been ill for two days, but a dose of Calpol has infused you with a temporary bout of buoyancy and a thirst for playtime. I can hear you shrieking with joy and jubilation as you progress through the game you're playing.

I'm desperate to join you. Early-childhood playtime is a precious and finite resource – I need to make every second count.

And it's not as if work is keeping me chained to my desk. I've had a productive day; there's no reason I can't go upstairs.

But I don't.

Why?

Because I'm choosing to prioritise a workout instead, and because this is the only time I can do it. In an hour, it will be time for me to end my working day, get dinner ready and then begin transitioning through your bedtime routine.

Part of my remit as a parent is to consider the actions that I perform away from you but that are still in service to you. *And that includes working out?* you say.

You're goddam right it does.

I owe it to both of us to be in the best shape possible so I can continue diving around in soft-play parks and throwing you up in the air, and so I can run around looking after my grandchildren if and when the time comes.

I often think about the indirect responsibilities of parenthood, and working out is undoubtedly as much a parenthood responsibility as it is a responsibility to myself. I'm obliged to do everything in my power to reduce the likelihood of you having to look after me when I'm old and frail. That's not a pride thing; that's a love thing. I owe it to Mummy as well. I don't want her to have to allocate a portion of her life to taking care of me in my later years. Of course, I know she'd do it, and I might have to rely on her to do that one day, and vice versa. But I'll be damned if my actions (or lack of actions) bring the timetable forward.

Arlo, above anything else, you must prioritise your physical health. For you, for your loved ones and even for the NHS. It's your body; you own it. But taking it for granted *will* have consequences for you and for other people.

So I'm not coming upstairs to play just yet. But it's only for a short while. Know that I will do whatever it takes to be the best version of myself so that I'm the best version for you. That's the version I want you to remember, to learn and to borrow from, for the betterment of your life and the lives of those around you.

Also, I'm not sure you want me upstairs because I know Nana is letting you do shit you're not allowed to do! So have a blast, and I'll be with you soon.

ZZZZzzzz
Tuesday, 4 October 2022

I wake up to Mummy showing me a picture of you lying on the floor next to your bed.

'I took that at three a.m.,' she says.

'Why is he sleeping on the floor?'

'He must have fallen out of bed and stayed there. I feel so awful.'

'I mean, yeah, I guess you should. Why didn't you hear him?'

'Did you?'

'You silly sausage. How could I have heard him when I had my earplugs in?'

One More Roly-Poly!
Wednesday, 5 October 2022

'Arlo, if you're not paying attention to the story, then I'm going to stop reading it,' I say.

In response, you remove yourself from your bedroom floor by way of a forward roll, bound over to me and then lean in close, crossing into my personal space. Our noses are touching. Your eyes are unblinking. You hold up a finger and whisper in a deadly serious tone, but one devoid of emotion – a robotic whisper, 'Just one more roly-poly, Daddy, then I will sit quietly for story time, and I will have my listening ears switched on, OK?'

'OK, son, sure,' I say, before breaking into a laugh. I mean, you've played that one like a pro. Everything – the speed of your reaction; your body language; your word selection; the pitch and tone of your voice – came together and hurled me off guard.

This is not the behaviour of a toddler; it's that of a preschooler ...

Clearing Out Toys
Thursday, 6 October 2022

Our house looks like a junkyard. The biggest culprits are your toys – they're everywhere! And most of them have remained stationary for months.

Stuff needs to go. We're having a clear-out.

We've explained to you that you've got your birthday and Christmas coming up and that we need to clear out the old and make way for the new – as it is with all things.

There was this daft and quite frankly horrifying suggestion that I should part with my books, but I shut that one down by whining like you do when I tell you it's time to switch YouTube off.

But while my books are staying, I have laid aside a load of other stuff destined for the nearest charity shop. So has Mummy. Now it's your turn.

'Mummy, I love those blocks.'

'You haven't played with them in over six months.'

'But I love them. Can I play with them now?'

'You can, but we need to give the stuff you don't play with to other boys and girls.'

'OK.'

'Good boy.'

'Mummy.'

'Yes, Arlo.'

'Can I play with my Dyson Ooofer?'

'The same Dyson you found on the street and haven't played with in forever? The one that's broken?'

'Yeah.'

'What about the other seven hundred vacuum cleaners in the house?'

'But I love this Dyson.'

It continues like that all morning. You home in on every item we select for donation, expressing a desire to keep it. We call bullshit and challenge your sincerity, but you defend yourself by playing with it for thirty seconds before picking something else up.

As parents, we find ourselves with our backs against the wall. I was the one who said we should involve you because they're your toys. You should have the final say. Mummy feels the same way, but she also knew how the situation would play out.

'This is why we need to do this when he's not here,' Mummy whispers.

I whisper back, 'Yeah, but soon as we get rid of something, he'll ask for it, even if he hasn't touched it all year.'

'Do we have any other choice?'

'I guess you're right.'

'I'll bag up everything he hasn't played with, and then it can go with the rest of the stuff to charity.'

'Can you take the crane?'

'Yeah—'

'Mummy?' you say.

'Yes, Arlo?'

'You know my crane?'

So much for whispering.

'I don't have to give it away, do I? Because it's my favourite toy, and I—'

'Love it?' both Mummy and I say.

'Yeah, I do.'

'You can keep your crane, but I want to see you playing with it for at least sixteen hours a day, OK?' I say.

'OK, Daddy. Erm, Daddy?'

'Yes, Arlo?'

'Can I keep that ball in your hand?'

'The one that *was* yellow but is now grey because of all the dust it's accumulated? The one you *never* play with?'

'Yeah.'

'Why do you want—'

'Because I love it.'

Wanted
Friday, 7 October 2022

October

Ashes To Ashes
Saturday, 8 October 2022

The grey skies and pouring rain reflect my sombre mood. The writing has been on the wall for weeks, and now the day has come.

I'm ill-prepared to confront such a bone-shuddering truth.

But death waits for no one, and, at 2.26 p.m., Mummy and I declared that your afternoon naps had officially died.

You've been fighting us all month. You take ages to fall asleep at night, insisting we all partake in your nightly ritual of silly buggers that goes on for far too long. And, despite our best efforts, you haven't napped since last Tuesday. So, when you said you didn't want to go down for a nap today, we didn't protest.

Here is my eulogy.

'It's never easy saying goodbye to those we care for the most. But all we can do is remember who they were and what they stood for. I'll admit that the prospect of life without Arlo's naps frightens me. I've grown utterly dependent on them, as plants depend on sunlight for food. No longer is lunch in peace a thing. No longer is there time to tidy up the sprawling mass of toys before another pile of toys comes crashing out—'

'Oh, piss off. As if you have to deal with any of that anyway,' Mummy shouts.

'Erm, it's rude to interrupt someone at the best of times, let alone a mourner performing a eulogy. Now, where was I …? Ah, yes. No resets. No restarts and no chances to decompress. No more solitary trips to the bathroom. Your absence is already laying siege to my sanity.'

The congregation stands and watches the coffin travel towards the incinerator.

The priest speaks. 'We now commit Arlo's naps to the fire, passing from this life to the next never to return, despite how much Arlo's daddy wishes it. And so, we say ashes to ashes, dust to dust. We bid you farewell. Now go you must. To the afterlife we send you, but despair not, for in your eternal slumber, you are free.'

Goodbye, old friends. It was great while it lasted. 'A toast to Arlo's naps, the greatest goddam sidekick a parent could ever wish for!'

Rest in peace.

Welling Up
Sunday, 9 October 2022

We're at soft play, and it's fucking chaos. Balls fly everywhere. Kids scream at the top of their voices while they dash every which way like particles in a hadron collider.

I need shelter. I build myself a little refuge out of large foam blocks. It's only big enough for me, so I'm afraid you'll have to find yourself another solution.

A four-year-old verbally spears me with a 'You suckerrrrrr!' admonishment before entering the blast-radius danger zone of a contraption that spits out white ball-pit balls like a volcano. Soft play is advertised as fun, but the marketing is misleading. It's not; it's dangerous. And I'm getting the shit kicked out of me being here.

'Daddy, shall we go on the slide?'

'Great idea, let's do it.'

As usual, I struggle to keep up with you. My back's in bits, and my neck isn't far behind. I ache everywhere.

We reach the slide and meet a young lady of about four who's crying. An older boy, her brother perhaps, is with her. He explains she had a falling-out with her friend. 'That's a shame. Can you find her and see if she wants to play a new game?' I say to her.

'Daddy, why is that girl sad?' you ask.

'She fell out with her friend, and it's upset her.'

'Come on, Daddy, let's you and me go and find her some new friends.'

And just like that, everything becomes still.

The noise has dropped; the chaos has reduced to a simmer. All my aches and pains have vanished.

I am left standing in the wake of your kind intention to find this little girl some friends.

I'm speechless. I've always suspected that you possess a great deal of empathy and the ability to be sympathetic, even at the young age you're at now, but this is the first time I've seen you take charge in designing a solution to relieve someone else – a stranger, no less – of pain.

I know I'm like a cheap broken record, always telling you how proud I am, but this is another huge moment for me as a parent. Tears have formed in both my eyes.

Well done, buddy. I've said many times that you are shaping up to become a fine addition to humanity. But that's not true. You already are.

Sympathy is vital to our survival. We need to receive it, and we need to give it. You won't always receive it, but you can always give it. How? With empathy: the process of stepping into the shoes of another and imagining for a second what it's like for that person to be that person and acting the way they are acting at this moment. Do that, and your stocks of kindness will never be exhausted.

You won't always get it right. Sometimes sympathy won't be your first reaction to a given situation. Sometimes you need to walk away, reflect and then act. Like so much in life, empathy and sympathy require practice. Like you've done today. Remember:

Kindness = Strength

I return to our table, find Mummy and recount the tale.

Now she's crying as well.

October Monthly Review
Wednesday, 19 October 2022

You don't nap. Neither do we take you for a dream wee any more. Bedtime has become fun again. You fall asleep quickly and without calling for a parent after we've said goodnight.

And we're pals again. Most mornings, you shuffle into the spare room (my temporary office) and hang out, before requesting that we go downstairs and open up the eyepatch and vitamin shop.

You use one of our phones to select songs on car journeys. Sometimes, you digitally stumble over to another app, and we have to course correct, but empowering you with technology means parenting in the car is less of an assault on our spirits. No longer do I compare carpooling with a toddler to waterboarding. We also allow you to have an iPad and headphones for longer journeys. You watch cartoons in silence. It's a mutually workable situation because you watch more cartoons than usual and we get to listen to songs we like. However, I've come to secretly love an orchestral version of the *Fireman Sam* theme tune.

Since our trip to Numatic International, you've gone even more Henry mad. You want to watch videos of the factory on YouTube every night. You love to organise your vacuum cleaners and their array of accessories, and you settle your toy Henry in your room each night for a sleepover.

Without tempting fate, I'm pleased to report that parenthood has become easier. It gives me hope for the next stage of our journey when you officially become a preschooler.

Not a day goes by without you making me laugh or impressing me in some fashion. I spend my life feeling tired but proud.

So that's it – the final monthly update of Year 3.

You've been awesome, and, as usual, words fail me when trying to express my gratitude for everything you contribute to my identity and the sheer fulfilment you bring to my soul each day.

You teach.

You tutor.

You instruct.

And you do it all brilliantly.

Thank you.

Thunder And Lightning
Sunday, 23 October 2022

I'm relaxing in the bath. One of our neighbours has decided to begin firework celebrations early. I can see flashes outside the window, but I can't hear the explosions, because I'm wearing waterproof headphones and listening to music.

After a few minutes ...

KNOCK KNOCK!

You come bounding in as I'm removing my headphones. 'Daddy, Daddy, Daddy, look outside right now. You have to see outside.'

Mummy follows behind. 'Have you seen it?'

'Seen wha— Woah!' Light transmutes the sky into a net of bright cracks.

'Daddy, that's called lightning. Did you know that, Daddy? Just look outside,' you say, words tumbling out of your mouth four times quicker than they normally do.

October

Rumbling. The unmistakable growl of deep, rolling thunder that sounds like tectonic plates arm-wrestling. It's monstrous.

More lightning. This time, the strikes are clearer. Branches of electricity dance above us in flashes, zigzagging in uncoordinated beauty. Nature's fury.

And rain. Each drop a paratrooper in an army of billions.

'There hasn't been a storm like this—'

'Daddy, Daddy. Excuse me, Daddy, but you need to stop talking to Mummy, so I can say something to you right now.'

'OK …'

'You need to get out of the bath, go downstairs naked and go outside for a shower – ha ha ha.'

'But I'll get cold.'

'You'll warm up.'

'OK, I'm getting out.'

This is very special for us as a family. First, we sit by the back door and watch the storm. I don't go outside for a naked shower, but I periodically lift you up, stick your head outside and ask you if it's still raining, even though it surely is.

'WHOA, Daddy, Daddy, Daddy, did you see it? Did you see that, Mummy?'

'We did, baby,' she says.

From the back door, we return upstairs, visiting the various windows on that floor to get the best possible look at the storm as it travels across the sky. Eventually, it trails off into the distance, departing for the next leg of its tour while leaving the three of us reeling.

For me, seeing your awe-infused eyes is the holy grail of parenthood. You must always prioritise the pursuit of these experiences over material things. That's lesson number one. And lesson number two is share as many of those experiences as possible with those you love.

Thank you, Mother Nature, for the fireworks; November the fifth has a lot to live up to this year.

One Ticket To Under The Bus, Please
Monday, 24 October 2022

Nana See-See has arrived to collect you for the day.

'Nana,' you whisper to her, even though I'm standing right next to you guys. 'Can we have ice cream when we get to your house? Mummy isn't with us, so she'll never know.'

Busted, Nana!

She doesn't even try and hide it. She doubles over laughing. 'Arlo, you've just thrown Nana right under the bus.'

'I know, Nana, but are we having ice cream?'

Daylight Savings
Sunday, 30 October 2022

'Morning, Daddy. Can we go downstairs?' you say, having arrived in our bedroom ready to begin the day. I check the time. It's 5.30 a.m.

'Arlo, it's still sleepy time, mate. Your clock isn't yellow.'

I pick you up and walk with you back to your bedroom. I'm surprised you haven't kicked off yet. Usually—

'See, Daddy? My clock is yellow. It's morning time!'

You have a clock programmed to turn from blue to yellow at a set time, signalling an acceptable time for you to get out of bed.

And you're not wrong. It is yellow. And I know why. The bastard clocks went back last night, and it would seem I forgot to change yours.

'It looks like Daddy made a mistake,' I say.

'Silly Daddy. Shall we go downstairs?'

'I guess that's exactly what we're doing.'

November (Again)

dad pride
noun

A type of satisfaction similar to normal pride but a trillion times greater in magnitude and density.

The Parenthood Dictionary
Adventures in Dadding Edition

Cyril 2.0 Delayed
Tuesday, 1 November 2022

I need to tell you something, but it won't be easy for you to hear. I have decided to postpone the creation of Cyril 2.0.

I know, I know – I'm a terrible father. Moreover, I'm a father failing to meet a deadline that I set myself. You don't even know about Cyril 2.0. Neither does Mummy.

When you get down to the nuts and bolts of it, it's really your mother's personality that's to blame. At the start of September, I walked past the biggest cardboard box I had ever seen and didn't take it. It was a box for a fridge, for God's sake – out on our street! The thing was maviss! I only had to drag it up the road a hundred yards, and it would have been mine to staple life into!

But, if you recall, Mummy was away, and before she left, she begged me to keep the house tidy. It was a pathetic display on her part: eyes wide and glossy, arms flapping like an ostrich shoved off a building – such was the desperation of her theatrical injunction not to trash our abode.

So, relying on my unfathomable reserves of maturity, excellent character and compassion for others, I told myself there would be no harm in postponing the project by a couple of weeks.

But then, we had the news about your eyesight, and I lost motivation. I got it back again but not until October, when Mummy and I agreed that extra leisure time should be devoted to clearing stuff out of the house, not bringing it in.

And now it's November, and we're prepping for your birthday. Next month, it will be Christmas. Do you see? It doesn't make sense to build what I'm sure will be my magnum opus.

I'm sorry I've let you down, son. It's harder for me to accept than it is for you. What can I say? Life throws curveballs.

But know this: my resolve has the power of a thousand strong men – Cyril 2.0 is still coming … just not in 2022.

The Magical Properties Of Vacuum Cleaners
Monday, 7 November 2022

'Daddy, that's a big mess, and now we have a situation.'

'And who's responsible for the mess?'

November (Again)

'This guy right here,' you say, pointing your thumb to your chest. 'I'd better get one of my Hoovers on the job! Daddy, you'd better get one of them as well.'

I'm gutted that you now pronounce 'Hoover' correctly.

Like last year, I'm surprised Henrys, Hettys and Hoovers have remained a constant in your life.

I'd love for it to continue, although I know it won't.

'Daddy, the hallway is very messy. We need to move all the Hoovers in there and get all the pieces, and then we need to clean the mess up.'

'That's fine, but don't we have a problem?'

'What problem, Daddy? Talk to me.'

'Well, you've set up a little shop in front of the doorway.'

'Oh yeah, I have. That's my shop.'

'So how are we going to get Henry and the gang into the hallway?'

'Hmmm,' you say, mulling over the predicament, running possible solutions through a simulation in your mind. Watching you engage your brain in this fashion is fascinating.

'I've got a good idea.'

'Hit me.'

'If I climb over the shop, you can pass my little Henry to me, and then you can pass all the pieces, and then you can step over the shop with the big Henry because you're taller. Is that a good idea?'

'It is. But we could just move the shop?'

'No, Daddy, you silly goose. That's not even the plan,' you say, like you're watching a clown perform a slapstick routine on stage. You're in on the joke, and you laugh because of it.

Scrape, thud, scrape.

'You OK, Arlo?'

'I'm fine. I'm just moving the pieces in the hallway so we can fit all of the Hoovers in here.'

Christ, more playtime damage to the house.

'Daddy, you forgot to get the Shark Hoover from upstairs.'

'We don't need the Shark as well, do we?'

'Of course we need the Shark.'

'But we've got your small toy Henry, the big Henry, the spare blue Henry base and all of the spare parts. There's not enough room.'

'Hmmm. I've got another good idea, Daddy. We need to take all the Hoovers upstairs to see the Shark, and then we need to do some hoovering.'

'Oh …'

'I will take my little Henry, and you can get the rest, Daddy. Quick, we need to hop to it.'

'Right away, sir.'

I carry out my orders efficiently and diligently, lining the Hoovers up next to each other upstairs.

'Daddy, do you know where the crevice tool is for little Henry?'

'Right by your foot.'

'Oh yeah, thank you, Daddy. What about the upholdery piece?'

'The upholstery piece? In blue Henry.'

'Got it!'

'Listen, Arlo. Nana See-See will be here soon, so we should really think about getting you dress—'

'Set the timer.'

'How long for?'

'For five minutes.'

'You're on.'

Set the timer – such an invaluable protocol to have in the parenthood toolkit. I'll be telling other parents about it until the day I die.

The timer goes off. We dance the 'timer dance', a slow, graceful swing with our arms stretched out, as if we were trying to keep steady on a ship in choppy waters. Next, you allow me to dress you and clean your teeth.

'We need to quickly dress the Hoovers.'

'Naturally.'

'Little Henry can wear this,' you say, adorning him with your Buzz Lightyear pyjama top. The other Henrys are too big for your clothes, so I dig out my *Peppa Pig* and Marvel pyjama T-shirts and dress both of the larger Henrys. By the way, my *Peppa Pig* – it's actually Daddy Pig – pyjama set was a present from you on Father's Day.

'Bye-bye, all you Henrys, see you later. Daddy, don't get them undressed. Just leave them there till I get back.'

'I won't touch them, I promise.'

Who knew I'd be so indebted to a bored Numatic International employee at a trade show one afternoon? But here we are. His actions have made my job as your father more enjoyable.

Hoovers, lawnmowers, construction vehicles – props you assign to yourself to help answer questions about the world while adding colour and vibrancy to your imagination. And the more questions you ask of the world, the more my world grows. *May it never stop growing.*

Almost A Preschooler
Tuesday, 8 November 2022

I'm on nursery pickup. I arrive, press the doorbell and announce who I am and who I'm here to collect.

'Come through,' the receptionist says before buzzing me in.

'Where is he, in the toddler room?'

'Nope. Today, Arlo's been in the preschooler room.'

'Oh, right,' I say, unable to decide if I'm about to burst into tears.

'Do you know where that is?'

'I don't think I do. I've never had to go there before.'

I'm directed through a route that I've not walked before, but it's one with which I'm about to become familiar. I head into the new room. The children here are louder, more boisterous and more confident. All 'bigger kids'. I hate admitting to myself that's what you are now, a 'bigger kid'.

I had mentally agreed that I wouldn't have to face the reality of your graduation from toddler to preschooler until you turned three. But the truth is that I've not thought of you as a toddler in months. Nevertheless, I'm going to keep pretending that you are.

You're sitting on a chair with a small chalkboard in your hand, drawing circles.

'Arlo.'

'Daddy! Hi, Daddy.' You put down your board and cuddle me.

'What are you doing in this room? This isn't your normal room. I don't even know what room this is,' I say with exaggerated shock and confusion.

'It's preschoolers.'

'Preschoolers! Wow. Have you had fun here? Would you like to come again?'

'Yes, I would. Look at this,' you say, thrusting the chalkboard into my hands for me to inspect your blue circles. 'I've been chalking.'

A staff member approaches. 'Hi, I'm Hannah. Arlo's had a wonderful day with the preschoolers, haven't you?'

You reply with a shy smile, validating Hannah's claim.

You belong here. It's bigger, with more stuff you're into, like construction toys and arts and crafts.

'He's such a smiley, happy chap whose enthusiasm rubs off on all his other friends. He's a wonderful influence.'

That, right there, is the single greatest compliment I've received about you. There is nothing I want more for you in this world than for you to live a confident, happy life, but one where you're giving back, inspiring those around you and bringing out their best selves – like you've done today.

Hannah explains that while you're not due to start in this room until January, you'll have several settling-in days to prepare. 'I think he'll settle almost immediately.'

'Come on, Daddy. Let's go home.'
'OK, mate. What do you say to Hannah?'
'Bye.'
'See you again next time, Arlo,' she says.

Annual Letter
Wednesday, 9 November 2022

It's 9 November, which means ... Annual Letter Day. You know the drill: do as you wish with this advice, but know it might one day help you as it's helped me.

Dear Arlo,

Change is inevitable. Whether you love, hate, accept or reject it, change doesn't wait. And it doesn't care. Humans experience time in a linear fashion. We're born, we age, and we die – nothing about our existence remains static, including our identities. What you believe today is unlikely to be what you will believe in the future. Our principles and beliefs are moulded throughout our entire lives, sculptured by experience. Crafted by change.

For the most part, if we look at change holistically over time, we see that it is for the best. Because change

November (Again)

means the world is evolving. Yes, we don't always take a step forward without sometimes taking a few steps back. We still have war and poverty and individuals in powerful positions who serve their own needs over the greater good. There is still much suffering. And, sometimes, change is slow to present itself.

But consider this: modern man is estimated to have evolved from our ancestors two to three hundred thousand years ago. We lived in caves and roamed the land for food and water, constantly in danger. Now we live in warm homes with high-speed internet connections, where a click of a button ensures we have whatever we can afford delivered to our doorstep. And we're living longer than ever before.

We take more steps forward than back.

Today, technology is enforcing change upon the planet and its inhabitants at a frantic and frightening pace, one our biological wiring was not built for. Our brains are similar to those of our ancestors born before the internet. Before the Industrial Revolution. Even before the agricultural revolution. Evolution can't keep pace with the progress our species has made.

For better or worse, we need to figure out how to prepare for and navigate a future that we cannot predict but that will no doubt continue to exhibit the rate and pace of change we've come to expect in modern times.

That is scary.

And so, we have a choice to make. We can embrace change, or we can run for it.

Arlo, choose option one. Embrace change. Keep your head above water and go with the tide. Yes, change can be scary and uncertain, but it can also be exciting and incredibly rewarding. It can lead to the most amazing forms of self-discovery and to inventions that benefit the world.

You've made major inroads already. Your attitude towards change is remarkable. But you may one day find yourself in a position where this is no longer the case. If that's so, then I hope this letter serves to aid you in steering you back on course.

If you asked Mummy, she would say that I love change. That's not true. I don't love *it. Not always, anyway. Change can be taxing and often draining. But so is remaining idle and pretending the need for us to adapt and change isn't tapping us on the shoulder, reminding us to take action.*

I don't always love change, but I embrace it regardless. Because it will happen to me whether I like it or not. Take you, for example. Every year I've commented on how I've been unable to reconcile myself to the speed at which you are growing. A part of me will always feel like that. And I will never enjoy the rate at which you are growing. But that doesn't mean I don't embrace your development. Because I can't stop you from growing up. I can either go along for the ride or spend my time wishing I could manipulate the laws of science.

Despite the difficulties, the rewards that change brings can be invaluable. Maybe you're scared to move jobs, to end a toxic relationship or to move to a new city. But once you undergo the transformation and come out the other side, you may find yourself happier than ever, and you will have learned something about yourself in the process. And if it doesn't work, then you have the power to change again. In that sense, change is a gift.

Technology will continue to change the world in ways we cannot foresee. Most of the jobs we do today will one day be obsolete. Many of us will need to adapt and retrain. Some will do this in time. Others will leave it too late.

Maintain your enrolment in the former camp. Learn new skills, and keep pace with the developing world. Allow your network to evolve. Accept that your beliefs and world views will do the same. Remember, nothing is static. Watch out for those who seek to protect the status quo, and be wary of those who allow their fear of change to blind them from making the right decisions, decisions that might in some way impact you.

Our ability to respond to change influences our ability to lead meaningful and successful lives. This is vital.

Use introspection to help you. Ask yourself questions: am I fulfilled in all areas of my life? Is this relationship healthy? Is the thing I wanted then the same thing I want now? How will I respond to the changes that the world has thrust upon me?

One of the guiding principles of stoic philosophy is training our minds to focus on what we can control and ignoring what we can't. You can't stop change from occurring, but you can determine how you react and respond to it.

Becoming a parent has reminded me of the importance of accepting change. You began this year as someone, and now, as we approach your third birthday, you end the year as someone else. You've changed. And so have I. And this time next year, we'll again be different people. This is something we cannot run from. So why try?

I hope this is a helpful framework.

Once again, you have been brilliant this year. That's something that hasn't changed. Long may that continue.

Love, Dad

PS: I can think of something else that hasn't changed: the level of contentment that my life has held since you were born.

The Things I Hate …
Sunday, 13 November 2022

I can count the number of lie-ins I've had this year on one hand. I hate that stat. And I hate the near-constant exhaustion that trails me wherever I go, no matter how early I go to bed. I hate cleaning your teeth; you've yet to master standing still for thirty seconds. I hate rushing to get out of the house on time. I hate parenting in the car. I hate it when someone gives you sweets or sugary food without my permission. I hate that I devote so much of my life to working rather than playing with you. I hate it when the weather messes with our plans. I hate that routine and consistency are so crucial for your well-being. Some days I'd love to let you stay up late and watch a film with us in bed. I hate looking at the bank balance the week before payday. I hate that you'll be starting school in less than two years. I hate it when Mummy tells me you got upset going into nursery. I hate it when you feel abandoned. I hate that you've had to start wearing an eyepatch again. I hate the jolt my chest makes when I see you have a near-miss accident. I hate it when I don't have to close the stair gate at night because you're not here. I hate it when you leave your listening ears behind. I hate it when I lose patience with you. I hate that large crowds and noise rock your confidence. I hate it when you turn the page of a book before I've finished reading it. I hate it when I accidentally hurt you when we're playing silly games. I hate it when you're in pain, and I hate that I can't take it away. I hate the phrase 'I don't want Daddy'. I understand it, and I don't take it personally. But I still hate it. I hate the thought of you being excluded in the playground from participating in a game or from receiving offers of companionship, romantic or otherwise. I hate it when grandparents tell me that 'it feels like only yesterday that my children were in nappies'. I hate that because I believe them, and I hate that I still can't accept the speed of your development. I hate that one day you'll learn that Santa isn't real. I hate that I can't protect you from everything. I hate that you're growing up.

... Are Outweighed By The Things I Love
Monday, 14 November 2022

I love how you refer to nursery as 'work'. I love being on pickup duty. I love how you come running up to me shouting 'Daddy' while exploding into my arms. I love how you're always encrusted in mud. I love your artwork and the excitement you display when you tell me what you've drawn. I love how much you enjoy looking out of the window at the binmen on a Monday morning. I love how much you like to help with chores. I love how you always ask for my food because you know I'll always give in. I love our sit-down wees, me on the toilet and you on the potty. I love how you mispronounce words. 'Maviss' instead of 'massive' is still my favourite. I love that you love to spin around in my office chair. I love the games. I love the walks to the park. I love that my life isn't about me any more. I love how you use my chin stubble to scratch your arms. I love seeing all our names on any gift cards we write. I love how radiant your smile is, and I love that you always use it. I love looking at your clothes; they're bigger than your baby clothes, obviously, but still small. I love that you love vacuum cleaners. I love how much you enjoy our family adventures. I love how wonderful your Mummy continues to be and how she allows me to enjoy the best of what fatherhood offers. I love that we have a support network. I love the special relationship you have with Nana Hoover. I love how much enjoyment and unrivalled meaningfulness she gets from being a grandmother. I love cuddles and snuggling on the sofa watching television. I love hearing the cartoons in the background because they always remind me I'm a dad. I love how wrong the doctor was who thought we wouldn't have children naturally. I love the near-constant levels of contentment I feel around you. I love how funny you are. I love how humour gives you confidence. And I love how warm it makes other people feel. I love how well you adapt to change. I love how you test boundaries because it means you're secure. I love it when you say 'Daddy'. I love it even more when you say 'my daddy'. I love that I'm a dad. I love you.

The Search For Sanity
Tuesday, 15 November 2022

I came up with the title of this book, *The Search for Sanity*, during our Covid-19 isolation period in December. You might say that it was early in the writing process to decide on a book title.

I'll admit it was something of a gamble, but I figured fate had stacked the deck in my favour. We were entering the terrible twos. The sheer volume of tantrums that other parents and the internet had me believe I was about to face left me feeling confident in a title like *The Search For Sanity*.

But I failed to consider a key variable. You. Following what has become common practice, you've done the opposite. You've had a handful of bad days where tantrums were prevalent, but no more. Most of the time, we've been able to step in and neutralise any emotional acidity before it spilt over into rage.

How do we do this? Simple: we talk to you.

That's seriously all we do. That's our big secret. Explaining. We bring you into the conversation when we're making our family plans. If those plans change, we sit down and discuss why. If something forces us to abandon our plans, we ask you to help us figure out new plans. Now, that might not be an approach that works for other families, but it works wonders for ours.

An example of this is when I took you swimming in the summer. We arrived and discovered the pool was closed. Now, you find me an excited two-year-old who won't kick off at that discovery. But you didn't. Because I explained the situation. Then I said, 'Arlo, I don't know what to do now. Do you think you can help Daddy come up with a new plan?'

The switch was visible in your eyes. You went from disappointment to problem-solving mode. You said, 'But, Daddy, the park isn't closed, is it? We could go there.'

'We could. That's a great idea.'

'I think that's the new plan.'

'I think you're right.'

Another example was when we lived out the most stressful part of our year, moving through JFK airport. You started meandering towards I'm-bored-let's-behave-in-a-way-that-tells-Mum-and-Dad-I'm-pissed-off until I explained our problem and asked for your help. You became an asset – a team player.

Mummy says I take this too far, that I'm an over-explainer, but I'm not about to change my approach.

November (Again)

Your comprehension of the world at such a young age is insane. To me, that fact alone justifies the book title.

And there are other things about parenthood that are insane, such as a parent's love for their children. It's beyond comprehension – trust me, I've spent enough time reflecting on it. Another is how I can feel I've done an entire week's worth of work before 8 a.m. on a Monday.

Every day, the muscles in my face contort and arrange themselves in ways that express the full breadth and depth of the human experience. That's what parenthood is to me: humanity stripped down to its core. And what a bright and beautiful core it is. It's sleep deprivation, sacrifice, love, joy, exhaustion, swimming upstream, frustration, reward, meaning, contentment and a million other combinations of emotions and feelings that we traverse on any given day.

But the most insane thing about parenthood is not that we willingly put ourselves through it – some parents do so multiple times – but that we tell ourselves and those around us that we wouldn't have our lives any other way. And those words are true. For me, at least. I wouldn't have it any other way. And I want it all. I want the tough days, the good days, the periods stuck in the trenches and above the clouds. I want the 'Santa isn't real' moments and the 'anything is possible' moments – the hard with the easy, the rough with the smooth. Give them all to me as they are.

My job as a parent is nothing but a long quest for sanity. It still blows my mind to have gone from being told we wouldn't have children naturally to everything we have today.

Something I've not spoken about before in these books is our future as a family. Will you become a big brother or not? The truth is we've wanted more children since you were a few months old, and we've been on Mission Sibling for almost two and a half years without success. It's been quite the journey for Mummy and me, though it's separate from the one we've embarked on with you.

Will it happen? I honestly don't know. Maybe the doctors were right. Perhaps you are that one-in-a-million miracle child they said you were.

I could spend hours speculating what life *might* have in store for us as a family, but I don't have time. Why? Because I'm busy. And so are you. We've got dens to build and sofas to trash. We've got parks to explore and carpets to vacuum, games to play and obstacles to climb. There's a big, terrifying mamma bear in the next room. We need to sneak up on her. There are things to reach for and places to travel to, experiences to collect and truths to learn, skills to acquire and questions to ask.

We've had a million adventures, but we're barely getting started. There's not a moment to lose.

'Are you coming, Daddy?'

'I am, son. I'm right behind you. Every step of the way.'

November (Again)

Tempus Fugit And The Small Things
Wednesday, 16 November 2022

I once told you that Mummy makes me a better father than I would be without her. But something I've never said is how you make me a better father.

Ultimately, I am a better version of myself because of you.

You adapt.

You learn.

You're fun.

You care.

You empathise.

You're affectionate.

You're kind.

You have a large heart that you share with those around you.

You're daring.

You're confident sometimes and reserved at other times. I'm not sure how environmental factors determine which characteristic comes out, but I know your inner voice calls the shots. It's a voice you mastered listening to at a young age.

If we are products of our environment, then I am better for having you reside in mine. Thank you for that.

I love to write about the big events and the major milestones in your life. And I love capturing all the funny stories that parenting you generates, along with Mummy's underrated mannerisms. They're creatively fun to document, and I never want to forget them.

So I use words to fix the memory of them on to the page, and then I share those words with the world to showcase what it's like to be a dad.

But I recognise now that I've led readers astray. Because the most meaningful element of parenthood is not the big stuff. It's the small stuff. The everyday stuff. The stuff in between. The stuff that most would consider mundane.

Every tea party. Every second spent walking to the park or reading the same book a dozen times or sitting on the sofa having a cuddle. Even sitting on the sofa and not having a cuddle but sitting side by side in each other's company, before transitioning to the next thing. Those are the moments where you fully discover the essence of what it's like to care for a child. Those moments sum up everything precious about parenthood because those moments *are* parenthood.

All time is precious. But the choice lies with us as individuals and as parents to see it that way. Life doesn't get any better than seeing your child take their first steps. But equally, seeing the look on their face when they're deciding if they want warm or cold milk can be just as special. Yes, one will give you that emotional electric thrill that gladdens your heart, but the other is no less rewarding.

To be custodian of another, to protect them and love them, to teach and learn with them, to endure the hard times while enjoying the good. It's all linked. It all comes wrapped up in the sacred, honour-bound gig we call parenthood. And if you go into the gig with both eyes open, you can find moments

November (Again)

of meaningfulness and a rich human connection everywhere you look. Yes, it's tiring and demanding, but aren't all the best adventures like that? Isn't life itself like that?

Every year I comment on the speed of your development, admitting how I've yet to come to terms with it. That's still true. But by paying attention to the small things, I can be assured I'm rewarded with the full experience. I'm not wasting time waiting for the next big thing, the next action sequence or the next major milestone. I'm focusing on the bits in between – the connective tissue. Small bits that join together big bits.

And when you stand back, you have a tapestry that captures parenthood in its layered and nuanced entirety.

Every morning, I wake up and walk down the hallway in our house and greet a young man whose choices, temperament and attitude to life allow me at times – *and I mean at times* – to breeze through parenthood simply by not doing anything. Simply by letting you be who you want to be. You could argue it's lazy parenting. If it is, then, parents around the world, please feel free to steal my approach.

If I die tomorrow, I die knowing that I have left the world a much better place than it was when I found it. And for that, you have my thanks. You are loved beyond measure; beyond imagination and beyond comprehension; beyond the laws of biology and physics; beyond the reaches of time and space. Beyond the known and the unknown.

Tempus fugit. Time flies.
So pay attention to all of it.
Especially the bits in between.
Especially the small things.

Cake
Thursday, 17 November 2022

It's evening, and you're in bed. I'm upstairs, but I can hear Mummy chatting to Nana Hoover downstairs in the kitchen, bringing her up to speed on your birthday party arrangements.

'We've finished the bath bombs, and they look great, but three haven't held their spherical shape. But that's OK, as we made extras. Also, I didn't make those three, so they were always likely to be rejects.'

Then they start having a good giggle – *pair of pricks*. I've never made bath bombs before, so of course I'm at risk of not nailing it first time. Who isn't?

'I mean, we've never made these before, but mine still turned out OK,' Mummy says.

I walk to the top of the stairs. 'How about you go fuck yourselves about my bath bombs? We don't know those were mine.'

'Have you seen them, baby? They're as flat as pancakes.'
Good joke.

The reason bath bombs feature in the arrangements is that I threw my toys out of the pram over the contents of your party bags. I didn't want sweets, and I didn't want plastic. Mummy came up with the

November (Again)

bath-bomb idea, which I thought was terrific, and I showered her with the praise she deserved because I'm a loving and supportive partner.

I go downstairs while Nana heads upstairs to bed. It's getting late, but we need to complete the second stage of your cake. Mummy insisted she should make it this year, and I insisted I should be part of that. You have a number-three-shaped chocolate sponge. The theme for your birthday is diggers, and Mummy's found some creative ideas to diggerify said cake.

'Right, I need you to add two hundred grams of chopped chocolate into the bowl. You need to be precise.'

'Am I allowed to break it with my hands?'

'I think that will be OK.'

'Are you sure? We don't want to get it wrong or the whole thing will be a disaster, and it will be all on you.'

'Let me recheck the recipe,' she says, scanning the page with that frown of hers that I've always found comical and endearing. 'It doesn't say, but I think it's fine.'

'Right you are. I'm on it.'

I weigh the chocolate but soon discover a problem. Mummy's busy cutting up chunks of butter, so I wait patiently with my hand in the air.

'What is it?'

'I've majorly fucked up.'

'Oh no. What? What is it? Tell me!'

'You said to add two hundred grams, but I've added two hundred and one. I'm so sorry. I'm such a piece-of-shit dad. Arlo will hate me forever.'

'Oh, you wally. That's fine.'
'But you said we had to be precise.'
'Just melt it in the microwave!'
'Aye, aye, Captain Boss.'

I add the chocolate to the microwave and then return to Captain Boss to await my next instructions.

'Can I leave you to mix the butter with the icing sugar and cocoa powder?'

'I will give it my all, though it's hard to get started.'

'Why?'

'Because you've currently got the bowl in your arms, and you're stirring. The whole thing is one giant mixed message. Pun intended. You're asking me to do something that you're doing. How do we move forward?'

'By you shutting up and mixing,' she says, thrusting the bowl into my arms.

I put everything into it: energy, enthusiasm, fire and spirit. I mix the shit out of this thing until it's ready to add to the food blender, along with the rest of the ingredients. Once the blender's done its thing, Captain Boss and I use spatulas to slather the mix all over the sponge before moving on to the next stage: adding the fence.

The fence is made from chocolate fingers, in keeping with the construction theme. But we don't have enough.

'You need to go to the shop and buy more,' instructs the captain.

'Now? But it's almost ten p.m.'

'So?'

'So, that's forty-five minutes past my bedtime. And it's cold outside.'

'Your point?'

'I want credit for how I'm a man who will go to extreme lengths for his son, and I also want you to admit that we don't know the reject bath bombs were mine.'

'The sooner you do this, the sooner you can go to bed.'

'I'm leaving now.'

'Hurry, I still need to sort pass the parcel out.'

Yup, that's right, Arlo. Despite everything that happened during your last birthday – the fuck-ups and the anxiety of having to coordinate such an endeavour while weathering stares, insults and 'helpful tips' from other parents – Mummy insists we once again wallow in the swamp of unpleasantness that is pass the fucking parcel!

I return from the shop with additional fencing materials. Captain Boss and I finish erecting the fence then call it a night. We won't do any more, as we promised you could help with the rest.

'I hope he loves his cake … and his presents and his birthday party. I just want him to have the best day.'

'Hey, come here,' I say, pulling Mummy in for a cuddle. 'He's gonna love it. You make everything special for him.'

'You think?'

'I know.'

Arlo, An Almost-Three-Year-Old
Friday, 18 November 2022

'Is tomorrow my birthday?'

'It is. How old are you going to be?'

'Three.'

'And that means you won't be a toddler … any … more.' Damn it, why is the day before your birthday always so upsetting?

'I'll be a big boy preschooler.'

'You sure will. Do you want pancakes for breakfast?'

'Yes, I do, Daddy.'

'No worries.'

You follow me into the kitchen and start yanking stuff from one of the drawers onto the floor.

'Arlo, do you think that course of action is healthy for Mummy's sanity?'

'Ha ha. I don't think this action is healthy for Mummy's sanity.'

'Shall we put those things away?'

'OK.'

I get started on the pancakes while you retrieve cushions from the lounge.

'I need to set up a pancake shop, Daddy. Help me.'

'OK.'

'First, we need to move these two chairs together, and then the cushions will be the walls. I need a blanket for the door.'

'What about this towel? Will this work?' I say, dragging one from a pile of washing on the dining-room table.

November (Again)

'Oh, yeah. That will work.'

I drape the towel over the chairs (they're stalls). Your new pancake shop, situated in the middle of the kitchen, is complete. You sit behind it, where you have access to our food cupboards.

'Come into the shop, Daddy.'

'OK.'

I crouch down and pull back the towel.

'Hello, Daddy. What would you like from my shop?'

'Well, obviously, I need stuff for pancakes. What have you got for me?'

'Let me have a look.' You turn around, open the nearest cupboard and extract a tin of pineapple, a tin of chopped tomatoes, a tin of beans and some lasagne sheets.

'Wonderful. How much?' *I bet it's two pounds.*

'Two pounds, please.'

'Here you go, sir.'

After actual pancakes, you hang out with Nana Hoover while I return to work and Mummy dashes here, there and everywhere to finalise your birthday celebrations.

In the evening, we sit you down and ask if you want to do something you've not done before.

'Arlo,' I say.

'Yes, Daddy?'

'Tonight, would you like to sleep in Mummy and Daddy's bed and have a sleepover?'

Your eyes widen. 'Yeah!'

'And would you like to watch a little bit of a film?'

'And then will I wake up in your bed, and will it be my birthday?'

'It sure will.'

'OK. Can we go now?'

'Sure.'

The three of us head upstairs. One unit. One team. Three human beings doing the best we can with what we've got. A family.

Your name is Arlo. You are 104 cm tall. You weigh 15.9 kg. Your sandy-blond hair is once again in desperate need of a trim. You love diggers, dinosaurs, vacuum cleaners and being outdoors. And you love getting up to mischief. You still spend most of your life smiling. Sometimes when you laugh, you do so while inhaling air. It has the effect of creating this inverted squeal-like noise that's the most unique sound I've ever heard. It's beautiful. And so are you. Mummy and I couldn't be prouder of the young man you've become, and I can't wait to see where you take us on the next stage of our parenthood journey.

Buddy, you fucking rock!

Toddler Inc.: Goodbyes

transition
noun

The act of moving from one thing to another thing, both physically and emotionally.

Toddler Inc. Employee Handbook
Fourth Edition

The Toddler Inc. building was a sight to behold at any time of the day. But at night, it was extra special. Lights danced in choreographed harmony on the front of the framework, portraying Toddler Inc.'s greatest accomplishments in dazzling, vibrant hues while music from hidden speakers lent emotional weight to the bright display.

Tourists would come from all over the world. They'd postpone their bedtimes and gather at the front gates to witness the spectacle.

The renovation project at Toddler Inc. had been completed last year, but the rear gardens, which the public couldn't access, were still left to do.

Mr Jacobs refused to rush. He had waited patiently until the right designs were presented to him. Eventually, they were, and he green-lighted the project.

And it was coming along nicely. The new polar-white porcelain pathways gleamed in the light from traditional Victorian lamp posts. There were automatic shoe buffers on every corner. Benches, each unique in design and adorned with a plaque bearing something memorable like an inspiring quotation or a funny joke, were bathed in the glow of the lamps. One had a rhyming tongue-twister about Billy Zane.

The landscaping was still in its infancy. Mounds of earth huddled together like piles of gold on a giant's desk. Bulldozers, front loaders, dump trucks and excavators worked together through the night to realise the complex designs promised to Mr Jacobs.

Arlo, wearing his snuggly sleepsuit, wended his way down the path and found Mr Jacobs sitting on a bench. He appeared as he always had done, without a coat. Arlo wondered if he was immune to fluctuating temperatures.

'Beautiful, isn't it?' Mr Jacobs said, watching the construction vehicles.

Arlo agreed. He LOVED construction vehicles.

'No one takes comfort in the process, Arlo. Everyone wants the end result. They show up for the grand unveilings, the ribbon-cutting ceremonies, the photos and the free champagne – not that I'm opposed to the odd glass of champagne, mind you.'

Arlo nodded.

'But it's the process where the work happens, the act of showing up each day and doing what needs to be done. That's what we should be recognising. That's the real success. It's all very well racing to the finish line, but for what? For a spike of satisfaction while you're awarded a medal? And then what? Arlo, learn to love the process, and you will live a life devoid of disappointment.

Toddler Inc.: Goodbyes

'Toddler Inc. has profited from parents not knowing that, but it seems times are now changing. Parents are embracing parenthood in its entirety. Bravo, I say.'

Arlo looked at Mr Jacobs, sensing a new direction in the man's life.

'Now that I've calmed down from my, err ... rare display of ... OK, I admit it, dreadful behaviour, I've done a spot of soul-searching, as one must from time to time, and I've decided to step down.'

Arlo was shocked.

'Come, come, now. I'm not quitting just because of ... What did the papers call it ...? My "first professional failure". Utter twaddle. My career is littered with failures. As it should be. If you meet anyone who hasn't failed, they're lying. Or they haven't pushed themselves and taken any risks. That is failure of a different kind – cowardice.

'Truth is, I should have left years ago. I didn't, because I was scared. Scared that I had become someone else who didn't know who they were or what they wanted. So I stayed. That's the true failure of my character. It's got nothing to do with the share prices tanking.'

'Will you find a big new office?' asked Arlo.

'I'm not sure what I'll do. I guess I need to shine the ol' shooter marbles and send them out on reconnaissance. But I'm in no rush. Arlo, you have been a great initiate, and despite our opposition to parents, I understand why yours feel the way they do about you. What's next for you? I don't know that either. But whatever happens, know that I'm rooting for you. And I'm rooting for your mummy and daddy.'

'Thank you.'

'I think being a parent isn't all that dissimilar from running a company. As a leader, you do the best you can with what you've got, accepting that mistakes and failure are a part of the way forward. So I wish you and your family the very best of luck. And now it's time for us to say goodbye.'

'Will I see you again?'

'You won't.'

'That makes me sad.'

'Then you are the richest little boy I know. Now then, let's me and you have ourselves one last high five, shall we?' he said, standing up. 'Put it there.'

Wearing his customary boyish grin, Arlo slapped Mr Jacobs' hand as hard as he could.

'Atta boy! Take care, Arlo.'

'Goodbye, sir.'

Mr Jacobs stood and looked down the path he had come from: a pristine, dust-free stretch of polar-white porcelain. The one he knew.

'I think I'll try another route.'

And with that, he stepped off the path and onto the development site. Within seconds his always-shiny jet-black steel-toecap boots were unrecognisable, transformed by the act of self-discovery and courage in asking what's next. He marched towards the horizon with a smile on his face and a spring in his step.

Arlo waved goodbye to his mentor and then settled to watch the diggers and bulldozers. He wondered whether he should wake up with his listening ears on and decided he would, but only because tomorrow was his birthday, and there was talk of cake *and* ice cream. If that wasn't worth the compromise, he didn't know what was.

Arloisms:
A Guide To Toddler Talk

Parents, write down every mispronounced word or misunderstood phrase your children say. In the years to come, you'll treasure the investment. Below is everything Arlo has said that's made me chuckle. Some words and phrases he only mispronounced for a short while. Others he was still saying when I finished this book.

Words

Aeroport: A cross between an aeroplane and an airport (I think). Or perhaps just an airport and not a port where they export Nestlé Aero chocolate bars.

Banamato: Tomato

Bagona: Granola

Bobs and bits: Bits and bobs

Booiful: Beautiful

Cat-pilar: Caterpillar

Deaf-in-ated coconut: Desiccated coconut

Fireman and Sam: *Fireman Sam*

Henmy: Toy Henry vacuum cleaner

Hosberbal: Hospital

Just-tend: Just pretend

Mash chay-choo: Mashed potato

Maviss: Massive (my favourite mispronounced word)

Onion: Union (as in who you'd contact if you were pissed off at work)

Tray-picker: Cherry picker

Tree grass: Tree leaves

Phrases

More See-Sees, please: I want more Weetabix (because 'See-See' means 'grandad' and apparently all grandads eat Weetabix).

Away, Mummy: Fuck off, Mummy, I'm playing with Daddy, and I don't want you to be involved.

Away, Dadda: Fuck off, Daddy, I'm with Nana, and she lets me watch YouTube videos on her phone, whereas you do not.

I'm going to work: I'm going to nursery.

I'm working here, Dadda: Daddy, get away from your desk and let me sit in your chair, trash your keyboard and then graffiti your desk with a biro.

Get on your marks, then get set, and then GO!: On your marks, get set, go.

Eh, hello, or Hello, every guys: Self-explanatory!

Finally, Arlo went through a period of saying 'I do', 'I don't', 'I won't' or 'I haven't' rather than plain old 'yes', 'no' or 'OK' when asked if he wanted something.

Acknowledgements

I'd love to take all the credit for writing this book, but I can't! I owe thanks to several people who helped me along the way.

To literacy magician, Ian McIlroy: you make me look like I know what I'm doing.

To literacy engineer, Ross Dickinson: everything reads better with your input.

To Chandana: you knocked it out of the park (again). Thank you for designing the book's cover art and interior artwork.

Numatic International – where do I begin? To Becky Coombes: thank you for graciously organising one of the biggest highlights of Arlo's life to date (and mine). To Paul Stevenson: your acts of kindness will never be forgotten. You're one helluva tour guide. And to the rest of the staff who played a small part in making our visit so memorable: thank you.

Mum, I'm sorry for the grey hair. I now understand how this was all my doing. Arlo and I are lucky to have you around.

Charlene, we completed Year Three of parenting! Well done us. But especially well done you. You remain, as ever, a wonderful mummy. But you're dog shit with finances. Please stop buying stuff we don't need!

Arlo – my torchlight, my mood booster, my recipe for happiness: each day you give me everything.

Thank you. You kept me on track by regularly asking me, 'Daddy, are you still working on the red book?'

And finally, to parents, the gatekeepers and custodians of the next generation of humanity: don't be too hard on yourselves, OK? No one finds our job easy. Try to remember that.

A Note From The Author

I need your help!

If you enjoyed *The Search for Sanity*, please consider heading over to Amazon or wherever you buy your books and leaving a review. Tip: you can copy and paste the same review on more than one platform.

I cannot overstate how valuable and important reviews are to an author, so believe me when I say that your support is greatly appreciated.

And if you're planning to tell your mates about *The Search for Sanity*, they can find it on sale at all the big retailers (Amazon, Apple Books, Google Play, Barnes and Noble, Kobo and many more outlets). It's available in paperback, hardback, ebook and audio.

About Tom Kreffer

Tom Kreffer is the author of the *Adventures in Dadding* book series, memoirs covering his son's early childhood. His books include *Dear Dory: Journal of a Soon-to-be First-time Dad*, *Dear Arlo: Adventures in Dadding*, *Toddler Inc.* and *The Search for Sanity: Life with a Two-Year-Old*. He is also the creator of the *Lessons in Dadding Newsletter: 'tried, tested and timeless wisdom to help dads become better at dadding.'* He loves *Star Wars* and Marvel movies, and he has a degree in film and television that he firmly believes to be worth less than a second-hand toothbrush.

He lives in Northampton, England with his family, whom he intends to exploit for many more story opportunities in the years to come.

Say Hello!

My website www.tomkreffer.com
email at tom@tomkreffer.com

Find Tom on social media

Want Free Stuff?

Free ebooks

I have created a series of ebooks to help parents, focusing specifically on dads. You can download these on my website for free at www.tomkreffer.com. They include *Pregnancy Guide for Dads*, *Labour Guide for Dads*, *Newborn Baby Guide for Dads*, *Sleep Guide for Dads*, *Toddler Guide for Dads* and *10 Things You Can Do Right Now to be a Better Parent*.

Lessons in Dadding Newsletter

Once a week (or so), I send out a *Lessons in Dadding* email featuring tried, tested and timeless wisdom to help dads become better at dadding.

Visit www.tomkreffer.com to join the fun and hone your parenting skills.

More Titles From Tom Kreffer

Dear Dory: Journal of a Soon-to-be First-time Dad

Partner Pregnant. Less than nine months to prepare. Holy s**t – you're going to be a daddy!

Now, a soon-to-be first-time father is charting a course through the perilous and choppy waters of living with a pregnant woman. He's dodging hormonal right hooks, evading emotional explosions, saying all the wrong things (like "Are you okay?"), and trying to figure out how the hell you install a car seat.

Written as a journal to his unborn child, *Dear Dory* is the unfiltered, irreverently funny, honest, and heartfelt account of one man's journey to fatherhood.

Superb read
★★★★★

It's funny, it's crude, it's heartfelt – worth a read
★★★★★

Loved it
★★★★★

Couldn't put it down!
★★★★★

Dear Arlo: Adventures in Dadding

It begins immediately.

There's no transition period, no trial run, no supervised training, no e-learning module and no simulation that you can f**k up as many times as you need to until you get it right.

As soon as the midwife hands you your newborn baby, you are responsible for keeping it alive.

Picking up moments after *Dear Dory* ends, *Dear Arlo: Adventures in Dadding* continues the story of one dad and his journal as he strives to survive the first year of parenthood, blundering his way through bottle-sterilising, night feeds and some cataclysmic nappy changes – all while a pandemic sweeps across the planet.

Absolutely brilliant – I laughed and cried!

★★★★★

Fantastic – couldn't put it down

★★★★★

Pure Genius!

★★★★★

Excellent

★★★★★

TOM KREFFER

Toddler Inc.

Toddlers are savages.

They scream, shout, rebel, slap, destroy, throw food and purposely withhold their love and affection – just to watch your soul snap and your spirit shatter. And all before 8 a.m.

And yet, they're also misunderstood creatures: funny and beautiful – endearing little marvels that brighten up your day. But mostly they're savages.

The Adventures in Dadding series continues with this highly entertaining third entry, captured by one dad and his journal. Blunt, honest and absurd – this is *Toddler Inc.*

Charming, hilarious and REAL
★★★★★

Brilliant and beautifully written
★★★★★

Fantastic read
★★★★★

Endearing and comical
★★★★★

www.ingramcontent.com/pod-product-compliance
Lightning Source LLC
Chambersburg PA
CBHW031053080526
44587CB00011B/663